THE LONG AFTERNOON

THE LONG AFTERNOON

BRITISH INDIA 1601–1947

BY

WILLIAM GOLANT

ST. MARTIN'S PRESS
NEW YORK

CONTENTS

v

LIST OF ILLUSTRATIONS

INTRODUCTION

[i]

BY THE TIME of the first voyage of the East India Company in
1601 the *idea* of India had favourably impressed Europeans. It
was a name to be used often. As late as 1614, over a century after
its rediscovery, India meant not only a particular place 'but all
farre-distant Countries'.[1] As a somewhat unreal place of fabulous
wealth, an El Dorado, it stirred men's enthusiasm. Columbus
named the islands in the Caribbean *Los Yndias Occidentales*
because he thought he had found a water passage to the east;
with the name of West Indies he sensed he could assert the truth
of his discoveries and impress his supporters in Europe. Even
with the increase in geographical knowledge in the sixteenth
century, the West Indies, the East Indies, and India shared a
common name. In time, the confusion of place became a confusion of meaning.

No other country discovered by Europeans has been the object
of such varying opinions as India. It resounded with illusive
characteristics, created false impressions, or became what the
visitor wanted to find. The early meeting of East and West led
to misinterpretation. In 1498 Vasco da Gama came to Calicut
where he and his men were taken to a Hindu pagoda which they
mistook for a Christian church resplendent with sculptural
adornments representing the Virgin Mary. Desirous to explain
any aberration, they concluded that the people of Calicut shaved
their heads leaving only tufts on the crown in order to indicate
they were Christians.

As men travelled east expecting to find the exotic and intoxi-
cating, they paused to be inspired in India by what would kindle
their imaginations. Falstaff in *The Merry Wives of Windsor* hints
at the Elizabethan idea of India. He has convinced himself that

[1] Purchas, *Pilgrimage*, 1614, p. 451.

Mistresses Ford and Page have flirted with him in order to be seduced, and since they control the purse-strings of their households, he hopes for excitement and profit. 'They shall be my East and West Indies and I shall trade with them both.' India easily became the outstanding example of the attraction of far-off lands where one could find an alternative to the mundane existence of home, where the differences in rules and the distance from traditional authorities offered a unique amount of freedom and irresponsibility.

The achievement of a British empire in India led the English to surround the country and their presence there with ambiguity, which, like a top soil, nurtured colonial self-deception and covered over the crude life processes on the sub-continent. The imperial idea itself, vague and well-meaning, was an over-estimation of the effects of British rule. There was little need to prove altruism. India was the brightest jewel in the royal crown no matter how its people lived. Before he left England to be a renowned viceroy, Lord Curzon spoke at an Old Etonian dinner in 1898 about his destination in the romantic phrases widely considered appropriate. 'He was going,' he said, 'to a temple where the suppliant adores but never catches sight of the object of his devotion. It is a journey the goal of which is always in sight but is never attained.'[1]

The 'mysterious East' euphemistically but aptly conveyed the confused feelings and impressions of travellers. The long, tiring journey frequently led travel-book writers of the late nineteenth century to observe the profound sense of distance from home which was felt in India. Fear of the unknown and the disturbing effects of separation from a familiar world led English men and women to carry with them to India as much of their personal belongings as space on board ship would allow. Steamship companies obliged by not furnishing passenger cabins, which allowed English furniture to accompany those who took up the white man's burden. Not to lose one's equanimity was the first imperative of the Raj. Accordingly the small band of servants of the empire preserved their self-identity by cherishing memories of home, observing the code of avoiding much unnecessary fraternisation with the natives, and appearing bored. For its

[1] *The Times*, 29 October 1898.

ability to represent all these qualities, the club was a fair symbol. 'India is a land in which it always seems to be afternoon. No one is energetic.'[1]

The history of Anglo-Indian relations was determined by the long-established attitude among the English that India was never to be their permanent home. The proportion of land mass to indigenous population in North America was favourable to European migration; the distance, though long, was not such as to be disorientating; the journey was drawn on early maps as an unbroken line, while European rulers granted land. The new world might adjust the discontents of the old and still retain a European culture. Points of departure from England like Plymouth became the name of the place of arrival. But India was never this kind of potentially permanent home for Europeans; the peninsula was crowded, the journey hazardous, while the Mogul ruler impressed foreigners as being richer and more civilised than many in Europe. The English quickly learned how hazardous to health a stay in India could be. In the seventeenth century the first four hundred out of five hundred residents in Bombay died. By 1907, after serious signs of unrest, the Viceroy, Lord Minto, wrote to the Secretary of State, John Morley, 'we all feel that we are mere sojourners in the land, only camping and on the march'. Morley answered, 'Your way of putting this helps me to realise how intensely artificial and unnatural is our mighty Raj, and to set one wondering whether it can possibly last.'[2] The English came to India to rule but not to live, an attitude which increased the distance between them and the ruled. In so far as the English were confident in India, they drew this confidence from a belief in their own impartiality and sense of justice, and the ability of example to educate backward peoples. To them India had the best possible paid administrator and therefore the idea of home rule seemed irrelevant. Home rule in the context of Indian history had a very literal meaning— the country should be governed by those who regarded India as their home. Since Britons did not, national leaders soon found it easy to condemn British rule as that of the foreigner, stranger, and enemy.

[1] P. Landon, *Under the Sun*, 1906, p. 171.
[2] Quoted in Ram Gopal, *How India Struggled for Freedom*, 1967, pp. 171–2.

The wish to have opinions about India did not only belong to those who went there. Europeans since the eighteenth century found India a place to confirm their own new ideas. The tendency of intellectuals to look for sources of evidence outside Holy Writ logically drew them to the pagan world which flourished untouched by the Gospel. Their universal ideas could not ignore the customs and peoples of the newly discovered world. Charles de Montesquieu argued in *The Spirit of the Laws* how climates affected society, its laws and its ethos. In India as in other parts of the world, hot climates produced passive men. In India 'rest and nothingness are the foundations of all things, total inaction [is] the most perfect state. They give to the supreme being the name "the immovable one" .'[1]

In the nineteenth century the German romantic Frederick von Schlegel further extolled the glory of nature by interpreting Hinduism as a religion with a wild and sensuous love of nature which God had implanted as a kind of primitive religion.[2] Less exuberant, Arthur Schopenhauer found in India a rich source for his own pessimism. What else was the conception of the transmigration of souls and the eternal cycle of birth and death but a judgement that everyday living was a great evil since it brought nothing but suffering? The life process was meaningless. The wisdom of the East asserted 'nothing at all is worth our striving, our efforts, and struggles. The world is bankrupt, and a business that does not cover the expenses.' The great Czech writer Franz Kafka was also drawn to Hindu writings and 'their icy hatred of life'.[3] His famous story *Metamorphosis* is a tale of a man who wakes one morning to discover he has become an insect. The protagonist is called Samsa which is a Hindi word for 'those who have been reborn into a new life'. Thus Kafka gave him a name which exactly described his condition.

It is well to keep in mind the rich and varied uses India has had in the intellectual history of Europe. The India of recent times is as complex as in the past. Social scientists measure disease, population explosion, food production and hunger, village communities, and the class system. Popular artists learn

[1] C. de Montesquieu, *Spirit of the Laws*, 1823, p. 228.
[2] F. von Schlegel, *The Philosophy of History*, 1847, p. 155.
[3] G. Janouch, *Conversations with Kafka*, 1971, p. 85.

the cadence of archaic Indian culture. The avant-garde of wealthy nations are attracted by the ideas of life renunciation and introspection to find new psychic experiences. As if a goddess from her own mythology, during the past few hundred years India has revealed something of herself, changed her form, and yet remains unknowable.

[ii]

By modern standards British supremacy in India lasted a long time, nearly two hundred years. The endurance of British rule was all the more remarkable given the physical size of their responsibility, 1,800,000 square miles, an area twenty times larger than Great Britain. The effects of government were further complicated and at times muffled by the variety of peoples, languages and customs in India which maintained an almost permanent lacuna between official intentions and local practice. Internal communications on which control depended were not good; the monsoons perennially dislocated telegraph and transportation while the basic unit of Indian life, the small village, was cut off from everything except its immediate surroundings. Some villagers by the twentieth century had not yet heard how Britain had replaced the Great Mogul; a measure of Gandhi's fame was that men of the village knew his name.

British ascendancy was 'an exception to all ordinary rules, a standing miracle in politics'[1] in that Britain remained in India, accepted the burden of ruling others and the mounting criticism of the ruled, without having a very clear or consistent idea of why it was there, what it aspired to do, or what advantages it gained. Forceful exponents of empire like Curzon, Joseph Chamberlain, and Milner were distraught by the loose purpose and lack of understanding of 'our undeveloped estate' which their efforts, mostly unsuccessful, tried to alter. With no specific goals, Britons arrived in India generally unprepared for their tasks, often finding no fixed procedure to build upon. Edmund Cox joined the Bombay police 'keen to do my best. Never once did I get any instructions in my duties. There did not exist in those days any compilation of rules and regulations for our

[1] J. R. Seeley, *The Expansion of England*, 1891, pp. 217–18.

guidance in the Bombay presidency.'[1] In such circumstances, by the rule of simple addition, all efforts could be quantified and translated into progress.

In other ways Britons were unsuited to govern India. They were racially sensitive and therefore uneasy in their everyday relations with the dark-skinned Indians. Logically they tried to keep the interaction of the two peoples formal to preserve their exclusiveness.[2] This exclusiveness, however, was at odds with the obvious need of the civil and military services to rely on native recruitment.[3] Distrust, manifesting itself as pique and irritation with India generally, made the few Europeans ill-at-ease in the 'sepia surround'. England's historical experience which praised the virtues of liberty over tyranny, the achievement of Parliament winning legislative power, the need for elected representatives to be sensitive to the wishes of the nation, and the responsible nature of all government institutions embarrassed the Government of India. It was accepted that this government was necessarily autocratic, unpopular, and not directly responsible to the people it ruled. The Secretary of State for India, Edwin Montagu, explained to the new Viceroy, Lord Chelmsford: 'The theory of India Office control is that it is parliamentary control over a Government in India which is not responsible to the people in India. We are here, I have always understood, to replace by the Houses of Parliament the "voiceless" people of India. We are trustees for them because they have no control over you and your Government.'[4]

Yet until the last decade of British rule those who came to India were not excessively disheartened. This was because at times people suspended or defied their rational assessment of problems, suppressed racial prejudice, and forgot the lessons of history. The excitement of being in India was sustained by the ethos of service which helped to ennoble work and the present. In personal and human terms there was something brave and

[1] Sir E. Cox, *My Thirty Years in India*, 1909, p. 92.

[2] As late as 1942 it was suggested: 'The average Bengali has never spoken to a British officer or soldier.' *The Transfer of Power*, Vol. II, 1971, p. 112.

[3] In 1929 the whole police force in India had 300 European officers and 800 European sergeants out of a total personnel of 187,000.

[4] E. Montagu to Lord Chelmsford, 3 August 1917. Chelmsford Papers, IOL.

courageous about Anglo-Indians, who, as pioneers pursuing their own interests, nevertheless were instruments of change making tangible achievements. Everyone contributed. Lady Chelmsford initiated an All-India Maternity and Infant Welfare League and Lady Reading started a National Baby Week to combat infant mortality. While the effects of British rule were contradictory, mixed, and many-sided, there was a substantial core of improvement which made even the first generation of Indian nationalists unwilling to sever the British connection.

This substantial core of improvements to which government reports and historians of the period referred, helped to sustain British rule. Beyond the benefits of law and order, an 'impartial' administration, and a judicial system there existed a relatively non-political area of activity which supported Britain's fundamental contention that India gained for its dependence on Britain. Private and public enterprise, committed to the strict principle of annual profit, effected changes in the Indian economy which probably would not have happened without British occupation. While these changes certainly fell short of the country's needs and served British as well as, if not more than, Indian interests, this was perfectly consistent with the sound business ethics of mutual advantage which officials, politicians, and entrepreneurs of the Empire accepted as practical and therefore irrefutable. Though it was always open to critics of government policy to argue that particular changes in the economy were never asked for by Indians, such a point of view missed what Britain rightly regarded as its contribution to India.

The expansion of the Indian railways occurred between 1879 and 1914 when the Government granted private companies free aid and guaranteed a profit of 3·5 per cent. By 1931 there were 31,710 miles of railroad open for traffic, usually owned by the state but managed by private companies. India had the longest line of state-owned railways in the Empire. In the years of railway development to 1900 the railways lost money, but from 1906 to 1926 the earnings on capital invested averaged 5·8 per cent. The railways made an annual contribution to the general revenue, one per cent on net receipts, and generally one-fifth of the net surplus profits.

Lord Curzon appointed an Irrigation Commission (1901–3) which made a comprehensive survey and recommended a twenty-year programme of development. By 1926 twenty-eight million acres or nearly 13 per cent of the total cultivated area of British India was irrigated by government works. Large-scale projects were completed: the Triple Canals in the Punjab, Sukhur Barrage in Sind, and the Sutlej Valley. These were classed as 'productive works' because charges for their use would cover all expenses, including interest on the original investment for some years. Most of the major irrigation systems were 'productive' and contributed to central and later provincial revenues.

Railway and irrigation expansion were in part a direct result of the Government's desire to develop a policy to counteract famine. Railways were used to rush food to stricken areas while a number of irrigation projects known as 'protective works', i.e. non-profit making, were to protect the farmers against drought. Important dams or canals were built at Godavari, Bhandardara, Bhatgar, and Sadra. The serious famines of 1876–8, 1896–7, 1899–1900 led the Government of India to develop a famine policy.

Famine Commissions helped to evolve a wide-ranging policy which included a famine code to provide work and relief to the needy and temporary suspension of land revenues. A Famine Insurance and Relief Fund was started in 1876. Government compiled vital economic and agricultural facts to anticipate the areas of vulnerability. Loans were extended for buying seeds, tools, and other farm necessities.

Agricultural research to increase the quantity and quality of production made some advance under British rule. The Pusa Research Institute in Bihar began in 1903, helped by the donation of Mr. Henry Phipps of Chicago of £30,000. It was a research station, experimental farm, and agricultural college. There was also an Institute of Animal Husbandry and Dairying at Bangalore, an Imperial Institute of Veterinary Research at Muktesar. In 1925 the Imperial Institute was created in London for the dissemination of information on the production and utilisation of raw materials. As a result of the creation of the Indian Central Cotton Committee in 1921, an advisory organisation to improve cotton growing in India, the Institute of Plant Industry at Indore, was founded in 1924.

After 1857 India became a favoured area for British capital investment. It is impossible accurately to fix the extent of this foreign investment; estimates vary from £365 million in 1909–10 to £829 million in 1939. The greatest share of this investment went into government, municipal, and railway undertakings no doubt because these had government-guaranteed returns. But whole new plantation industries grew as a result of British investment—coffee, rubber, indigo, and tea. Tea plantations, the most lucrative of these, were begun by retired government officials and army officers. In 1930 around £90 million was invested in tea companies, three-quarters of which were registered in England. The average dividends of eight companies between 1926 and 1929 was 38·5 per cent. British enterprise and money went into manufacturing industries as well. The extension of railways into Bengal led to the formation of big coal companies. In 1904 82 per cent of Indian coal production was owned by Europeans. Jute manufacture was started in Bengal by George Acland in 1854. Profits even by Indian standards were sometimes staggering. One estimate put jute mill profits from 1915 to 1924 at 90 per cent per annum of their capital.

The Raj lasted as long as it did not only because of cash profits, an army of over 200,000, a favourable balance of trade to Britain, or because India paid for British rule. India contributed to Britain's image of herself as a great power and world leader. The Indian Empire enlarged the scale and purpose of affairs of state, providing a place to tour with style, a colourful addition to any pageant, and a mission worthy of effort. Even Britain's enemies believed India gave Britain a world view and therefore a reason for respect. Hitler wrote in *My Struggle*: 'It is childish to assume that in England the importance of the Indian Empire for the British world view is not appreciated.' With so many reasons to stay in India, Britain became dependent on those it ruled to provide evidence for self-respect. When Indians evolved a basis of self-esteem in their own national identity, Anglo-Indian relations in the twentieth century took on many of the aspects of an unhappy marriage where scenes of disagreement predominated, words failed to create understanding, and relations became permeated with hopelessness which only divorce could change.

I wish to thank Lord Radcliffe for helping me procure the Boundary Commission Awards, 1947, Sir George Abell for answering my many questions, Mrs. Pat Taylor for making the maps, and Mrs. Linda Thomas for typing the manuscript.

ONE

MOTHER INDIA

[i]

AT THE BEGINNING of the seventeenth century, the English East India Company was cautious. The group of City merchants decided to risk their capital only after there had been favourable reports about trade prospects in the East, a number of successful voyages, and the high price of spices on the London market seemed to assure good profits from quiet trade. No doubt the defeat of the Armada and the adventures of Drake and Raleigh heightened national self-confidence, which among London merchants meant a will to speculate. But still they sought a direct guarantee from the Crown that they would be the only English company in eastern trade. The new company received the royal charter granting the exclusive right to trade in the East and to transport goods and spices from Java, Sumatra, and the Moluccas. The Company was not conceived as a vast enterprise to outdo foreign companies already in eastern trade. Each voyage was sponsored from money raised by special subscription which allowed individual members of the company the option not to invest in every voyage undertaken. Since the return voyage would take all of three years and it was less profitable to dispose of the imports at one time, the founding members of the Company expected to make profits from their investment only after several years.

An exclusive English charter did not affect foreign competitors. The Dutch East India Company, established six years before the English, already had considerable control over the Spice Islands. They regarded their eastern trade as more than merchant adventure. State and private money was consolidated in the hope that large profits would become the financial basis for Dutch independence from Spain. With ample funds and a

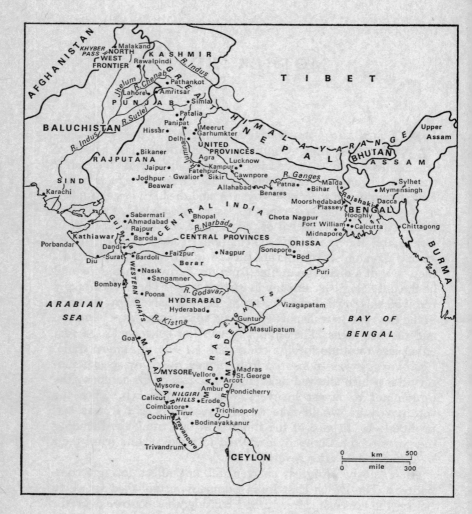

Places mentioned in the text

policy aimed to repel enemies, the Dutch opposed the English company when it began to set up trading stations. At Amboyna, an island east of Java, in 1623 the Dutch Governor, Herman van Speult, tortured a Japanese soldier from whom he 'learned' how the English were plotting to overthrow by force the Dutch fort on the island. In fact the mere presence of Englishmen on his island convinced the Governor of the necessity to destroy would-be conspirators. Eighteen Englishmen were arrested and tortured by ducking and burning until they confessed; ten of the arrested were executed in public. The English public was angered and out-raged, but the East India Company responded according to the law of least resistance, and decided it more prudent to build trad-ing bases on the mainland of India. Whereas their activities could be easily discovered by the Dutch on the small islands, the vast-ness of the Indian sub-continent might provide them a safe niche.

In 1613 the English received permission from the Great Mogul, ruler of India, to found a trading station or 'factory' where servants of the East India Company could live and work. A year later the first Indian cargo of cotton and indigo reached London. With only little fluctuation, profits of the company were high. They rarely fell below 100 per cent of the capital raised for each voyage, and in general they were over 200 per cent. By 1647 the Company had twenty-three Indian factories and ninety employees. The favourable return on money naturally led the Company to think in terms of expansion. The major factories became the walled forts of St George in Bengal, Fort William in Madras and Bombay Castle. The forts were not yet centres for conquest but shelters for Englishmen from the strife, famine, and disease beyond their walls. The servants of the Company took their pleasures as they came. The Reverend Patrick War-ner, Company Chaplain at Fort St George, wrote to the Court of Directors in 1676: 'There are also some of the Writers who by their lives are not a little scandalous to the Christian religion, so sinful in their drunkenness that some of them play at cards and dice for wine that they may drink, and afterwards throwing the dice which shall pay all, and sometimes who shall drink all, by which some are forced to drink until they are worse than beasts.'[1]

India was a strange mixture of chaos and inertia to the early

[1] Quoted in H. Brown (ed.), *The Sahibs*, 1948, p. 13.

English businessmen. The vast spaces, slow communication between forts and between India and England, the variety of customs and peoples soon suggested to them that here was a place where the pre-established European standards need not apply if only because the enforcement of laws was remote. The East India Company believed in its right to a monopoly of trade but could not curtail the temptation of private trade among its own servants. It was not until later in the eighteenth century that the English established a semblance of law and order over most of the sub-continent. Until then the country was an entrepreneur's frontier where fortunes could be made if one had a dose of shrewdness about the ways of the world, a combination of daring and self-reliance, the ability to devise and personally administer clever schemes, and good health. An age that understood the gains to be had through bribery produced men who willingly took risks for the many glittering prizes. The career of Thomas Pitt, doyen of the Pitt family, impressed his contemporaries as an example of how fabulous wealth could be made in India. He was an individual example of what was to become a popular conception of the benefits from association with India, that wealth came easier to Englishmen in India than anywhere else.

Thomas Pitt (1653–1726) was the the son of rector of Blanchford St Mary in Dorset. As a boy he went to sea to learn about life and earn a fortune. Still a teenager he settled in India and engaged in trade, flouting the Company's monopoly. By purchasing goods from Indian craftsmen and traders and transporting them to other parts of Asia, he made considerable profits. He was caught by the Company's agents and fined but did not change his methods. From 1677–80 he traded in horses and sugar in Persia, and in 1682 negotiated with the Nawab of Bengal for the right to establish a trading station on the banks of the Hoogly. When Pitt returned to England the following year he was arrested and fined £40,000. For the next decade Pitt was engaged in litigation with the Company, but his wealth and influence made him a formidable opponent. As M.P. for New Sarum in 1689, he was becoming too important to oppose. The directors of the Company decided to turn the poacher into gamekeeper and sent Pitt out to India to be nothing less than Governor of Fort St George. He was a predatory example of the modern tycoon whose instinct for gambling for high stakes was tempered only by cunning. By flouting the business conventions of the day he established his own domain, and in the end showed the wide latitude permissible in Indian affairs.

Even while Governor of Madras Pitt could not resist a profitable transaction. In 1701 an Indian merchant brought him an uncut diamond weighing 410 carats. A native had found it years previously near the Patreal mines on the River Kristna and had hidden it by forcing it into a wound in his leg. The diamond was then stolen by a British sea captain who sold it to the native merchant. Pitt bought the diamond for over £20,000 and gave it to his son Robert to smuggle into England. It took five years to cut the stone and was sold to the French Regent for £35,000. In 1791 it was placed, somewhat ominously, among the French Crown Jewels, and valued at £480,000. It is among the few crown jewels to remain unsold to this day.

The England to which Pitt returned in 1709 had a recognised style for demonstrating success. The elegance of life was measured in country houses, titled friends or better still relations, and involvement in the affairs of state. 'Diamond Pitt' became a landowner. He bought and refurbished Mawarden Court at Stratford, Down at Blandford, Boconnoc in Cornwall, Kynaston in Dorset, Bradock, Treskillard and Brannell in Cornwall, Woodgates in Wiltshire, Abbot's Inn in Hampshire and Swallowfield in Berkshire. In 1678 he had married Jane Innes, a descendant from the Earls of Moray. His eldest son Robert married Harriet Villiers, daughter of Lady Grandison of the noble family of the Dukes of Buckingham, and was the father of William, Earl of Chatham. His second son was made Lord Londonderry, his second daughter married General, later Earl, Stanhope. In a letter from India written in 1706 Pitt explained his motivation. 'What have I fateagued for after this manner and lived soe many years in exile from my country and friends . . . but to make my children easy in their circumstances and mee happy in their company; and having by God's blessing acquired such a competency as I never expected or could hope for, so as that I shall have been able to establish a family as considerable as any.'[1]

[1] Sir T. Lever, *The House of Pitt*, 1947, pp. 23–4.

Another merchant adventurer was Elihu Yale (1648–1721) who, by the presentation of a few of his many souvenirs of India, gave his name to the famous New Haven university. Yale's family for a time lived in Boston, Massachusetts but decided to return to England because they disliked the Puritan community. They secured for him a position as a writer with the East India Company in 1671. To augment his meagre salary Yale began to explore new ways of earning money. He bought cloth in India on his own and arranged for it to be shipped to Java in exchange for spices that were in turn sold in London. This trade was so lucrative that he eventually bought and ran four ships. Like Pitt he exported diamonds, became Governor of Madras, and married his children into the aristocracy. One daughter married Sir Dudley North, nephew of Lord Guildford, and another married the brother of the Duke of Devonshire. In 1691 while still Governor of Madras he admitted that 'in twenty years' diligent service in India and trading he had an estate of about five million dollars'.[1] Relieved of his post as Governor in 1692 because of his interloping in Indian trade, Yale stayed on until 1699 to enhance his wealth. When he returned to England he brought with him 'three chests, two escritories, and seven boxes', so much booty that by his death in 1721 a new method of sale—the auction—had to be used to dispose of it. In this way some ten thousand articles were sold, including eighty-five paintings.

The excitement and notoriety that surrounded the careers of Pitt and Yale in India reaffirmed the popular notion of India as a place of unique opportunity for Englishmen. The formal if remote rule of the Great Mogul and the native princes gave the fortune hunters a protective covering for their shady dealings. Yet, India herself felt only slightly the presence of these men, who, limited by the technology of the pre-industrial age, negotiated in relatively small quantities, since schemes revolved around themselves and a few others, because there could be no effective control and communication if the organisational structure were too large. As long as trade was possible within the existing political and military authority of Indians, Europeans

[1] See H. Bingham, *Elihu Yale*, 1938 and E. Yale in *The Dictionary of National Biography*.

had little reason to view India as anything other than an economic asset which was most efficient when operating costs were low.

Two broad events in the eighteenth century changed the position of the English in India: the Mogul Empire, divided by internecine warfare and unable to withstand the foreign invasions from the north-west, collapsed; England's economic and military power, especially at sea, outpaced that of her European rivals. The century which saw England begin the industrial revolution and consistently defeat her European enemies also saw the founding of the Indian Empire, as a prize of battle. Other European countries, each in their own way, experienced what proved to be insurmountable obstacles before they could control India; for them India became a too expensive luxury. For the English an empire in India was a logical extension of their growing power.

The Portuguese, helped by their considerable skills in navigation and exploration in the late fifteenth and sixteenth centuries, had been the first Europeans to have a permanent settlement in India. Goa on the west coast of India was the administrative centre of a trading empire that spanned much of the known world. But geographers' abilities did not meet the needs of administration and human relations—so much the issue if such an empire were to succeed. Trading in India led the Portuguese to wreak a missionary's vengeance on the native peoples; an aggressive idealism hoped to convert or destroy the heathen. The Inquisition was launched in Goa in 1560, designed in principle to forbid non-Christian practices or punish deviations so natural among the newly converted. In reality the Portuguese felt no restraint in annihilating the indigenous Indian culture under their domain. In one year alone 280 temples were pulled down. The Viceroy, Albuquerque, wrote in a letter: 'I leave no town or building of the Mussalman's. Those who are taken alive, I order them to be roasted.'[1] Tension between Portuguese and Indian became so great that an order was issued forbidding any Christian from being shaved by an Indian barber. By the early part of the seventeenth century, however, Portugal was no longer pre-eminent over other European countries. Lacking energy, wealth,

[1] R. P. Roa, *Portuguese Rule in Goa 1510–1961*, New York, 1963, p. 43.

and commanding authority at sea, the Portuguese were continually defeated by the Dutch and English. After losses to the English in 1612 and 1630, the Portuguese in 1642 entered into an alliance with the East India Company to counter the growing power of the Dutch.

During the seventeenth century the Dutch were able to form their empire by combining military and navigational skill with a flair for administration. No small amount of care was necessary to arrange the shipment of merchandise between Japan, India and Europe. Committed to the development of the Spice Islands and the Malay archipelago as the main source for goods to be imported into Europe, the Dutch relegated their stations on the east and southern coasts of India to a secondary importance. These stations were intended for the acquisition of goods for trade to the Spice Islands so that the Dutch did not use their own capital to buy the spices they exported to Europe. By selling copper from Japan and fabrics from China to the Indians, the Dutch company could in turn procure cloth and indigo to sell to the islands. However, by the end of the century the very elaborateness of the Dutch system, which spread from Holland to the Cape of Good Hope, India, Ceylon, the Dutch East Indies and Japan, forced the Dutch to abandon their Indian stations when decline in military strength and the cost of operations were too great. Involvement in wars with local princes, as well as with the Portuguese and English, and the slowness of administrative decisions, led the Dutch instead to consolidate their holdings in the East Indies.

The French were reluctant imperialists. During the sixteenth century only sporadic contact with India occurred. Separate companies sailed from St Malo and Marseilles only to be regularly repulsed by the Dutch. Much later than their competitors, a French company was formed by Colbert in 1664 under the patronage of Louis XIV who granted to subscribers special privileges. Then as later, the French felt a certain lassitude about foreign adventures (as Richelieu noted, they had a temperamental weakness—the desire for a speedy realisation of their wishes—so that 'long voyages were not for them'). Instead of seeing the foundation of a national company for eastern trade as a way to greater profits, the French bourgeoisie believed that the subscriptions called for in the name of the king were a form of taxation. In such unsettled times the new company was under-subscribed so, in the hope of allaying doubts about distant expeditions in the East, the French adopted a step-by-step policy of colonising stations along the trade route. Madagascar, Mauritius, East Africa, Arabia, Réunion furnished French naval bases. In 1674 they established at Pondicherry a factory of six men 'to do what they could'. Other enclaves were at Surat and on the Malabar coast.

The death of Aurangzeb in 1707 threw the Mogul Empire into civil war. Europeans witnessed the disintegration of indigenous Indian authority; a feudal system based on loyalty to the head was overrun when local potentates asserted their independence; the Viceroy in the Deccan claimed the independent state of Hyderabad; central India was ruled by the Hindu Marathas; the Sikhs carved out a kingdom centred around Lahore. In 1739 the Persians, coming through the Khyber Pass, invaded India, defeated the Mogul's army and plundered Delhi. Among the ashes of one dying empire another could now rise.

The final struggle for the mastery of India was between the French and the English. The French were at a considerable disadvantage because, unlike the English, they did not have enough capital to support the vicissitudes of war, so that a series of misfortunes could quickly bring final ruin. The main French centre, the coastal city of Pondicherry, was susceptible to attack from the sea, and could be easily starved of supplies during a long siege; English superiority at sea guaranteed the effectiveness of this extra weapon. While the French possessions clustered around Pondicherry, the English had other important bases of operation in the north at Bombay and in Bengal. The French also regarded their Indian stations as less important than the ones in North America (by the middle of the eighteenth century these were quite extensive). For the sake of the western hemisphere France was willing to sacrifice advantages in the East, as was shown when, in 1748 at the Treaty of Aix-la-Chapelle, they returned the city of Madras, whose capture was the greatest French victory in India, to the English in exchange for Louisburg in Canada. India, unlike Canada, did not lend

itself to colonisation, and this fact may have deterred the French
from regarding it as anything other than an impermanent base
for trade. Nor did the French find it easy to turn their Indian
presence into sources of great profit. In these circumstances,
daring schemes in India had to be trimmed to sound economy.
Victory had to be quick, inexpensive, and directly leading to
wealth. When it was not, the French colonial empire in India
was foreclosed. Dupleix, the French Governor at Pondicherry,
worked brilliantly within these limitations. He meddled in
Indian politics, allying himself with prince or usurper until he
could find someone to supply him with men and resources to
fight the English. The tumultuous political situation in India
gave him ample possibilities for manoeuvre.

In 1740 the Marathas invaded the Carnatic, the Indian
province which included both French and English settlements.
Dupleix opposed the invasion, and was rewarded by the Mogul
Emperor in Delhi with the office of Nawab. Now, with Indian
sanction, he was able to train a native army in European methods.
With this army Dupleix defeated the English in Madras, and
the Nawab of the Carnatic, in 1746. After the pillage of Madras,
Dupleix proceeded to Fort St David, the other English fortified
city, a few miles south of Pondicherry. The abortive siege
lasted eighteen months. In the course of the campaign the
French fleet had been damaged by hurricane and retired from
the Indian seas. This left Pondicherry open to English attack
from the sea and prevented Dupleix from committing himself
totally in the land battle. The treaty of 1748 ended the fighting
and compelled the French to return Madras to the English, but
Dupleix had succeeded in opening wide areas for further ex-
ploits. He had trained an excellent fighting force, large and
effective enough to master Indian opponents. By his daring he
was now to involve the English in the politics and intrigues of
native Indian princes. Dupleix, in short, prodded the East
India Company into conceiving of their trade and treasure as
secure only when opponents who threatened English power
were defeated.

Dupleix's immediate aim was to extend his authority to the
areas surrounding French bases in the south. Two unique
opportunities arose in 1748. The ruler of the Deccan died and his

throne passed to his son Nasir Jang, but the grandson Muzaffar Jang also claimed the throne. In the Carnatic, Chanda Sahib the son-in-law of the previous Nawab was released from prison by the Marathas and conspired to overthrow the present Nawab, Anwar-ud-din. The three opportunists joined forces, fought and killed Anwar-ud-din at Ambur in 1749. A year later Nasir Jang was assassinated. Muzaffar Jang became Subadar of the Deccan at Arcot and Chanda Sahib Nawab of the Carnatic at Hyderabad. For a time Dupleix knew the rewards of an Indian empire. The new and grateful rulers gave him land encompassing eighty villages round Pondicherry, the towns of Divi and Masulipatam, £50,000 for the French Company, and the same amount for the troops. Dupleix himself received a large grant of money and an income of £10,000 a year.

The English could not but see the danger. The French policy of alliance with native rulers achieved a pinnacle of success, and success could stimulate ambition. If Dupleix were not stopped British power in the Carnatic and throughout India would be undermined. Accordingly, the British sought out the illegitimate son of Anwar-ud-din, Muhammad Ali, who had fled for his life to Trichinopoly. Backed by British arms, money, and encouragement, Muhammad Ali delayed Dupleix by long negotiations until the British could send him a proper fighting force.

Robert Clive, a young clerk with the East India Company, turned soldier, set out with five hundred men to attack Arcot and thus lure Chanda Sahib from the siege of Trichinopoly. Chanda duly withdrew his forces from the south to defend his capital. Clive took and held the city in 1751, and began what he was to finish in 1765: the assertion of British supremacy in India. The French General, Law, was unable to capture Trichinopoly. Most significant of all, Dupleix, his reputation tarnished by these military and financial failures, was recalled to France, his policies were reversed, and the French agreed in 1754 not to interfere in the affairs of the native rulers.

The consummation of British ascendancy in India was the dual success in the Carnatic and Bengal. In Bengal the hardship of war, the frequent plundering by the Marathas, and the lack of an accepted system of accession made the power of the ruling Nawab Siraj-ud-daulah, ineffective. The British incurred his

dislike when they fortified Calcutta without permission and also
aided the Nawab's enemies. He promptly attacked the British
fort in Calcutta. The Governor and other prominent men fled by
ship, but some of the captured prisoners were placed in a small
room, the famous Black Hole of Calcutta, where according to
one account 146 men were cramped into a space eighteen feet
long and fourteen feet wide. The East India Company appealed
to the Nawab to restore its city and its privileges while the
Council in Madras prepared a large military force to assure such
an outcome. This expedition was led by Clive on land and
Admiral Watson at sea. They recovered Calcutta in January
1757 without real opposition, and then proceeded to the town
of Hugli in search of plunder. It then became the British aim to
replace the Nawab of Bengal with a ruler disposed to favour
them. To achieve this the Company wooed one of the Nawab's
Generals, Mir Jafar, to conspire against his leader. In the
mango groves of Plassey in June 1757 a British force met the
Nawab in a battle that was to determine events far into
the future. At a crucial stage in the campaign Mir Jafar advised
the Nawab to retire, causing the troops to panic and giving the
British victory. A few days later the Nawab was murdered and
Mir Jafar was enthroned triumphant.

The French Governor of Pondicherry, Lally, mounted a final
attack against the British in Madras in 1754. He failed and
suffered one defeat after another. At the Treaty of Paris in 1763
peace in Europe and Asia was restored; the French agreed to
use their stations only as trading posts and not to maintain
troops there.

In two eventful decades the English had secured for themselves the gratitude of native rulers and the defeat of the French
as contenders for influence and control in India. Clive helped to
negotiate peace between the Mogul Emperor and his vassals,
and in return received the diwani, or right to collect and manage
revenue in Bengal, Bihar and Orissa. At the death of Mir Jafar
in 1765 the succession of his son was sanctioned by British
authority. The East India Company was acknowledged as the
authority with rights over the total administration of Bengal.
Trade receded before the Company's new role as Indian administrator; profits derived from the collection of Indian revenue,

while Company troops maintained the peace of India at the native ruler's expense.

That an English Company should become a governing body, owning and administrating lands in India, was an anomaly Parliament looked to control. After 1765 the British Government regulated the amount of dividends the Company could pay, and from 1767–9 demanded that it disgorge £400,000 for two years to the Treasury and export a fixed amount of British goods to India. In return the Company was allowed to keep its possessions. Though the Company paid lucrative dividends, and its servants literally took fortunes from India, its finances as a whole were unsound, since the military and administrative costs, plus the debt to the Treasury, imposed heavy burdens a private company was unable to carry. Accordingly, the directors appealed to Parliament for financial aid. This request led to the passing of the Regulating Act of 1773, which asserted the legal right of the Company to administer the territories in India, but with the proviso that this right emanated from Parliament. The office of Governor-General was created and he and his council were appointed for five years, with control over the territories in Madras and Bombay as well as Bengal. The Company was still managed by the Board of Directors, though Parliament had to be informed about military, financial and civil affairs. The Crown claimed the right to administer justice, but in suits between British subjects and natives of India it could only do so at the request of the defendants, and it would not hear claims by natives against British subjects. Generous salaries were also fixed, and the accepting of bribes by servants of the Company forbidden. Thus the British Government sought to make the Company less a commercial enterprise than a uniquely respectable delegated authority of itself. To organise this effectively in the context of eighteenth-century politics meant that Parliament had to regulate the Company's policies from the top and in this way overcome its very real powers of direct administration and patronage.

With this object in mind Pitt's India Act of 1784 introduced a Board of Control, headed by the Chancellor of the Exchequer, with powers to modify Company orders and make its own. The system of dual control, that of Company and Crown, worked for the next seventy-five years, until the Mutiny, when Parliament took over complete responsibility for the Indian Empire. Pitt's Act also established the office of Governor with a council in the presidencies of Bombay and Madras.

After 1793 the Company's charter was renewed every twenty years, allowing Parliament further opportunity to investigate and reconsider affairs in India, a power that would certainly limit the Company's plans. When the charter was renewed in 1813, commercial interests in Parliament, smarting from the fall in European trade caused by the Napoleonic Wars, were able to end the Company's trade monopoly. They showed that the profits of the Company came not from trade but from government. To soothe the hurt feelings of the directors, the Company was allowed to retain a monopoly on tea, its major item of profit, but India was now opened to trade under government licence. Parliament also spoke in the language of righteous benevolence, when it resolved 'to promote the interest and happiness of the inhabitants of India'.

The process of turning the East India Company into a delegated political authority was completed in 1833 when Parliament finally made the Company relinquish both its monopoly of trade in China and the tea trade in India, and wind up all its commercial business. The Governor-General in Council was now empowered to make and regulate laws affecting all British India, though Parliament retained overall control. Slavery was abolished, and an Indian Law Commission was formed to survey existing police and judicial procedures and report on ways in which India might obtain a codified system of law and justice. Finally, in 1853, the Company was reduced to acting in trust for Parliament over no fixed period. The Mutiny in 1857 allowed Parliament to end the system of dual government. The Company was required to sever its connections with India and the Crown took over the Indian Empire.

It was no poetic licence that justified the writer who portrayed India as a place of lusty adventure and heroism, where 'rapine and war suspended the labours of industry'.[1] The consolidation of British power after 1765 was made possible by a persistent willingness to engage in war against Indian states.

[1] Sir Walter Scott, *The Surgeon's Daughter*, 1897, pp. 130–1.

With bases in Calcutta, Madras and Bombay, a relatively efficient system of training native troops, the navy, and wealth generated by a presence in India, the English over the next hundred years weakened all possible rivals to their power. The right to dominate the Indian people and native rulers was a trophy of the battlefield.

The acquisition of India by military means often did not appeal to the conscience of some in Parliament, particularly in the early stages of aggrandisement. There were frequent complaints that wars which resulted in conquest were started with that precise end in view, and wars were expensive and irrelevant to the trading purposes of Britain. Ultimately, however, the combination of the presence of the French, enemies of Britain in Europe and America, and the turmoil within India itself could justify a bold military policy. Inefficient government and dangerous alliances between Indian states threatened to keep the sub-continent in a state of chaos far worse than the clinical operations of the British which were intended to bring an enduring peace. It should not be forgotten that the spoils of war in India were considerable, that the defeated enemy often paid the costs of war, and lost land or financial power.

The Maratha Wars (1775–82, 1803–5, 1817–19) illustrate how British power led them to interfere with the succession of native rulers, since the continual threat of war between usurper and usurped made peaceful government and trade impossible. The fact of British ascendancy in India made the East India Company the policemen for the native rulers. By a policy of supporting contender or ruler according to how one or the other viewed the British, the Company was able to prevent the Marathas from extending their alliances to challenge the position of the British. In any case the Marathas did not have the financial resources to finance an extended campaign, nor a system of succession that assured united support behind one leader. Disputes between Hindu chiefs coupled with quarrels and intrigues made the Maratha federation susceptible to the skilful British diplomacy of dividing the enemy by drawing off a section of his support. Defeat on the battlefield led to the loss of Marathan territory and revenue. Later, easier methods of acquiring territory were found. The doctrine of lapse, introduced

by Dalhousie in the middle of the nineteenth century, laid down
that princes who owed their existence to British power but left
no natural heir had their lands annexed. Eventually all the
native states of the Maratha confederacy came under the control
of the British.

Similarly, the Mysore Wars (1767–9,1780–4, 1790–2) were
caused by the threat of adventurous Indian rulers seeking to
extend their possessions and thus endangering the supreme
position of the Company. The rulers of Mysore, Hyder and his
son Tipu, took territory at a time when the British and the
Nawab of the Carnatic were distracted by the French Wars. At
various times the British entered alliances with the Nawab of
the Carnatic, the Nizam of Hyderabad, and even their old
enemies the Marathas, in order to prevent the ruler of Mysore
from ever winning a decisive victory. With Tipu's defeat in 1799
the Company gained more territory, extracted from the
defeated state a subsidy for the British military force, and the
right of the Governor-General to take over the administration
of Mysore should he believe it necessary.

As if they were reaching the end of a chess game, the Indian
rulers lost their possessions by the logic of past defeats; their
resources were insufficient to weaken the British. Britain's
powerful military force won victory after victory. Even the
Indian feudal ruler could tire of battle. And the Company's arms
did increase the security of life and property (for instance when
in 1817 and 1818 the marauding hordes of central India, the
Pathans and Pindaris, were suppressed). In the first half of the
nineteenth century increasing portions of the sub-continent
were brought under Company rule: the Rajputana states, territory in the north and north-west, acquired as a result of the
Nepal Wars, Jaintia annexed in 1832, the Sind in 1843, Nagpur
and Berar in 1853, and Oudh in 1856, gave the British Indian
Empire a patchwork appearance on contemporary maps. For
the next hundred years administrators and imperialists sought
to make from this diversity some discernible pattern.

Successive defeats of Indian armies and British consolidation
of territory gave the latter broader opportunities to scrutinise
the people now under their jurisdiction. No doubt the extent
and manner of the defeats, the chicanery and fickleness of the

rulers, the irresolution of the troops, the decadence and corruption of the courts, disposed them to be suspicious. Tales of oriental splendour might still stimulate European writers, but the administrators had to look at the country from a practical point of view. Inevitably, as the British assumed the role of potentate over an Indian Empire, they acquired a stern and arrogant attitude. As Englishmen gazed at the people of India from the height of the dais, they did not like what they saw.

[ii]

At the turn of the nineteenth century English writers began to disparage the moral character of the subject peoples. It was as if they searched to find noble reasons for vicious deeds, so to give a righteous glow to the expansion of British power in India.

In 1813 Parliament published a report of replies by English magistrates in India to questions posed by the Governor-General in Council in 1801. The Governor-General asked what was the moral character of the inhabitants in their districts. The learned justices vied with one another to find the most absolute phrase of condemnation.[1] A farrago of vituperation claimed that Indians were 'depraved and proliﬁgate, having a feebleness of mind which fosters the baser passions and criminal indulgence'. 'Selﬁshness, low-cunning, litigiousness, avarice, revenge, disregard for the truth, and indolence are the principal features to be traced.' Particularly repellent was their indulgence in 'every species of voluptuousness and sensuality'. Mr Beecher, Justice of Moorshedabad, was perhaps the most conclusive: 'I can scarcely name any virtue they may be said to possess.' The court at Dacca actually included a list of the number of persons committed for trial, but not of those found guilty, a misplaced

[1] However, one justice, Mr H. Stracey of Midnapore, found the natives 'mild, humane, and placable', suggesting that 'the vices and crimes of the people proceed from their poverty and ignorance, and I do not conceive that they are likely to grow much richer or wiser, while the present state of things exist. . . . Where labour is amply rewarded, where all can easily get employment, and where the poor are provided for, the people lead industrious and virtuous lives'. See the answers to question 15 in East India Affairs, *Answers to Interrogatories of the Governor General*, Vol. IX, 1813.

emphasis that shows a disposition among the magistrates to make numbers appear to support their extravagant assessments. Even so, the numbers tried hardly justified the conclusions of the magistrates. Dacca, with a population of about 200,000, showed the following number of commitments for 1801, not an untypical year.

Numbers tried for:[1]

Murder	1	Forgery	0
Perjury	8	Rape	0
Robbery	0	Fraud	6
Burglary	0	Receiving stolen goods	5
Arson	2	Plundering, Assault,	
Theft	16	Breaking the Peace	4

Also in 1813, the British Government published Mr Chas. Grant's (1746–1823) *Observations of the State of Society Among the Asiatic Subjects of Great Britain* written in 1792. Grant was a member of the East India Company's Board of Trade at Calcutta and favoured sending missionaries to India. The publication of the replies by the magistrates, Grant's *Observations*, and James Mill's famous *History of India*, in the same decade indicates that the denigration of Indians had become an accepted and acceptable point of view.

Grant's *Observations* were the first extensive criticisms of the people, in many ways setting the tone for later writers. The society he described aroused in him passionate disgust. He begins with what is common knowledge: all Indians are depraved. 'In Bengal, a man of real veracity and integrity is a great phenomenon.'[2] With little wish to argue a case, Grant cites random examples and takes his own generalisations as facts. He judged the whole of Indian society by the testimony of witnesses in court; that two witnesses contradicted one another showed a people's fundamental mendacity. Grant went little further than pointing to the fact that women argued in the streets, or merchants delayed or misunderstood, or many turned to the

[1] *Ibid.*, p. 104.
[2] C. Grant, *Observations On the State of Society Among the Asiatic Subjects of Great Britain, Particularly With Respect to Morals; and on the Means of Improving It*, 1812–13, x, p. 56.

law courts, to assert the underlying wickedness of the 'Asiatic subjects of Great Britain'.

He does give some interesting glimpses into Indian life, however, and shows how relatively easily the new ruler could misinterpret events. During the famine of 1788 a gentleman from Calcutta asked his servant to go among the poor to buy their children. The servant was instructed to tell the parents 'when the scarcity should be over, they might receive their children back'. Twenty children, mostly girls, were thus humanely preserved from the scourge of famine. Grant stressed the end of the story, that only three of the parents of the twenty ever enquired after their children. 'The unnatural parents cannot be supposed to have perished from want, for each received money for her child, and by the liberal contribution of the inhabitants of Calcutta, and chiefly the Europeans, rice was distributed daily to the multitudes at various stations in the city.'[1]

Grant passed over without comment how the gentleman acted with decency in rescuing the children; he did not expect the parents to buy back their children. Though he condemned the parents he could not be sure that they were not struck down by famine or some other illness or that they in fact received the charity of the inhabitants of the city. Rice may have been distributed daily but it was unlikely that this was enough to sustain all needy families in a period of shortage. Most likely the poor families thought their children were in better hands than their own, in the care of a gentleman.

Ultimately Grant's condemnation of Indians was justified because of the existence of widespread poverty. Good men should not be poor; poverty, on the other hand, only proved the social effect of moral weakness. The Asiatic peoples of India were 'a race sunk in misery by their vices'. Grant put into words a typical British response to life and ways in India. The 'absolute worthlessness of their culture' kept Indians sub-human, with the 'insensitivity of brutes'. Grant asserted that racial and moral categories were related, that the difference in colour between Europeans and Asiatics, white and black, expressed the difference in moral complexion. 'The universality

[1] *Ibid.*, p. 59.

of great depravity that is here insisted on—a moral hue, between which and the European moral complexion there is a difference analagous to the difference of the natural colour of the two races.'[1]

Grant concluded that Indians were fortunate in possessing a natural passivity which would in the future lead them to accept the benevolence of British rule. The people wishing to be protected, rather than trouble to protect themselves, would welcome moral enlightenment. Throughout the next century it suited the British ruler to give moral explanations to Indian conditions, since the task of changing a nation's morals was slow and relatively inexpensive. The title of the official government annual report published from 1859 to 1937, *The Moral and Material Progress of the People of India*, suggested that the one, material progress, derived from the other, moral progress. What kind of moral education should the Englishman introduce in India? Missionaries arrived, church schools were started, barbaric native customs were outlawed, but in fact nineteenth-century Englishmen who came to India believed that the way to improve the character of the natives was for them to live there. Mere presence was a sign of sympathy, an example of a superior moral life for natives to emulate. The great prize for a reformed native was an educational stay in England where he acquired the finishing touches to his new standing as a 'gentleman'. For many of the English who lived in India in the nineteenth century it was tedious and difficult to retain the pose of sympathy. A knowledge of untamed India could lead the new rulers to despise those they ruled, and to show it.

Racial hatred need not always be expressed crudely or cause many and frequent incidents of brutal oppression. The circumstances of British rule militated against a too-outspoken hostility. The conqueror was concerned with good and peaceful administration. Overt and vehement abuse was muted by the fact that a virtual handful ruled over millions. Unrest and rebellion increased operational costs. Thus the racial antipathy Englishmen felt towards Indians was sometimes subtle and indirect. Whereas 'sympathy and understanding for the peoples in the Indian empire' were the often-claimed intentions, lack of

[1] *Ibid.*, p. 61.

sympathy and considerable misunderstanding prevailed. To
penetrate some British attitudes towards Indians is to begin to
explain the origins of the acrimony which affected Anglo-
Indian relations in the twentieth century. To counteract the
low opinion Indians knew the English had of them, nationalists
had to attack English pride and raise high the traditions of their
own culture. The Indian leaders had to formulate a theory of
race favourable to themselves and to balance the prevailing
English one.

Recent psychological research suggests that the white man
associates the dark skin with excrement, 'the unwanted thing';
he frequently describes the peoples of Asia and Africa with
adjectives of uncleanliness like dirty, filthy, smelly. 'The
presence of a native in the same carriage with you doubles the
disgust one feels for a long, hot, tiring journey.'[1] The standard
of hygiene has not infrequently been a standard of measurement
of civilisation. Nineteenth-century sanitary reforms in Britain
heightened English awareness of the appalling conditions in
India. The image of people and place quickly became one of a
nation sunk in its own filth. The Report of the Indian Plague
Commission 1898–9 quoted the Report in a Sanitary Survey of
Calcutta made in 1896.

> The condition of the house drains and 'down pipes' which were
> intended to convey latrine and house and sullage water, were in a
> deplorable condition. In a large number of cases, the down pipe was
> broken at from five to fifteen feet from the ground, and the water,
> urine, and liquid sewage from the houses was simply splashing on
> the ground, fouling the whole gali or lane, and soaking the walls of
> the houses which, in many cases, were thickly covered with filth.
> Many of the interiors of the dwellings were pitch dark even in broad
> daylight, the rats ran about fearlessly as if it were the middle of the
> night. Walls and floors alike are damp with contamination from
> liquid sewage which is rotting, and for which there is no escape.[2]

The responsibilities which took English men and women
away from their homeland and brought them to India had the
effect of dislodging conventional security. The tension which

[1] H. Compton, *Indian Life in Town and Country*, 1904, p. 183.
[2] *Plague Commission*, Vol. V, Summary with Appendices, 1902, Cd. 810, lxxii,
pp. 446–7.

resulted from dissociation from the familiar was increased by the general English reaction to India as uncongenial. Dislike of the Indian people was a corollary of feeling 'out of place' in India. Home was not here but in a land far away. The unending conversations about 'foul weather' were symptomatic of deeper discontents with immediate surroundings. Unable to have a natural rapport with the Indian world around them, the Raj had to rely on its own small community to reiterate the values of England, though this might only be a memory of people and places. Ultimately, Indians could be blamed as the cause of their misery, for India 'called' them and alienated them. 'Here we stand on the face of the broad earth, a scanty pale-faced band in the midst of three hundred millions of unfriendly vassals.'[1]

In one sense the Englishman's life in India induced a return to childhood, a time of fears when a person is dependent on others and insignificant. The average English household had eight servants, with the family dog having a servant of its own, while the school-age child had a 'boy' to carry his satchel.[2]

An English family might live in child-like dependency on native servants, which sometimes undermined normal adult self-reliance. If childhood is a major source of all human anxiety, it may be that reversion to childlike dependence on servants transformed the Indians into hated parental figures, in other words the men and women who performed household tasks.

It was also the case that much in India engendered fear among the English. The 'dark horde' might at any time rebel, and the small European community would have to rely for protection on the police and army who were largely made up of Indians. Rebellions at Vellore in 1806 and at Cawnpore and Lucknow in the Mutiny of 1857 showed the precariousness of British rule. Particularly unsettling were the terrors of the Great Mutiny, the ghastly deaths of English women and children 'foully murdered' and thrown into the well at Cawnpore. One way the English in India could stave off their own fears and instability was to denigrate the Indian race. Racial hatred and physical revulsion transformed a potential or real enemy into simply an unworthy opponent, thereby suggesting, 'you need

---

[1] F. H. Skrine, *Life of Sir W. W. Hunter*, 1901, p. 68.
[2] W. Wilkins, *Daily Life and Work in India*, p. 57.

have no worry about these people for see how weak, fearful, and dishonourable they are'. To denigrate the races of India also made possible the elevation of the British, for the same reasons. Racism not only lessened the threat from the millions, but also became a prop to the ruler's self-confidence; it was a source of stamina amid a potentially terrifying and desperate situation.

The British presence in India was engulfed in miasma. Some who contemplated life there were struck by how unreal it all was, 'the strong flavour of Gilbert and Sullivan which lay at the back of it all'.[1] Victorian feelings, gentility and refinement, could be abruptly challenged in India. Pagan sculpture, even the life of the streets, showed human animality and its coarse, primitive aspects, which the sensibilities of the age tried to deny. The 'sub-human' Indian native hinted at an earlier stage of human life which, if too compassionately viewed, might cast doubt on the nobler values of England. These noble values, belief in the British Empire itself, were too necessary for sustaining the British in India for them to be compromised by objectivity. Sensing danger, both real and symbolic, proper English ladies protected themselves from 'the harsh Indian light', remained behind drawn curtains during the day, rode in the sun wrapped from head to toe and crowned by large umbrellas. The memsahibs were famous for their lily-white skins since 'the merest touch of the tarbrush is sufficient to create a stigma'.[2]

In the unconscious, hatred can be a form of hidden affection. In an uncanny way India became Mother India to Englishmen there. As forbidden voluptuousness and banned sensuality, it tempted them as a precious and unattainable loved one. The primitiveness of life could be an enticing veil arousing desire, feelings not unlike those of the normally repressed child towards its own mother. Mother India beckoned indulgently and stimulated fantasies, for transformed into mother nature, resplendent, fecund, and violent, India gave Englishmen opportunities to assert human dominance and aggression with every tiger hunt. Psychoanalytic methods do explain how India could excite the imagination, for in India the wayward son could possess and dominate a dreamed-of mother, which he could not

[1] Lord E. Hamilton, *Forty Years On*, n.d., p. 123.
[2] H. Compton, *Indian Life in Town and Country*, p. 154.

do in real life, in the mother country. Mother India was also a passive and accepting mother, who allowed a considerable amount of deviant behaviour and aggression.

Commentators have had little need to use depth analysis in explaining English attitudes towards Indians. Nineteenth-century writers preferred depicting everyday events to illustrate the debased and therefore unsuccessful life of the people. For example, Indians spoke imperfect English, which led to considerable, and often amusing confusion. A good tale, even if incriminating, found its way into the sketches of nineteenth-century India.

> A European out shooting peppered a villager with snipe shot and compensated him with ten rupees. In order to retain a written record of the transaction, he ordered his clerk to obtain a receipt for the money. (The native scribe wrote): 'To compounding one bloody murder, ten rupees. Omissions excepted.'[1]

Europeans mistreated Indian servants who were frequently beaten. Hurting them may have provided some form of psychological relief which reassured the master of his superiority; whipping could give him a sense of his wilful control over reality. Europeans also showed a remarkable disregard for the death of natives. The early history of the tea plantations in India reveals the indifference planters showed towards their labourers.

Tea was found to grow wild in Assam in the 1820s. Planters were granted by the Indian government special privileges in the form of tax relief and rent-free land to encourage development of the industry. Tea companies were founded in 1839. By 1865 one company alone grew 327,000 pounds of tea. As the drink became popular in Europe, from 1860 to 1865 company dividends rose from five to thirty-four per cent. At first, labour was imported from China in the belief that only there they knew how to grow tea. But Indians were soon used in large numbers to clear tracts of jungle in Assam and work the fields. These labourers were known as coolies, the name of a tribe in the Gujerat in western India. One government commissioner reported 'scenes most revolting to humanity. The fate of the

[1] H. Compton, *Indian Life in Town and Country*, pp. 183–4.

majority of the unhappy people was truly sad. Those who survived the epidemics which broke out on the passage up and sometimes carried off as many as twenty per cent of their number during a voyage seldom exceeding three weeks, were landed in a country utterly strange to them, with a climate which in their weak state was particularly calculated to generate disease of the most virulent and fatal type. They were often conveyed to gardens where no arrangements had been made for accommodating them, and where no medical aid of any kind was available. In one extreme case the mortality in the garden was so excessive that their manager deserted it, 'leaving the dead unburied and the dying without help'. [1]

With few amenities, inadequate food and housing, the 'coolies' died of dysentery and malaria. The Commission investigating the plantations in 1868 complained that many gardens failed to submit returns; among those that did the acknowledged incidence of mortality was very high. The number of deaths was given as half-yearly totals, while the 'total strength' of labourers does not make clear if it represents replacements for those who have died in the half-year: we cannot know if this number represents the garden population before death. Below is a chart of some typical examples of population and death in the tea gardens of the Upper Assam. [2] These are not the worse cases.

Name of garden	Half year	Total strength	Number of deaths
Nagagholee, Upper Assam	2nd of 1865	659	107
Rungolating, ,, ,,	,,	36	14
Gilladharee, ,, ,,	,,	282	111
Cherido, ,, ,,	2nd of 1866	301	110

In many of the plantations reporting, over one third of the existing work force perished in half a year! The planters did not question their right to procure labour for these unhealthy regions, and the extension of tea gardens was not delayed until medical treatment would mitigate the effects of malaria and

[1] Mr Campbell's 'Report on the Tea and Tobacco Industries in India', in *Tea Commissioner's Report*, 1874, vol. XLVIII, c. 982, p. 35.
[2] Sir P. Griffiths, *History of the Indian Tea Industry*, 1967, p. 351.

proper habitation facilities could be built. The 'coolies' were an expendable labour force; they were virtually nameless.

It is less important how true some of the British judgements of the moral character of the people of India were than to comprehend that there existed a deep animosity. Nineteenth-century tensions and convictions cast a permanent shadow on events into the twentieth. Future political and social intercourse between Indians and Britains was soured by these memories. India was by no means free of crime and unsavoury customs; criminal castes (Mang and Ramosh) were tolerated in society. But the British often saw what they wanted to see, as the statistics of indictment from Dacca in 1801 show. A nation, famous for its practical political wisdom at home, too quickly generalised about life and people in India. The general sullenness and docility of the Indians had been noted by many contemporary writers; only a passive and moderate population could be ruled by a small handful of civil servants. Extreme poverty weakened the resolve of the many to complain. Considering the unsatisfied wants of the people, it is surprising that there were not more sustained attempts to take by force what was denied by right.

[iii]

The end of the Great Mutiny saw the passing of the East India Company and the beginning of a relatively calmer period of Indian history. After 1858 there were few wars of aggrandisement, while the princes of the native states drew closer to Britain. The tranquillity of British rule lasted for nearly fifty years, disturbed only by the militancy of the movement for national independence. In 1909 the British Government scanned these fifty years in a report, *Some of the Results of Indian Administration during the Past Fifty Years of British Rule in India*. It quoted the uncritical words of Edward VII: 'We survey our labours of the past half century with a clear gaze and good conscience.' The needs of the people were met by 'a widespread and open-handed charity'. Echoing the optimism of the East India Company before it, the Government claimed the British Indian Empire embodied the purest intentions, 'the most benevolent in act ever known among mankind'.[1] Self-praise by the rulers of India was also displayed in pageants. India gave governors and viceroys splendid opportunities for theatrical demonstrations of greatness.

One Vicereine, Lady Dufferin, acclaimed for starting a hospital for sick animals during her husband's term as Viceroy, described the meeting of her husband and the Maharajah of Jodhpur in 1884, observed from a seat hidden behind a screen.

[The rank of the Maharajah required that] the Military Secretary, the Under-secretary in the foreign department and an A.D.C. to the Viceroy should drive to his residence to fetch him. Scarlet cloth was laid down for him; a guard of honour was at the door; a band played on the steps, and between each pillar down the hall stood a gigantic trooper of the body-guard, in his scarlet uniform, holding a lance in his hand. As the Maharajah arrived a salute of twenty-one guns was fired from the fort.

A still grander throne than usual was placed for the Viceroy—it was a silver one, with large gold lions for arms; an attendant with a white yak's tail in his hand stood by, lest a fly should trouble His Excellency's composure; a gold embroidered carpet was laid before the dais. . . . Some attendants held bunches of peacock feathers set in gold, and others had very big gilt maces in their hands. . . . When the Maharajah reached the door the Viceroy got up and walked to the middle of the room to meet him, shook hands with him, and motioned him to a chair on his right. . . . The Maharajah's dress was green and gold; he spoke through an interpreter, and the dialogue with him went pretty well. No one else attempts to speak. 'After a short conversation' say the regulations 'the Maharajah's attendants are presented to the Viceroy and each one holds out to him one gold mohur [the chief gold coin of British India] which he touches, thus politely expressing, 'You may keep it, though you are so anxious to give it to me.' Then there was another short conversation before the leave-taking. At a signal the Viceroy's attendants brought in two silver vessels; one contained attar of roses, the other some very sticky leaves wrapped up in a silver and gold paper. I believe that when carefully unwrapped a small piece of betelnut is found in each. The Viceroy puts a small spoonful of attar of roses on the Maharajah's hand, and gives him a sticky thing to take away with him. . . .

---

[1] *Memorandum on Some of the Results of Indian Administration During the Past Fifty Years of British Rule in India*, 1909, Cd. 4956, Vol. LXII, p. 479.

The Viceroy again takes a few steps to conduct the Maharajah to the middle of the room.[1]

The Vicereine, exhausted just from watching this ceremony, and knowing she must that evening make several hundred curtseys, retired to rest in her rooms.

The social centre of British India was wherever the Viceroy made his home, Government House in Calcutta or Simla. The European community took considerable pleasure in meeting each other in the sanctified surroundings of a government palace. These gatherings inevitably took on the formality of an important ceremony. In order to make ladies feel welcome in India, the 'Drawing Room' was introduced, an afternoon event where 'it was hoped trains and feathers would be worn'. To the observant, nuances of colour and length of gown gave indications of character and social status. Some ladies had the privilege of coming early, which allowed them to make 'first bows to the Vicereine and introduce their menfolk'. These first ladies and their gentlemen would stand on either side of the Viceroy's throne, 'in a sort of sacred semi-circle', to await less favoured guests. Ladies without the private entrée were later presented to the Vicereine and Viceroy as they arrived. In the background were long buffet tables, and a military band played gentle music.[2]

A much grander event, the highest in the social season, was the Viceroy's levée and 'the Dignity Ball' with its twelve hundred invitations. Europeans and Indians came, though the latter did not bring their wives or daughters, and thus could not participate in the dancing. 'Therefore his presence in a ballroom is unnecessary.' Elaborate ceremony is always susceptible to embarrassing moments. As people passed the Viceroy, who stood at a precise figure in the carpet, at the rate of twenty-five a minute, there was little opportunity for idle banter. When the Viceroy recognised someone he wanted to be particularly gracious to, he put forth his hand to be shaken, but this could cause the next man also to put forth his hand, 'but meeting with no reciprocity, he slinks off in dismay'.[3] There was perhaps no

---

[1] Marchioness of Dufferin and Ava, *Our Viceregal Life in India*, 1890, p. 12.

[2] C. T. Buckland, *Sketches of Social Life in India*, 1884, p. 10.

[3] *Ibid.*, p. 13.

moment more awkward in Anglo-Indian society than when at the levée the European line finished and the Asian one began. It was noticeable that the smart ladies and their gentlemen near the end of the European line crushed forward, while the Indians, like athletes in a race, sought to run to attach themselves to the end of the European line.

A more relaxing social event was the Sonepore Race Meeting which lasted for ten days. It was akin to an extended picnic, with everyone living on the course in pitched tents. These were placed in separate camps so as to make up different parties. Each camp contained its own badminton and lawn tennis courts. Since boredom too often filled the hours for families in India, the opportunity of pleasure was seized with vigour. One day at Sonepore tells something of the zest for life. Cannon blasts would announce the dawn, followed by a band parade when 'your man' tells you it is time to get up. Mornings were a cool and pleasant time of the day. Events began early. After coffee or tea, the races started at 8 a.m. and finished at 10. A champagne breakfast followed the races and then social meandering, visits to other camps, or the bar, or seeing the native fair. Lunch was at two. The time till tea could be filled with sport or rest, but few after that missed the carriages which took everyone to the race-course for polo, 'Public schools vs. the World'. Dinner was at eight, but women at times withstood the pangs of hunger in order to be dressed in time for the ball. There was refreshment in the al fresco drawing-room to crown a lovely day.[1]

It was the consistent impression among visitors to India, that life among the Europeans 'is very monotonous, life slips away at a wonderful rate, it is like tobogganing down the vale of years'.[2] With so many servants the wives had little to do. Domestic architecture strove for a style that conveyed peacefulness, grandeur and permanence. Homes were 'Bourbon', a variant of the classical eighteenth-century Doric style, with broad verandahs on two or three sides and massive pillars. The flat roofs provided a place to walk or rest in the early morning or early evening. But the houses gave a false impression, for the people inside them often longed for the time when they could

[1] Buckland, *Sketches of Social Life in India*, p. 62ff.
[2] A. M. King, *The Diary of a Civilian's Wife in India 1877–1882*, Vol. II, p. 133.

leave. They felt irritated at having to put up with imitations of things English and being away from the mainstream of life. Living in India put a great deal of strain on Europeans; there were health risks, the unhappy experience of departure of one or more of the family, long separations from loved ones, while the heat always made them tired.

Suspicion and dislike of the Indian environment forced the British to withdraw from the external world and to heavily rely on their own community. Many were bored and frustrated. Natural curiosity had to be thwarted. The lure of opium dens and night haunts had to be suppressed. To allay any confusion about their intentions the British community strove to give an appearance of rigid dedication. It occurred to more than one writer that Anglo-Indian society was divided into castes as precise as those of the Hindus. Civil servants and administrators were Brahmins, with special privileges and authority over others. The military were the warrior caste. The merchant caste included plantation owners, businessmen, and European workmen like foremen on the railways. The pariah and lowest caste of Anglo-Indian society was the half-caste Eurasian. Though no social structure can expect absolute conformity, Anglo-India did possess a strict etiquette which gave some clarity and purpose to everyday life. Anglo-India was 'a land of dinner parties', of shallow gossip and petty ambitions. Amateur theatricals and concerts were given mainly at home. The daily routine was austere, as befitted the servants of empire. Since the early morning was a time 'before the fierce sun rose', the Englishman woke at 5.30 for tea and toast and fruit. Exercise was solitary, a ride on horse or bicycle, or a walk; before breakfast at nine, a bath and the papers; work until five, dinner at seven followed by reading, cards or billiards. Beneath the surface there was a great deal of heavy drinking and some promiscuity, yet the facade of respectability remained, for in India appearances mattered.

For those who breached the rules and 'went native', that is for those who showed too great an interest in Indian ways, there was exile. The deserter from a community was considered not unlike a deserter in wartime; both put personal wishes above those of the community when it was threatened.

Rudyard Kipling, the greatest writer about Anglo-India, devoted several stories in his first series, *Plain Tales From the Hills*, to the experiences of people who test the existing social conventions only to learn that the prohibitions which keep natives and Englishmen apart are right and practical. 'Beyond the Pale' asserts this moral as a preface to the parable story. 'A man should, whatever happens, keep to his own caste, race and breed. Let the White go to the White and the Black to the Black. Then whatever trouble falls is in the ordinary course of things neither sudden, alien, nor unexpected. This is the story of a man who wilfully stepped beyond the safe limits of decent everyday society, and paid for it heavily. He knew too much in the first instance; he saw too much in the second. He took too deep an interest in native life; but he will never do so again.'

Christopher Trejago, a civil servant, wanders into the heart of the native quarter. Behind a grated window the pretty Bisea, a widow of fifteen, sings verses from the Arabian Nights. Their eyes meet. Next morning he finds an 'object-letter' in his dogcart. The letter was made up of a broken glass bangle, one blood-red flower, a pinch of bhusa (a food given to cattle), and eleven cardamons. Trejago's first error is that he knows enough of native customs to interpret the letter. He understands that the broken bangle means a Hindu widow, the flower to write or come, the bhusa signifies he should stand outside the widow's window where there is a pile of bhusa, and the eleven cardamons mean eleven o'clock.

That night he visits the girl, detaches the grating, and makes the girl his lover. For some weeks Trejago strides two worlds; by day he carries out his office routine, by night he wears native dress, a boorka, and visits his loved one who makes 'funny little gestures with her rose leaf hands', whose little feet are 'light as marigold flowers that could lie in the palm of a man's hand' but who is 'as ignorant as a bird'.

One day the widow hears that her lover has been seen out walking with an English lady. Confused and jealous, she sends her Englishman away. After a separation of three weeks, Trejago decides to visit Bisea again. He begins to remove the grating, as he has done in the past, when the girl thrusts out her hands in the moonlight. Both hands have been chopped off and the stumps are nearly healed. As Trejago peers into the darkness of the cell something sharp like a knife or sword strikes him on the leg. He limps away. He is unable to learn what has happened to Bisea. Did the master of the house gain knowledge of their affair or was there some other reason?

There are limits to how much an Englishman can understand the life of the natives. 'He lost her in the City where each man's house is as guarded and as unknowable as the grave.' The grating is walled up, the barrier between native life and the Englishman's made more solid and permanent. But Trejago has learned enough for himself; he throws away his boorka, the false native costume which symbolises his adoption of native ways. He returns to the official routine, 'he pays his calls'. His sleep at times is disturbed, but the only strange thing about him that others can notice is the slight stiffness in his leg, thought to be a riding strain.

Here are some of the fixed ideas of Anglo-India: the barbaric but sensually attractive native world might lure an Englishman but never keep him; for being tempted Trejago was punished; he limped because he had lived amid the natives as someone other than a representative of the ruling caste; the English community could still accept him, for no one knew of his nocturnal escapades; they explained his stiff leg in terms of what was familiar to them.

Many of those who went out to India were courageous. As a 'heroic little band' they knew the discomforts and ravages to health. No matter what their opinions about India and the Indians they had left a familiar world for a foreign one. Many wanted to believe in the grand purpose, the noble calling of service for the empire, the great civilising force. Yet, most had to come to terms with the feeling of insignificance, of being 'little bits of dirt on the hillside'.

In these circumstances public ceremonies were specially important. A public event made for cohesion in the British community. The grandeur and splendour asserted what everyone in India wanted to believe: British rule was glorious and just. That English statesmen who acted in these ceremonies linked older political traditions with present rule in India.

The greatest of these spectacles was the Royal Durbar of 1911

when George V was crowned King-Emperor. When the King
and Queen arrived for their ten days' stay, it was described as
'a splendid dream', in which twenty thousand workers prepared
the site. 'But today the dream has come true.' A million pounds
was spent in building drains and polo-grounds for 233 camps
spread over twenty-five square miles. The King's camp covered
eighty-five acres and had red roads, green lawns and specially
transported English roses.[1] The *Times* correspondent could not
disguise the emotion of the day:

> One is forced to write mainly of its spectacular side, but no one who
> stood on the plains of Delhi today can have failed to feel that it re-
> called and symbolised the long and majestic story of two races whose
> fate has been interwoven, that it expressed the promise of a still more
> glorious and more closely united future. It epitomised the centuries;
> it made visions of the years to come seem real and immediate. Ships
> sailing into unknown seas, handfuls of men battling amid myriads,
> had set in motion a train of events culminating in this mighty gather-
> ing; all the past strife and turmoil of India, the splendour and the
> misery, the conquests which flowered and bore fruit and were over-
> whelmed in chaos, had been a preparation for this day of days, in
> which Princes and peoples gathered, after more than fifty years of
> tranquillity, to do glad homage to a British Emperor who came as a
> guarantor of peace and upholder of justice and freedom. One felt,
> as one gazed upon the scene, that the Durbar was not the apo-
> theosis of a tinsel Imperialism, it was the ritual of the unreasoned
> but increasing faith which has linked the people of a distant island
> with the ancient nations of the East in a common striving towards
> an exhalted end. Despite past differences, the mutual aims of Indians
> and Englishmen today found united expression in joyful devotion to
> the Crown.[2]

No one at the Royal Durbar could have imagined that George
V would be the first and last British monarch crowned in India.

[1] Hardinge of Penshurst, *My Indian Years*, 1948, p. 42.
[2] *The Times*, 13 December 1911.

TWO

INTRACTABLE REALITIES

ONE OF THE BY-PRODUCTS of the Industrial Revolution has been the growth of a heightened social conscience. The conditions of people working and living in the manufacturing cities could not forever remain hidden from social and political writers, government officials, and church leaders. The first 'white man's burden' was the cause of alleviating the suffering and discomfort of the working class. The European's religion, his trust in the progressive improvement of life through the application of science and technology and natural human compassion, helped to forge this conscience into a practical desire to know by statistical measurement the extent of human problems. Philanthropic and charitable institutions hammered at some of the bulges in working-class poverty, while government investigators reported in commission after commission about the practices of the new industrial society. People became trained to take up the cause of raising the standard of living for everyone within his own society, and all political parties in their own way took some interest and then pride in social legislation.

Could this heightened social conscience extend towards India? There, peculiar problems beset the most zealous reformer. Most of the population lived in some 450,000 villages which had not yet been touched by metalled roads or railways. Government reports in the nineteenth and twentieth centuries consistently remarked on the incomplete and tentative nature of their information. It would have been necessary for the British to establish a police state of unprecedented efficiency just to gather definite statistics about the population. In the end the very enormity of the problems discovered even from inadequate reports acted to discourage the planner. This is not to suggest that no attempt was made to improve the life of the people under British rule. Spurred on by utilitarian ideas, changes in the judicial and administrative systems were introduced in India during the nineteenth century. Yet, in the natural course of events, the Imperial Government might have been expected to try to increase efficiency by introducing reforms that were compatible with English practices or current 'advanced' thought. For example, the Indian Penal Code, enacted in 1860, made no attempt to codify Hindu and Muslim law but instead merely 'rationalised digests of English law and practice'.[1]

Besides the *Moral and Material Progress of the People of India*, 1859–1937, the British Government published regular reports on *Sanitary Measures*, 1900–1918, a *Quinquennial Review of the Progress of Education*, 1884–1919, *Railway and Irrigation Works*, 1899–1916. Though it suited the British Government to record what progress had been made in India as a result of their rule, social and economic reform never became the major preoccupation of government. The above-mentioned reports were more concerned with measures taken or in progress than an assessment of distressed areas. Significantly, the reports on sanitation, education, and irrigation ended after the First World War when constitutional reform became Britain's main policy for India. In the decades before 1918 concern was always circumscribed by caution. Lord Dufferin, speaking at the St Andrew's Day Dinner in 1888, explained:

> If ever a political organisation has existed where caution is necessary in dealing with those problems which affect the adjustment of the administrative machine, and where haste and precipitancy are liable to produce deplorable results, it is that which holds together our complex Indian empire: and the man who stretches forth his hand towards the ark, even with the best intentions, may well dread lest his arm should shrivel up to the shoulder.[2]

Practices of the Hindu religion particularly offensive to Victorians such as suttee (a widow's suicide at her husband's funeral pyre) were proscribed, though they were never wholly abolished. The annual reports of the Indian Government are

[1] E. Stokes, *The Utilitarians in India*, 1959, p. 225.
[2] B. L. Glover, *British Policy Towards Indian Nationalism*, Delhi, 1966, p. 187.

filled with items of improvement like the opening of an irrigation system, land reform, famine relief, the building of a school
or hospital. Yet considering the scale of problems, it never
seemed possible for the British fundamentally to alter the
conditions of Indian life, if only because the amount of money
required for major welfare legislation was seemingly beyond the
capacity of the people of India to pay or the British Government
in London to approve. Therefore, one improvement or a dozen
would eventually be swallowed up by the enormity of the
material needs of the people. Anyone who had stayed in India
for long was soon swept up by the feeling that there was nothing
to be done that would not seem insignificant in a decade. In one
of Rudyard Kipling's Indian stories, 'Thrown Away' from *Plain
Tales From the Hills*, a character expressed the despondency and
inertia that could take possession of the English in India:

> Now India is a place beyond all others where one must not take
> things too seriously—the midday sun always excepted. Too much
> work and too much energy kill a man just as effectively as too much
> assorted vice and too much drink. Flirtation does not matter, because
> everyone is being transferred, and either you or she leave the station
> and never return. Good work does not matter, because a man is
> judged by his worst output, and another man takes all the credit of
> his best as a rule. Bad work does not matter, because other men do
> worse, and incompetents hang on longer in India than anywhere else.
> Amusements do not matter, because you must repeat them as soon
> as you have accomplished them once, and most amusements only
> mean trying to win another person's money. Sickness does not
> matter, because it's all in a day's work, and if you die, another man
> takes your place and your office in the eight hours between death and
> burial. Nothing matters except home—furlough and acting allow-
> ances and these only matter because they are scarce. It is a slack
> country, where all men work with imperfect instruments; and the
> wisest thing is to escape as soon as ever you can to some place where
> amusement is amusement and a reputation worth the having.[1]

If the actual experiences of Viceroys, Governors, and civil
servants did not dampen their will to reform, there existed no
less an authority than a venerable conservative ideology to halt
innovation. Edmund Burke had played a leading role in the

[1] R. Kipling, *Plain Tales From the Hills*, 'Thrown Away', 1890, pp. 15–16.

prosecution of Warren Hastings and his policy of amassing Indian territory. For the same reasons that he opposed the French Revolution and defended the rights of the Irish and Americans, Burke asserted that no government or body of men was ever sagacious enough to alter the existing fabric of society, neither its own nor, least of all, someone else's. 'It is with infinite caution that any man ought to venture upon pulling down an edifice which has answered in any tolerable degree for ages the common purposes of society.'[1] The nature of man and society was so complex that no simplification—and all reformers must simplify by proposing some gross philosophical principle—could possibly supersede the positive advantages of current practice. Custom, morality, religion, class division, as they functioned in India, were logical, practical solutions to the needs and history of the people. That it took centuries to evolve such a society was for Burke an affirmation of the fundamental necessity of the institutions.

The source of Burke's ideas was his religious ideas. Since an omnipotent God extended laws to Asia as well as Europe, the sanctity of society was a universal truth. For individuals or a party to reform society was arrogantly to propose that ordinary men should be free to offend a portion of the divine moral order. Reformers teach men only a 'servile, licentious, and abandoned insolence'.

While it would be wrong to suggest that Burke anticipated the whole British attitude towards India, his ideas, however, were prescient. He confirmed that there was something inappropriate and wrong about Englishmen ruling Indians, a realisation felt by some administrators and visitors.

When the High Anglican Viceroy, Lord Irwin, later Lord Halifax, met Indian poverty face to face for the first time, what impressed itself on him was the reflection that the extent of the misery made 'silly and inapt' any idea of reform. It would be difficult to understand the reason or logic behind this attitude if it were not for the conservative predisposition to distrust reforms that try to change society. On 3 August, 1926 Lord Irwin wrote from India to his father:

[1] E. Burke, *Reflections on the Revolution in France*, New York, 1955, pp. 91–2.

After Church on Sunday morning I went to see the quarter in which
the depressed classes or 'untouchables' live. You can have no conception of the squalor—real pigsty fashion, and I have no doubt the
people who live in them are real pigs. But the classes of their own
countrymen just above them are almost wholly devoid of social conscience in the matter and I am told that oddly enough the depressed
classes themselves have a superstitious fear of coming into contact
with those above them. It is a very astonishing state of society and
makes all the theories of liberal reformers look silly and inapt.[1]

Though conservatism urged the Englishman to leave alone
the deep-rooted, cherished religious customs of the people, there
were also other motives. Far from subverting Hinduism, the
East India Company, quick to see profit, went into the business
of protecting Indian religious festivals. The Company levied a
pilgrim tax on visitors to Hindu shrines. From the festival at
Jagannath alone, from 1814 to 1831, the company showed a
profit of £99,000, though some of the money collected was
used to maintain the temples.[2] When Lord Curzon, Viceroy
from 1899 to 1905, preserved and refurbished Hindu and
Muslim monuments he was consistent with the conservative
view, that an English administration must respect the culture
of the country it rules.

Still consistent with conservative ideas, it was even possible
to accept that India must some day be self-governed, for no
matter how innocuous the British administration and prescribed
its powers, one people could not forever rule another. Rather
than fundamentally change the society they found, no mean
undertaking for a country the size of India, settled opinion
could take solace in the conviction that the Englishman's
presence, his style of life, manners, let alone business enterprise,
were all contributing to the education and development of the
native population.

Inevitably, such a point of view led to a certain over-playing
at being English among the Raj. Some of the scenes from the
imperialist's life might have been taken from *opéra-bouffe*. There
were interminable quarrels over precedence in British India.
The Government found it necessary to issue a table of etiquette

---

[1] Lord Irwin to Lord Halifax, 3 August 1926. Irwin Papers (IOL).
[2] R. Ingham, *Reformers in India*, 1956, p. 38.

and precedence which became a charter for English men and women. The Oxford University Press published in 1904 *Hints for the First Year's Residence in India*, presumably for those of the middle class sent out to India but unfamiliar with the 'correct' way to treat native servants:

> Never let any servant enter your presence coatless, or *en deshabille*, or when in full toilette, carrying a duster, as a badge of office. Discourage any tendency on his part to wear one end of his turban down his back. He should never wait at table without wearing his kamaband. Trifling as these offences are, they indicate a want of respect. No one understands better than an Indian the maintenance or loss of prestige.[1]

Strands of a more obvious conservatism blended into the careers of the Viceroys who went to India in the twentieth century. Of the eight appointed between 1900 and 1943, six were associated with the Conservative Party, six were the sons of peers, and seven had gone to public schools, five to Eton, one to Harrow, and one to Winchester. No Labour Party members were sent to India. One of the Liberals, Lord Reading (1860–1935), was a Liberal Imperialist with no small admiration for the Empire. On leaving India in 1924, he said: 'I return with a deeper realisation of the beneficent outlook of the British Empire. . . . I glorify in the high purpose it is our duty as citizens of the Empire to seek to achieve.'[2] The other Liberal, Lord Willingdon (1866–1941), wrote to Harcourt Butler his hopes for the future: 'The world is certainly topsy turvy but I hope the end of it may prove for us to be a Great Empire Federation when we can snap our fingers at the rest of the world.'[3]

The Viceroy occupied the most 'responsible, picturesque and distinguished office'[4] in the Empire. He had absolute powers of veto as well as the absolute right to pass legislation. The men sent to exercise this formidable authority were nurtured in upper-class privilege. They were chosen because they could be trusted to use such powers hesitatingly and only when law and order were threatened or when by their use a political crisis

---

[1] A. C. Wilson, *Hints for the First Year's Residence in India* ,1904, p. 36.
[2] H. Montgomery Hyde, *Lord Reading*, 1967, p. 393.
[3] Lord Willingdon to H. Butler, 9 April 1932 (IOL).
[4] *Indian Statutory Commission*, Vol. I, 1930, p. 177.

could be averted. None was dedicated to social reform. These men frequently likened their period in office to the management of their country estates. They vaguely believed in the moral purpose of empire, and nationalism was a nuisance to administration. India seemed to allow them to make personality more important than policies. By ceremonial tours, public utterances, interviews and conversations, the Viceroy made his mark. Lord Cromer described in 1918, in the language of the leisured gentleman, the prevailing twentieth-century conservative attitude to change in general, and with India in mind:

> I always bear in mind an axiom of Eastern administration that my father constantly quoted, and which was, that progress in all Eastern countries should be made at a steady jog trot, and that either a walking pace or a canter were equally disastrous to those who tread either of these paces. The tendency in most things today is unfortunately to canter. . . . I confess that I am a strong adherent of the jog trot principle of progress, which obviates all ill-considered projects passing into law.[1]

In government financial policy, a 'step by step' advance was judged more appropriate than a 'jog trot'. Financial orthodoxy as practised in England was a weight against all flighty government projects requiring expenditure. The impact of government on the impoverished millions was limited because British Rule flourished during the heyday of relatively laissez-faire ideas about the financial role of government. These ideas, reaffirmed by important government committees in London, the Geddes Committee (1922), the Macmillan Committee (1931) and the May Commission Report (1931), called for low taxation and government expenditure, balanced annual budgets, respect for the sinking fund and debt repayment; while development and investment should come from private enterprise, government-assisted projects, like the railways and irrigation in India, were expected to be economic and self-supporting.

Conservative financial ideas restricted the amount of help the Imperial Government could give the people of India. An *a priori* commitment to short-term financing with limited government expenditure made it unthinkable for the British or Indian Governments to develop a large national economic plan which

---

[1] Lord Cromer to H. Butler, 8 October 1918, Butler Papers (IOL).

assessed Indian needs and special problems. It was also firmly
believed that Britain could not be expected to finance from her
own revenues Indian social reform. The structure of the
imperial, central, and provincial finances after 1919 was so
complicated by different authorities and interests that it was not
possible to create very efficient or far-reaching social welfare
schemes.[1]

Financial orthodoxy had a sombre and cautious tone which
always warned, puritanically, against 'extravagance'. Extravagance was usually defined as a term of criticism against proposals
which asked for large capital expenditure. In 1935 the British
Government asked Sir Otto Niemeyer, a former Treasury
official and director of the Bank of England, to consider the
financial implications of the new Indian constitution. While
finding it just possible for the financial requirements of the new
constitution to be met by the existing structure and sources of
revenue, he could not resist cautioning the provincial governments not to expect the central government to support or carry
large deficits.

> It is necessary, however, to add a word of warning, lest the provinces
> be tempted to mortgage in advance these prospective additional
> resources. No one can say in present circumstances that this pro-
> gramme will with certainty prove feasible, and it must be regarded
> as subject to the important reservation that if necessary the
> Governor-General will have to exercise his delaying powers under
> the second proviso to sub-section (2).[2]

When the Secretary of State weighed the implications of Sir
Otto's report and the requests from the provinces for additional
money, aspirations were judged to 'outrun financial possibilities.'
Only disadvantages were seen to result from anything but a
severely limited policy.

> We wish to make it clear beyond peradventure that we see no pros-
> pect whatever of being able to undertake additional burdens of this

[1] 'How a Minister for Industries can co-ordinate his work in industrial development with a ban not to touch any of the subjects (factories, boilers, electricity,
waterpower, mines, and labour) so intimately connected with it, and without the
least power to have a hand in them, it is impossible to conceive.' Memorandum by
Sir K. Reddy (Madras) to the Reforms Inquiry Committee (1924).

[2] *Financial Inquiry, Report by Sir O. Niemeyer*, 1935, Cmd. 5163, ix, 669, p. 18

magnitude (1 crore of rupees a year), or indeed as we have previously tried to show, of any appreciable size at all. This means that if concessions are to be made to individual provinces, it can only be done at the expense of the other provinces, and not of the centre. And, for our part, we see great difficulties in any redistribution of relief, which may easily create more discontent than it alleviates.[1]

[ii]

Geographically, India is set off from the vast expanse of Asia by the snow-peaked Himalayas that contain within and around them jungles, deserts and swamps. The lesser mountain ranges of the Western and Eastern Ghats, along the coast of the southern half of the peninsula, girdle the gentler hills of the Deccan and the plains of the Indus and Ganges. The physiognomy of the land is among the oldest on earth. Like an enormous cow, the melting snows of the Himalayas feed the great rivers of the Indus and Ganges. The Indus with its fewer tributaries waters only a relatively small proportion of the land surrounding it. This semi-arid region has low, unreliable rainfall and rocky, uneven ground which adds to the difficulties of cultivation. The plains and the plateaus watered by the Indus system are spotted with oases of fertile land on which are grown cereals, rice, pulses, millet and cotton. The proliferation of tributaries and gentler sloping of the Ganges helps it to disseminate the heavy rainfall of the Gangetic plain. Here is the most highly agricultural land in India with more than half the total area under cultivation, producing rice, wheat, pulses, cotton, tea, jute and cereals.

Climate and weather fix the rhythm of the Indian seasons with the extremes of aridness or monsoon rains. It is possible to hear in Indian music the dramatic themes of the land: stillness, tension and explosion.

Most of the Indian sub-continent is marked by a predominantly dry climate in which the long and severe dry season is not offset by adequate rainfall. Only in eastern East Pakistan (Bangladesh) and a strip of land running from Bombay to the tip of the peninsula is there enough heavy rainfall to compensate for the dry season. India, lying in the monsoon belt, is

---

[1] *Other Official Views to Sir O. Niemeyer*, 1935, Cmd. 5181, xix, 111, p. 12.

lashed from mid-June until October by torrential rains coming from the north-east and south-east. The onset of the monsoons may vary considerably, as well as the amount of rain they bring. There has been as much as a thirty per cent difference in the amount of rain between one year and another. The heavy, concentrated downpour often gluts the parched land with too much water, washing away precious top-soil and accelerating the dilution of nutritive organic and mineral compounds in the soil. As the rain subsides a long dry season follows with a parching of the land. Life noticeably wilts, the soil surface is baked hard and even the light is dust-tinted.

The constant warmth and long periods of high humidity speed up the chemical process which forms the soil. The torrential nature of the monsoon rainfall also acts to increase soil decomposition with a corresponding lessening of the soil's fertility. Many sections of the land are susceptible to drought either by the late arrival of the monsoon or simply when there is less rainfall in a season. Heavy rainfall on dry, hard soil can make the land so waterlogged that it is unfit for cultivation, while water evaporation leaves salt deposits on the top-soil which mar crop production. In West Pakistan alone 50,000 to 100,000 acres deteriorate each year. During the intervals between wet and dry weather low pressure over the Bay of Bengal creates cyclonic storms of hurricane and typhoon intensity. As the high winds strike the coast they can drive large quantities of water over low-lying areas. In 1876, it has been estimated, over one hundred thousand people were drowned in less than half an hour, and perhaps an equal number died from an epidemic of fever caused by effects of the storm. Since cyclones of great severity occur about once in five years, the Indian finds not only his land, his food, but also his life constantly threatened by these disastrous alternations between drought and flood.

The general climatic conditions prevailing in India demand great effort for low yields. In some areas it takes four thousand tons of water to grow one ton of rice, a thousand tons of water to grow one ton of corn. This same climate stimulates the spread of weeds, fungi, and insects which interfere with plant growth. Even before men organise and structure life on the sub-continent, the harsh and dramatic aspects of the landscape are fixed like a deity, ruling imperiously.

The population of British India and the Indian states was 388,988,000 in 1941. The people of the sub-continent have at different times represented between one-fifth and one-sixth of the population of the earth. The pattern of habitation has followed the human suitability of Indian geography. The highest densities are in the Gangetic plain where the alluvial lowlands have either ample rainfall or significant irrigation systems. Here in 1941 there were on average between 500 and 750 persons per square mile. The southern tip of the peninsula, in the provinces of Madras and Travancore, was almost as heavily populated. The other most populated districts were on the eastern and western peripheries of the sub-continent, while large regions in the centre and north-west had between 0 to 250 persons per square mile. Thus there was considerable variation in the amount of congestion from region to region. The average for the whole of India was 246 people per square mile.

The absolute ratio of land to population when Britain ruled India does not point to a country bursting at the edges. Most of the population was spread over the country in small villages, with under 500 inhabitants. In 1941 there were 450,000 such villages. Only 12·8 per cent of the population lived in towns of any appreciable size. This was the picture of India in 1941 even after the country had seen a rapid increase in population since 1891. In fifty years India's population had grown by almost 110 millions, an increment of fifty millions from 1931 to 1941 alone. Population dispersion helped to give the impression that 'Indians were everywhere' but illusive. 'Have you ever met an Indian? Met an Indian. An *Indian?* How many Indians had I met? To speak to . . . at least a thousand. But it would be hopeless to try to remember them individually.'[1]

The lack of concentration in the Indian population helped to confirm for Western observers the lack of unity in the country. Like its population India was a 'variegated assemblage of races', diffused and fragmented. The existence of some six hundred native states of varying size introduced further political subdivisions in the country. Language added its own complication.

[1] B. Nichols, *Verdict on India*, 1944, p. 11.

There were some 222 vernaculars in India. English was spoken among a small educated minority, while most of the people spoke Hindustani. Muslims used the Urdi script and Hindus Hindi. In the south, languages belonging to the Dravidian family, Telugu, Tamil, Kanares, Malayalam, prevailed. Bengali was the natural tongue for the people of Bengal, Western Assam, Bihar and Orissa; Marathi in parts of Bombay, Central Provinces, Berar, and Hyderabad; Punjabi in the Punjab and Kashmir; Gujerathi in Gujerat and Baroda State; Rajasthani in Rajputana and Central India; Sindhi in Sind, and so on. Inevitably the English came to believe that whatever they did in India, they were making some contribution to breaking down the many disuniform aspects of Indian life by giving their language to the country.

A high absolute ratio of man to land is not in itself inimical to economic self-sufficiency. A large population is a form of natural resource possessing skills, a capacity for labour, and a consumer market for production. In modern times people in industrialised countries have preferred to live close to one another in conurbations; high population densities demand considerable organisation of human activities, but this has not been insurmountable everywhere. For India, what has always been crucial is whether the large population can sustain itself through sufficient production. Yet the poor soil and adverse climate undermine the success of human effort. Yields in food production are low. The average annual yield of milk per cow in India is forty gallons, in the United States it is 495 gallons. Whereas the yield of corn is ten to fifteen bushels per acre in India, in Western Europe it is forty. With the majority of the population making a living from agriculture, the peasant farmer or ryot embodies the plight of his country.

The overall increase in population which has occurred in India in the twentieth century intensified the pre-existing struggle for enough to eat. More people created a greater demand on food production while paradoxically more people living in the villages and working the land caused the holdings to be fragmented, which in turn reduced the amount produced per person. A society that lives at the subsistence level finds it difficult to make adjustments for eventual efficiency. Cow dung instead of being used as a fertiliser was dried for fuel. Religious traditions and the low level of education prevented peasants from adopting new machinery to aid production. To harvest a crop with a scythe was almost unknown in India, and oxen were used to tread out the grain, which was then winnowed by the wind. Though irrigation systems were extended in British India (use of which was an important source of revenue),[1] the amount of land under cultivation was enlarged, and alterations in crops helped to increase overall production, these changes never satisfied the nutritional demands of the country, nor were they able to accommodate a larger population. Only the mechanisation of farming and the development of strains of seed and livestock suitable to conditions on the sub-continent would have been able to improve yields and production dramatically. However, an expanding labour force stimulated the use of manpower instead of machines, while throughout the century the fall in farm prices in Europe meant that the English felt little urgency to invest in Indian agriculture in the circumstances of world over-production of food. The change-over to machinery and scientific agriculture occurred slowly in Britain in the 1920s and 1930s. Being reluctant modernisers at home and relying on cheap foodstuffs from Australia, New Zealand and South Africa, the English were unwilling to be large-scale experimenters in agricultural efficiency in India. Besides, there were other more profitable enterprises open to Europeans. The advances that occurred in agricultural production and marketing in Europe and America did not happen in India.

India has experienced varying degrees of famine throughout her history. The late arrival or early departure of the rains meant that survival was a gamble against the rains. Drought in 1896–7 affected at least 225,000 square miles and threatened 62,000,000 people with starvation. In the last three decades of the nineteenth century four severe famines struck the country,

---

[1] 'The country we have been passing through is cultivated, and looks green, entirely owing to the irrigation works. Two million pounds have been spent upon a canal, 40 miles long, bringing water from the river Chenab, and the land now, instead of being a barren waste, pays the government 25 per cent, so that in a few years the outlay was repaid.' Lady Minto, *India, Minto and Morley 1905–1910* (1935), p. 61.

while in the twentieth century the Imperial and Indian Governments had to allot money annually for famine relief. Even when there was enough to maintain life, the people of India were always deficient in protein and fat-rich foodstuffs. In the past as in the present the Indian consumption of animal fat, protein, calories, and vitamins is among the world's lowest, a fact which is attested by the distinctive Indian physique which expresses the genealogy of under-nourishment. The frail body-type, delicate bone formation, slim figure have been conditioned by generations of inadequate diet. One investigator wrote, 'One could swear that the enormous eyes, admirable in themselves, have eaten up the thin faces.'

India's climate, if less than perfect for men, is nearly ideal for many micro-organisms which are harmful to health. The monsoon rainfalls, which wash away land and flood out the inhabitants, leave cesspools for organisms to multiply. Under these conditions and with the normal bodily functions of the millions of people living in villages, an extensive system of sanitation was essential. Yet it was and is possible to find the same water tank used for drinking and washing, or lavatories drained into the water supply. As a result India for most of her history has been ravaged by disease of all kinds, but especially cholera. In addition the religious fairs which brought millions of pilgrims to be purified by ritual cleansing in the waters of the Ganges have aggravated the possibility of infection, whilst the river itself became a van sending the pollution hundreds of miles away. One has only to compare India with Europe to see the nature of the problem. Whereas by the end of the nineteenth century the cholera bacillus had been virtually eradicated in Europe, in India it continued to reap an appalling harvest. In 1900 at least 800,000 died of it in British India alone. By 1943 the number was 460,000. Calcutta was known as the 'world headquarters of cholera'. It lacked any system of filtered drinking water and forced thousands of people to use a few water closets. Open drains spilled into water holes from which people drank, and rubbish decayed in the street. In some Indian villages cholera is worshipped as a fierce goddess. Animals are slaughtered until the ground is drenched with blood in the hope that the hungry goddess will be satisfied. Plague was also endemic in India. The bacillus which enters the blood is carried by a rat-flea. On the death of the rat it attaches itself to another living organism. A chain of infection thus begins, especially in the unhealthy sanitary conditions of India. From 1896 to 1921 at least 33·6 millions died of the plague.

However fragmentary the information about the general life of the masses of people in India, evidence about the diseases of poverty during the years of British rule exists. Added to the figures of deaths from plague and cholera, those of normally non-fatal illnesses like smallpox, fever, dysentery, and diarrhoea, also figure in the official government statistical abstracts as causes of death. Before the Second World War malaria caused twenty per cent of all deaths, tuberculosis around fifteen per cent for urban dwellers. Those who survived lived to suffer:[1] at least five per cent of the adults had venereal disease; there were a million lepers; perhaps half a million blind or with defective vision from trachoma. Diptheria, whooping cough, pneumonia, meningitis, rabies were common health risks. Malnutrition, inadequate housing and clothing increased the susceptibility of people to illness. There were not enough doctors, nurses, or hospitals to treat the whole population.

Historians must appear callous towards the poor of India.[2] Often the only way they have to describe the conditions of life is through neutral but malleable statistics. Conclusions are

---

[1] Illness was one of the main causes of suicide. 'The reason in most cases was a state of mental depression due to disease.' K. R. Eates (Indian Imperial Police, Sind): 'Memoirs Grave and Gay of Crimes, Criminals and Court' (unpublished), India Office Library.

[2] Indifference to the weight of numbers also permeated official reports. See Sanitary Measures:

1899–1900. 1902 Cd.

Land Revenue Report 1902 lxxi 527.

'The year 1899 was generally a healthy one, though the failure of the monsoon rains in Western and Central India changed in climatic conditions of the last quarter for the worse, and terminated the prosperity which the two previous years had established.'

Total deaths: Cholera	169,000
Smallpox	48,000
Fevers	4,000,000
Dysentery and Diarrhoea	243,000
Total	6,460,000

difficult to draw because the numbers in themselves do not state from how many thousands dying or suffering from a malady one is justified in making a judgement. Neither does the emotional reporting of the passing Western visitor tell the story of the life as lived by the poor who do not live among the statistics or adjectives because they are locked in the unrelenting conditions which keep them poor. While statistics help anyone to comprehend social life by gaining distance and perspective, the poor lack this very distance.

The last statistical abstract for British India gives some glimpses of the magnitude of the nation's health problems. In Calcutta in 1938–9 there was a total population of 1,100,000 within the municipal limits. Nearly the whole population, one million, were treated in hospitals, no doubt because the sick were brought to the city from outlying districts. For all of British India in 1938, eighty-seven million people were treated in hospitals. Yet it is probable that only about a quarter to a third of the total population ever entered hospital.[1] The majority of the population, though suffering from illnesses, received no treatment or went to the village medicine man, herbalist or witch doctor. Hospital care was not free, which would discourage the poor, while it was commonly believed that to enter a hospital was to die because it was 'the place where people died'.

The chart below gives the number of people treated in hospitals for some, but not all, illnesses. It is a sample, and a conservative one, of the extent of illness. If the numbers below are multiplied by four, since only a quarter of the population probably used hospitals, a crude estimate can be made of the amount of illness in British India in 1938.

TABLE I

Diseases treated in 1938 in hospitals

Dysentery	1,499,619
Malaria	13,163,203
Animal parasites	4,604,691
Diseases of the nervous system	2,105,258
Eye	9,300,142

[1] In 1925 the municipal nurses of Bombay visited forty-five per cent of the registered births in the city. Twenty-seven per cent of these births took place in hospitals, confirming the figure of twenty-five per cent to thirty-three per cent as a reasonable estimate of those using hospitals.

Diseases treated—*cont.*

Ear	5,205,659
Respiratory, excluding pneumonia and tuberculosis	6,038,952
Dyspepsia	2,413,367
Diarrhoea	1,670,973
Digestive	5,279,231
Ulcers	5,037,131
Skin	6,565,966
Injuries	4,391,369[1]

The treatment of the mentally ill describes an aspect of hospital policy. Most of the mentally ill lived among the normal population either undetected or in some way accepted in village life. It was clearly the hospitals' aim to discharge each year very nearly the same number of people admitted. In 1938, a typical year, 2,589 were admitted into mental hospitals. In the same year 600 died, nearly twenty-five per cent, while 1,077 were discharged as cured, and another 863 were classified as 'discharged otherwise'. As a result of death and discharge, 2,540 left mental hospitals, or nearly the exact amount admitted.

The limitations and hazards of the Indian environment place unusual burdens on human resourcefulness, ingenuity, and intelligence. Western education, if it was going to offset the debilitating environment, had to replace the informal learning habits of caste and village with a system of learning rooted in science and technology. In many ways the small units of Indian life, the family and village, that comprised the bulk of the population, suited a policy of improvement through education. The agricultural cycle left much free time to learn, the uses of knowledge could be demonstrated in the gains it brought to everyday life. A practical education if on a sufficiently wide scale could not but help assist national development. As people learned rudimentary facts about hygiene, diet, and cleanliness, illness could be curtailed.

Yet under British rule the vast majority were left ignorant and illiterate. The Government of India spent around 4 per cent of public revenues on education in the twentieth century. Just over 3 per cent of the population were under instruction. 'The bulk

[1] *Statistical Abstract for British India, 1930–1 to 1939–40*, 1942–3 Cmd. 6441 pp. 115–17.

of the pupils do not study beyond the lower primary standard or
its equivalent, and the actual length of school life is about four
years.'[1] The 1931 All-India Census showed that the number of
children in schools decreased from the ages of ten to fifteen from
those enrolled from the ages of five to ten. Since students were
the most numerous group convicted of revolutionary crimes,
there were political as well as financial reasons for curtailing
education expenditure. In 1937 the Government of India conceived its most valuable contribution to the proper development
of education in India, not to build more schools or reduce the
90 per cent illiteracy, but 'to provide a clearing house for ideas
and a reservoir of information on the subject'.[2]

Instead of an army of technocrats and doctors slowly com-
bating the handicaps of the environment, the English education
system produced droves of lawyers and lesser civil servants.
Ironically it was the trained lawyers, Gandhi and Jinnah, who
led the national revolt against British rule. The British system
of education in India indicated that the political and administrative needs of ruling India took precedence over the social and
economic ones, with the result that the life of ordinary people
remained the same as it had always been. India's 'dumb
millions' under British rule did not acquire the special training
they needed to cope with their many problems.

There was no minimum age educational requirement in
India. The insufficient number who passed through the system
were not trained in ways to aid the country's development.
Macaulay's famous education minute of 1835 set down the
broad purpose of Indian education, which was to create a class,
or small élite, 'Indian in blood and colour, but English in taste,
morals, and in intellect'. Presumably, this élite, by its example
and moral probity, would act as a beneficent influence on the
bulk of the population. The statistics of passed candidates in
medicine in 1939–40 show that there were just over eight
hundred trained medical staff for the year, with no Doctors of
Hygiene, seven Bachelors of Hygiene, and four Bachelors of
Sanitary Science. This was not enough to sustain the existing

---

[1] *Education in India*, Cmd. 256, 1919, xxxviii, p. 4.
[2] *Moral and Material Progress and Condition of India*, 1936–7, xx, 1041, pp. 125–
126.

deficient medical system, let alone affect the nation's health in broad terms.

The higher rate of illiteracy among Indian women made it less likely that they would change unhealthy family habits. The tendency of Indian women to regard their husbands as 'lord and master' was part of the habit of mind that induced them to accept the fixed practices of traditional marital life with little questioning. The Hindu wife was taught social customs and religious rites. Her practical or useful knowledge was such that it supported the existing way of things. The custom of child marriage and early motherhood placed a special kind of hazard on women and their children. A girl became a mother often before she had either the mental or physical strength. When the raising of the age of consent was debated in the Indian Legislative Assembly in 1922 it was estimated that 3,200,000 mothers died in the agony of childbirth in each generation. In 1931 there were over 4,000,000 married girls aged five to ten and 105,000 widows of the same age. As we have seen, a stern kind of determination asserted itself on the Indian children who survived birth, in the form of an unhealthy environment, inadequate diet, and the inheritance of a physique with few immunities or overall strength to repel illness. Early marriage also contributed to deformity at birth. Since male offspring were needed for religious ceremonies, caste rules made marriage obligatory; woman's importance was mainly as mother of male children. Parents were eager to marry off their daughters to rid themselves of a financial burden. They preferred to make some marriage in preference to none. It frequently happened that young girls married men of fifty and over. Inevitably there occurred early widowhood. In 1929 there were 26·8 million widows in India. The widow was maintained by the family of her former husband but not allowed to remarry. Placed in a position of servitude since she was no longer the deliverer of male offspring, she was expected to take up the innumerable household chores.

Muslim women, though marrying later than Hindus, suffered the peculiar effects of the system of purdah. Living in a fixed quarter of the house, the women had little education to lighten the strain of seclusion. There was also a high incidence of rickets, tuberculosis, and osteomalacia because confinement deprived the women of enough air, light, and exercise.

[iii]

Generations brought up under the influence of the idea of religious toleration have found it easy to blame the Hindu religion for the continuation down the decades of India's backwardness. The Reformation and the virtual separation of Church and State anticipated a general liberalisation of life which was followed by scientific and technological changes that raised men's ability to sustain more people in a better standard of living. The very importance of Hinduism as a social organisation and a system of ideas speaks to these critics of a fundamentally reactionary society, mesmerised by unconstructive feelings that are sanctified by tradition, antiquity, and ceremony.

Institutionalised religion need not always address itself to the 'eternal human questions' which all men share. Man's religion is an explanation, made acceptable because it is inherited as a part of the social framework, of what he finds mysterious, frightening, and painful. The ideas and the ceremonies of the religion are acceptable because ultimately they organise and control human uncertainty and fear. Religion by explaining things makes life easier; it is the expression of how men have adjusted to the universe they live in, and at times it interprets everyday experiences. Even if religious duties are arduous, and religious ideas inconceivable, the faithful receive deep satisfaction from the knowledge of how life works, and the personal possibility of attaining salvation.

Though the physical environment of India may not have been as harsh in prehistorical times as today, nonetheless nature's capacity to be arrogantly indifferent to men's needs must have impressed itself on the minds of the people at an early date. Hinduism is pervaded with a consciousness of the environment. As in other primitive religions it tries to understand wind, heat, and water through its near-mystical powers to dissolve, restore, destroy, and cause to reproduce and grow. The historical and geographical changes undergone by the peninsula have not radically altered a sense of the dominating presence of nature in everyday life.

One way in which Hinduism respected the forces of nature was to give to all the creatures of the earth a portion of the essential universe. Man could be understood as a literal microcosm of the world. Since human organs are in continual contact with the external world, the function of vital organs like eyes, feet, mouth, nose, genitals form a link to a cosmic reality. Breathing organs accept the atmosphere, the feet are moulded. to the earth on which they move. In the hymn of the Purusha in the *Rig-veda*, man is pictured transformed into the features of the physical world. 'His head becomes the heaven, the navel the atmosphere, his feet the earth, his eye the sun, his manas (mind, will, libido) the moon, his mouth Indra and Agni (fire), his ears the heavenly regions, his breath the wind.'

One of the most prominent gods of the *Rig-veda* is Indra, who, by manifesting himself as thunder and lightning, is made the war god of the heavens, dedicated to fight the demon who strives to prevent the monsoon waters from reaching the thirsty earth. Considering the vital role of the monsoons for Indian agriculture, it is not inappropriate that this god, sung by poets as the creator and director of all things, should give his name to the sub-continent.

The Indian view of nature responds to the activities of climate. Organic life, plants, animals, and men, are wandering souls, that is they contain within themselves some cell-like substance that passes from one life or body to another at death. 'The self at death approaches another body just as a caterpillar passes from one blade of grass to another.' All the creatures of earth are linked by the process of disintegration, transformation, and rebirth which happen to them. Inorganic forces, on the contrary, earth, fire, water, and wind, are ruled and protected by divine rule, Brahman. This inorganic structure is the stage erected by Brahman on which the organic souls must struggle and act. Creation means *srishti*, a discharge, emission, or setting free, coming from Brahman, passing through the inorganic bodies, and falling on organic life, an almost metaphysical conception of rain.

Though it has often been seen as the cause of the continuance of conditions of poverty, Hinduism originated as a response of men to an environment which they were powerless to change.

Indians do not feel any less than other people the sorrows of infant mortality, illness, deformity, sudden and unexpected death, or lingering human decay. On the contrary, they are more aware of sorrow because the incidence of events causing human sadness and misery has probably been higher in India over a longer period of time than in any other country. But so many of the tragedies of Indian history occurred before the Industrial Revolution, that is before men had the power on a large scale to control the forces of nature or to avert the consequences of natural disasters, that the religion which developed on the sub-continent was entirely peculiar to the area. Any attempt to understand Hinduism must relate it to the special features of India, a view which Hinduism confirms by asserting that the religion belongs only to the people of India who live in India. Hindu religious ideas can be studied as a human reaction to the generally negative character of the physical environment. By examining the religion one can measure the mental effects of continual hardship imposed by the activities of nature in India. One can weigh the cumulative effects of hunger, disease, frequent bereavement, illness, upon a culture that must, like any other culture come to terms with its own experience.

Hinduism begins with a keen awareness of the omnipresence of human suffering. The second *Brahmana* describes the nothingness before the creation of the world, when there was 'nothing whatsoever', in the language of poverty. Before genesis the universe 'by death indeed was covered, or by hunger, for hunger is death'. To be alive, according to the ideas of the religion, is to be chained to the endless procession of birth and rebirth, the recurring process that inherently has no meaning. Death starts again the cycle by which the soul forms and enters into a new body which must experience again anxiety, woe, and unfulfilment.

One of the main purposes of the religion is to turn the disadvantages of life on the sub-continent into the spiritual ideal of life renunciation. That life is hard assists the believer to take interest in his spiritual soul, since he is enjoined to bear the sorrows of the world lightly in order to free himself from caring about worldly success and striving, and devote himself to the perfection of his soul. Salvation is made possible by an inward concentration and the performance of Hindu ritual, which lead to a knowledge of spiritual reality. The frequency of external failure is thus sublimated as the inwardly attainable dreamless sleep of psychic stillness and peace. Detachment is one of the highest virtues for it indicates that the soul is above caring for the things of this world, that it is no longer concerning itself with what is selfish, materialistic, and transitory.

One of the ways to find release from the physicality of existence is the technique of Yoga, whereby an 'apathetic ecstasy' is induced by exercise and breathing. By a sort of auto-hypnosis, yogins concentrate on inner psychic experiences generated in the unconscious. To be ready to accept the irrational sensations, all conscious, rational thoughts are systematically purged. Eventually even the normal pain felt from lying on nails cannot disturb the inner concentration. Asceticism can lead the practitioner to a state of nirvana when, wanting nothing, the self strives for nothing. Self-mortification, self-sacrifice, sexual abstinence, silence, fasting are acts of self-control that bring the practitioner to 'truth'.

Marx has written that 'man makes religion, religions do not make men. Religion is the sigh of the oppressed creature, the sentiment of a heartless world, and the soul of soulless conditions'. Nowhere does his judgement seem more apt than in India. The austerity of the religious ideal responds to the insurmountable difficulties of the Indian environment. Men must have often felt themselves helpless before the chaotic events of wars, disease, and an inhospitable climate. Hinduism strives to compensate for this by turning human energy inward to find, in the cauldron of the unconscious, sensations of such intensity that they become the meaning of life.

Hinduism, however, did not attach itself to the consciousness of people through its metaphysical ideas. The ideas were reinforced by the social structure, the system of caste. The religion conceded a great deal of toleration to local sects and allowed the development of sub-castes. Hinduism was essentially a religion bred on ritualism. Ceremonial observance became the way a person carried out his duty of *dharma* towards the Hindu community. Since the country defied permanent centralised organisation, the religion had to be self-regulating, as each person, by accepting his caste designation and the corresponding obligations, fulfilled his holy purpose. The four major castes, Brahmans or priests, Kshatryas or military and political, Vaishyas or merchants, Shudras or labouring, structured a formal order on the chaos in the country. Caste *dharma* fixed tribal territory, social status, occupation, marriage partners, diet and at times guaranteed subsistence to its members. The immediate community, therefore, acted as an affirmation of inherited caste status. The economic and social result of this system was to uphold never-changing traditional methods. It imparted an essentially negative and melancholy attitude towards all worldly changes.

An analysis of the physical environment alone does not reveal all of India's intractable realities. Though Hindus out-numbered Muslims by about three to one over all of India, in some areas, Bengal, the North-West Frontier, Baluchistan, and the Punjab, the majority of the population were Muslims.[1] The failure of the two largest communities in India to live and work together as one added danger and tension to any change or event.

One of the early analysts of the communal problem between Hindus and Muslims suggested that economic hardship created among the Indian people a sense of frustration and a readiness to simplify all problems by avenging the wrongs done to them through rioting. 'An analytical study of the Indian social mind reveals the deep impress of the logic of the stomach upon the Indian people.'[2] The existence of the two religious communities, in many ways antithetical to each other, transposed the struggle to exist on to another plane. This new plane released non-social instincts which led one community to attack the people and places of worship of the other, as if flying at 'one another's throat[s] would satisfy the demands of hunger'.[3]

Some explanation for Hindu-Muslim hostility lies in the history of India. Muslims raided northern India on a large

---

[1] Division of the population in the four Muslim provinces, 1931.

	Hindus	Muslims	Sikhs
Bengal	21,570,407	27,497,624	10
Punjab	6,328,588	13,332,460	3,064,144
North-West Frontier	142,977	2,227,303	42,510
Baluchistan	41,432	405,309	8,368

[2] N. Banerjea, *Psychotherapy of Indian Riots*, Calcutta, 1941, p. i.

[3] *Ibid.*, pp. 6–7.

scale since the first millennium. The weak and disunited Hindu kingdoms lost successive battles to the invaders. By the beginning of the eighteenth century most of India was subject to the rule of the Mogul Empire. Mogul rule could be beneficent. Akbar (who ruled from 1556–1605) not only built sumptuous palaces at Agra and Fatehpur Sikri, but established a rule of religious toleration, accepted the advice of both Hindu and Muslim nobles, abolished tax and other privileges based on race, encouraged inter-marriage, and even established a religion *Din Ilahi*, to incorporate different practices into one acceptable religion. When, however, Aurangzeb succeeded to power (1658–1707), fanatical bigotry revived. Hindus had to pay a special tax, were excluded from office, and had many of their sacred temples destroyed. In the Hindu villages life and property were insecure. As a result Hindu society drew inwards, making more strict the social organisation by preventing inter-marriage with the conquerors. The two separate communities lived uneasily together. Under British rule the two religions had separate electorates, education, press, literature and languages, which contributed to an aggressive and uncompromising attitude towards the other community. When many low caste, 'untouchables', and other 'unclean' castes converted to Mohammedism, Hindus, if they were to survive, had to sever normal relationships.

Nor was it difficult in the course of everyday life for the two communities to antagonise each other. In the 1920s it was headline news if a Hindu married a Moslem. The heroes of one people were enemies to the other. A communal riot occurred when a procession called out the name of a man who was an assassin to the other community. Hindus worship idols, Moslems forbid their worship. The Koran enjoined their destruction. Moslems destroyed or mutilated Hindu graven images, and converted temples into mosques. Historical monuments often commemorated a humiliation for the other community. These reminders, like the famous Shiva temple of Benares, half of which remains in its original form as a Hindu temple, the other half a mosque, was 'a standing disgrace to all Hindus of all times'.[1] Ceremonies offended religious sensibilities. The cow, worshipped as a mother in Hinduism, was used for a sacrificial

---

[1] R. Agarwala, *The Hindu-Muslim Riots*, Lucknow, 1943, p. 10.

death in the Bakra Id festival of Moslems. Fireworks exploded at festivals could puckishly be directed towards the property of the other community. One Hindu custom, the throwing of coloured water on passers-by, could be less than fun to a non-believer. Certain trees were sacred to Moslems, but Hindus felt that when a tree grows too large and obstructs the road it should be removed. The polluting of water, a very sensitive issue in a hot and dry climate, could occur for Hindus if Moslems used a leather bucket to draw water from the well. Bitterness could also have economic causes. Hindus, who had earlier than Moslems taken advantage of the English educational opportunities, got government jobs and were in a position to assist through official patronage their own people. Hindus were also village financiers, or *banias*, who were notorious for exploiting the small landholders and tenants who were mainly Moslems.

Riots between different Indian communities, like natural catastrophes, periodically swept India in varying degrees of ferocity. Wild gangs could find reasons for aggression in the extremes between rich and poor, the fervour of religious passion, and disdain for authority. A communal riot could happen in almost any part of India, though some areas were more susceptible than others. One such area was Malabar between the western face of the Nigiri Hills and the Arabian Sea. From 1836 to 1853 there were twenty-two outbreaks of violence, from 1858 to 1921 thirty-five. In 1911 Hindus outnumbered Muslims by three to one, but in some towns such as Erode and Walluvanad, Muslims or Moplahs outnumbered Hindus. These were the chief areas for outbreaks.

The Moplahs were descendants of Arab traders and sailors from the ancient period when Malabar was the trading centre for pepper. They married low-caste Hindus and openly received converts. Frugal, hard-working, but poorly educated, the Moplahs took on heavy unskilled manual labour such as clearing the jungles. Few had substantial property while the large families they produced sub-divided what land they did own. As a result the Moplahs were poor, leasing land from and paying tax and rent to Namburdiki or Hindu landowners. They belonged to a fanatical religious sect, the Sunni, which revered the Sultan of Turkey; they believed that to die fighting a non-believer was to gain heaven and luxury. Homicidal riots usually started when a convert to the sect decided to return to Hinduism.

In 1921, inspired by the Khilafat movement to believe that the British Government was against Islam, the Moplahs declared 'swaraj' and formed gangs with makeshift uniforms and assorted weapons. Some assembled at Tirurangadi where in 1894 the bodies of Moplahs had been burnt during an outbreak of violence. They picketed the police headquarters and went on to assault a number of Tiyya toddy drawers, breaking their pots. The district magistrate attempted to arrest the leaders of the gang, but they were protected by the mob. In the course of searching for the leaders a mosque was entered and, according to rumour, defiled. This was enough to create a holocaust. Mobs of between 5,000 and 10,000 attacked post offices, railway stations, houses of officials, liquor shops and plantations. Arson and murder were committed; 'almost every Hindu house where loot could be obtained was attacked and plundered'.[1] There were a number of cases of forceful conversion and women appropriated as wives. At least a thousand people died during the Moplah rebellion.

It was never easy to understand the Indian problem. The pressing social and economic needs were on such a scale that it was necessary for political rulers to adjust their scale of values to weigh Indian realities. The world-famous Indian poet and artist Rabindranath Tagore spent a considerable amount of his creative life seeking to evoke strong national images. He chose to symbolise India as a primal, splotchy-skinned beast, over-grown with its immense body, both powerful and awkward yet still tied to a docile harmlessness. The ungainly proportions and clumsiness continue, however, to engender in the artist feelings of tenderness towards this overgrown child. 'When they get wild, they are furious, but when they calm down, they are peace itself. The uncouthness which goes with bigness does not repel, it rather attracts.' About the painting 'Agonised Cry' (*c.* 1928–30) he wrote: 'Life chained to an imperfect mind sends its agonised cry.' This bulky, misshapened child, the great mass of the Indian people, eluded the understanding of British rulers, but never-theless became the inspiration to the Indian nationalist movement.

---

[1] *Moplah Rebellion*, Cmd. 1552, 1921, xxvi, 237, p. 38.

THREE

REBELLIOUS NATIONALISM

[i]

REBELLIOUS INDIAN NATIONALISM as it passed from the nineteenth to the twentieth century resembled the pre-natal human embryo; it developed slowly in order to gather within itself the older traits of its culture. Just as the human foetus by six weeks passes through a fish-like phase, thus suggesting an earlier stage of pre-human life when the species lived in water, so Indian nationalism accumulated previous stages in the history of its consciousness until it found a near reincarnation of archaic India in 'Mahatma' Gandhi.

Gandhi's first political principle was for Indian political leaders to identify with the village peasants and by this to find real India, 'to see how we would like to drink water from the pool in which the villagers bathe, wash their clothes and pots and in which their cattle drink and roll. Then and not till then shall we truly represent the masses and they will . . . respond to every call'.[1]

Gandhi adopted the dress of the ryot, the loin cloth or dhoti, and his frugal diet. At his trial at Ahmedabad in 1922 for writing three seditious articles he gave his profession as farmer and weaver though he was of course a London-trained barrister. The ashrams or religious retreats he built in India were economically self-sufficient model villages where non-violence, truthfulness and hand-weaving were practised. For him the struggle for Indian independence was a private test in the quest for truth.[2] For millions he embodied a simple, pre-industrial

---

[1] *Young India*, 11 September 1924.

[2] The four photographs of Gandhi, between pp. 62 and 63, show something of the process of physical and spiritual self-transformation which he passed through to

India. Gandhi conformed to the established religious idea of saintly leader and as such mixed an essentially political demand for independence with a moral fable where the lowly confronted the great to teach how affairs of state should be settled. Gandhi wished the claims for political justice to be subservient to *satyagraha*, where the claimant used the cause of independence as a process towards his own self-purification through personal suffering. Passive resistance expressed the 'force' of love and truth, the literal meaning of *satyagraha*. The freedom fighter had to attain a high level of self-discipline to welcome the blows of his enemy and make no effort to restrain him. Non-violent civil disobedience was an 'all-sided sword' which eventually would dissolve the will of the user of violence, in the context of events the British ruler. Gandhi explained the special kind of courage expected of the *satyagrahi* with a question: 'Wherein is courage required—in blowing others to pieces from behind a cannon, or with smiling face approach a cannon and be blown to pieces?'[1]

To accept suffering was one of the oldest tenets of Hinduism. To experience and submit to pain, even to induce it, was an effective means to escape from the physical present into a higher spiritual state. Gandhi dramatised the struggle against British rule by conceiving it as the triumph of the soul over the body. One of his messages from prison called for 'peace, non-violence, suffering'. At times he longed for the martyr's end. 'I have some time prayed God: Give Thou to me death by the hands of this Government. . . . We must willingly receive bullets in our bodies.'[2] British officials were dismayed by Indian tactics because these ideals were so completely foreign to them.

Under Gandhi's influence Indian nationalism became an alliance between middle-class, professional leaders and the poor peasantry. Leaders and masses shared beliefs. Cow protection was adhered to as a religious duty because this taught reverence

make himself a worthy opponent of British rule. For him, the struggle for political independence could only come *after* casting out the foreigner in one's self.

[1] M. K. Gandhi, *Hindu Swaraj or Indian Home Rule*, 1909, quoted in H. Jack, *The Gandhi Reader*, 1958, p. 114.

[2] *The Times*, 14 February 1922 quoting from *Narjivan*.

1a. J. Gantz (1802–1862) 'View of the Banqueting Hall, Madras', c. 1826. Drawing and watercolour capriccio. By kind permission of Lord Dufferin. The European section of the picture on the right is classical, neat, and vigorous. The native section by contrast is dishevelled, with buildings fading into ruins, and people inert. The rich foliage of the 'European' tree almost shames the scraggy, unkept trees and shrubs which crown the squatting Indians

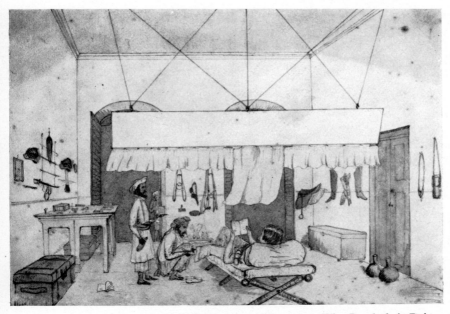

1b. G. F. Vesey (1839–1899) 'My Room at Dinapore. The Punkah is Being pulled from the back-room', c. 1876. Pencil and ink drawing. The young officer in spartan surroundings and with modest possessions maintains the traditions of learning while native servants administer comforts

2. Coronation Durbar, Delhi, 1911. Their Imperial Majesties, King George V and Queen Mary, arrive at the Central Pavilion. See pages 32–33

3. M. K. Gandhi, see pages 102–107, in 1886 (top left), in 1888 as a law student in London (top right), in 1906 as a barrister in South Africa (bottom left), in 1914 as a satyagraha marcher (bottom right)

4. R. Tagore (1861–1941) 'Agonised Cry', *c.* 1928–30. See page 60

for lower animals and thus life itself. The cow was not slaughtered for food but admired as 'a poem of pity' which inspired non-violence. Gandhi gave up drinking milk when he learned how milk was taken from the cow by the process of pookha (the cow had air or straw forced up its organ of generation to prevent any milk from staying in the udders). To revere the cow as a mother also attached people to the soil, for even in towns and cities the presence of cows roaming the streets unmolested was a reminder of the countryside and India's ancient heritage.[1]

To end rural poverty Gandhi advocated the making of homespun or *khadi*. Though he had not seen a chakka or hand loom in 1908, and later his supporters roamed the countryside to find a usable hand loom and someone who knew how to operate it, Gandhi thought making homespun would be a profitable means for peasants to fill the months of enforced idleness between the planting and harvesting of crops. The rural community had to be self-sufficient. Home spinning would restore the prosperity of former times when the villages and towns 'smiled with plenty'.

By 1920 the spinning-wheel had become the symbol of simplicity and economic freedom, the practical embodiment of an ethical system which rejected British rule by boycotting British cloth. It asserted Indian self-sufficiency, and revived an 'ancient rustic art and rustic song'.[2] When Gandhi became president of the Congress Party he made the wearing of khadi a strict condition of membership and advised Congress members to spin for an hour a day. Thus, demand for homespun was stimulated and the equality of all classes was established since bodily labour, in this case spinning, could be practised by all.

Gandhi taught how nationalism and cultural self-awareness were inextricably bound together. The traumatic events which preceded the birth of nationalism in the nineteenth century— the dissolution of the Mogul Empire, the atomisation of political life, the dominance of the British—placed obstacles before any Indian who wanted to find his identity in his own history. Since many British officials disparaged Indian languages, customs,

---

[1] C. F. Andrews, *Mahatma Gandhi's Ideas*, 1930, p. 33.
[2] *Young India*, 17 February 1929.

and philosophy, the first nationalists had to look past these criticisms to find pristine India. Initially it was easiest to look for some compromise between English and especially Christian judgements of India and India's own 'eternal truths'.

Ram Mohan Roy (1772–1833) has often been cited as the father of Indian nationalism. Yet his ideas were more an attempt to reconcile British criticisms of Indian society, Western rationality and Hindu spirituality. Roy was born to a wealthy Brahmin family in Bengal. He acquired a broad knowledge of Persian and Arabic languages and studied Buddhism in Tibet. From 1809 to 1814 he was the native assistant to the collector of revenue in Ranpur. In 1814 he inherited his family's wealth and retired to Calcutta where he devoted himself to the translation of sacred Hindu texts into the vernacular, social reform, and the creation of a common universal religion based upon the unity of God. English rule, though a foreign yoke, he thought would benefit the inhabitants of India. He opposed suttee and polygamy and showed that they were not enjoined in the ancient Hindu texts. He favoured the remarriage of widows and went so far as to see in Christianity a code of morality which was best calculated 'to elevate men's ideas to high and liberal notions of God'.[1] His major work, *The Precepts of Jesus* (1820), denied the divinity of Christ and the miracles attributed him but accepted the moral code as the 'guide to peace and happiness', the nirvana of Hinduism.

While making concessions to British ideas, Roy subtly rebuked English arrogance by suggesting that truth and the true religion were not the exclusive prerogatives of 'high names and lofty places'.[2] Roy conveyed his thought in high-flown rationalism as in his essay *The Missionary and the Brahman Being a Vindication of the Hindu Religion Against Attacks of Christian Missionaries*.

In Bengal, where the English are the sole rulers and where the name Englishman is sufficient to frighten people, an encroachment upon the rights of her poor, timid, and humble inhabitants and upon their religion cannot be viewed in the eyes of God or the public as a

[1] *English Works of Raja Rammohun Roy*, Allahabad, 1906, p. 483.
[2] *The Missionary and the Brahmin, Being a Vindication of the Hindu Religion Against the Attacks of Christian Missionaries*, Calcutta, 1821, p. 138.

justifiable act. For wise and good men always feel inclined to hurt those that are of much less strength than themselves, and if such weak creatures be dependent on them and subject to their authority, they can never attempt, even in thought, to mortify their feelings.[1]

Roy took at face value English professions of good will. From the association with Englishmen Indians would gain useful assistance: improved methods for cultivating the land and deliverance from rank superstitions and prejudices. India, governed in an enlightened manner, 'will feel no disposition to cut off its connections with England'.[2]

Christianity and Hinduism were clearly united in the religious society Roy founded in Calcutta in 1828, the Brahma Samaj. Roy took the content of the new religion from ancient Hindu texts while the methods of devotion were very like the weekly Christian service. The society met once a week from seven in the evening until nine during which time a service divided into four parts took place. The first part was the recitation of texts from the ancient Vedic hymns, then followed a reading from passages from the Upanishads translated into Bengali. A sermon was delivered in the vernacular, and finally the congregation sang hymns, some composed by Roy himself, with musical accompaniment. Though Roy believed that the future religion of India would make Jesus supreme, Jesus would also be loyal to Hinduism. Careful to conform to Hindu orthodoxy, Roy had the sacred Vedas chanted in a special ante-chamber so that they might not be polluted by contact with the vulgar; he himself took great care to maintain Hindu dietary laws.

Ram Mohan Roy was a major figure in the Hindu renaissance of the nineteenth century. His religious writings and translations into Bengali of the ancient Hindu texts and the New Testament established him as a scholar of world reputation. He was made a maharaja by the Emperor at Delhi and went to England to advise Parliament on judicial and revenue systems operating in India. He was the first Indian accepted as 'a gentleman' in Britain. This kind of eminence has made him seem the first example of a new India. Though no rabid patriot, Roy did anticipate in a sketchy way the pattern of later nationalism. He

[1] *Ibid.*, p. 137.
[2] Raja Rammohun Roy, *Remarks on Settlement in India by Europeans*, 1832, p. 4.

admired ancient Hinduism; he believed in partial reform of 'superstitious practices' of the religion, he created a special institution to incorporate his ideas, and he asserted the immutable character of India. 'India would remain Indian no matter what the influence of the West.' Roy also indicated how any awakening of Indian consciousness must primarily take place within the context of Indian religious ideas, for spirituality was the country's primary cultural force. An Indian could criticise the Hindu religion, as did the Christian, without losing respect for or belief in Hinduism.

Nationalists might want to glorify their country by rekindling the lamps of Indian culture but first it was essential to find that culture lost in sculptural adornments, a vast literature, and an obscure history. The genes of rebirth were formed from the innocuous curiosity about Indian fauna and flora, languages, poetry, and painting. Scholarship and research, like courtship, provided a necessary phase to accumulate knowledge which prepared for the consummation of the Indian renaissance in the independence movement. One of the ironies in the history of the British in India was that Britons were the midwives of Indian nationalism, since it was they who began and stimulated research about the country they ruled.

William Jones (1746–94) was the first great British scholar to read and write Sanskrit with ease. The early culture of India, to a century trained to admire the classical eras of Greece and Rome, stimulated him to 'know India better than any European ever knew it'. In 1783 he was made a judge of the high court at Calcutta, and in the following year founded the Bengal Asiatic Society which published his discourses on Indian subjects. These included the study of Indian chess and music, the orthography of Asiatic words, a comparison of the gods of Greece, Italy and India, Hindu chronology, and local botany and zoology. He made translations of literature and wrote poetry which emulated the delicate and florid style of Indian writers. His Hindu teachers paid him the highest compliment when they called him 'a Hindu of the Military tribe'. He planned, but did not have time to finish, a comprehensive digest of Hindu and Mohammedan law which might become the standard of justice for the 'millions of innocent and useful men' under British rule.

Some of the servants of the East India Company could not help but bring with them the curiosity about the natural world which affected men of intelligence in the eighteenth century. Books of drawings and descriptions of Indian natural history, often executed by native artists, were published in the *Annals of the Royal Botanic Gardens*, Calcutta. Contributions to knowledge were made by books like R. Russell's *An Account of Indian Serpents* (1796) and *Descriptions and Figures of Two Hundred Fishes Collected at Vizagapatam on the Coast of Coromandel* (1803); W. Roxburgh's *Plants of the Coast of Coromandel* (1795–1819); and J. Royle's *Illustrations of the Botany and Other Branches of the Natural History of the Himalayan Mountains and the Flora of Cashmere* (1833–9).

Literal descriptions of what existed suited the abilities of the amateur artists and scholars who first portrayed India. James Fergusson (1808–1886) retired from indigo farming to travel throughout India from 1835 to 1842 to draw and measure buildings and monuments. He published *Picturesque Illustrations of the Ancient Architecture in Hindustan*, and *The Rock-cut Temples of India*. A paper he gave before the Royal Asiatic Society in London so stimulated interest that servants of the Company were officially instructed to measure and draw antiquities in the different presidencies of the country.

Educated Indians soon joined or founded societies for the study of their country. The questioning, curious, and critical attitude demanded by study did not remain confined to historical and environmental subjects. The very nature of British rule led a number of associations to become political, either to act as a pressure group on the British Government or to propagate a new religious view, which because of the marriage of Hinduism and the institutions of society meant resisting the encroachments of government or missionary. Typical of this self-interest was the British Indian Association founded in Calcutta in 1851. Financially supported by wealthy landowners it struggled to defend the landowner's interest, especially when the Government tried to control rents or tamper with the permanent settlement. The Arya Samaj was founded in Bombay in 1875 to reassert Hindu orthodoxy in the face of westernising tendencies. The Theosophical Society established branches in India after

1879. Admiring the mysterious powers of Hinduism the spiritual East became a combatant against the practical and rational West. Two prominent theosophists, Annie Besant and A. O. Hume, helped to found the Indian National Congress in 1885.

The Indian National Congress, like the Indian Renaissance in general, owed much to the activities of the English. A. O. Hume joined the Indian Civil Service before the Mutiny. He took up the radical position that Indian loyalty to the Empire would only exist when British rule was seen to be just, impartial and efficient. Much that he saw caused him to worry. Hume tried to bypass the officials who labelled him 'a mischief-monger' and 'an Indian Parnell' to influence directly decisions at the top. He expressed himself with nervous excitement; his criticisms had a bluntness and urgency that made him seem more anti-British than he really was. He wrote to Lord Dufferin in 1886 warning him of how little about what truly existed in the country reached him.

> You do not get the truth—that virtually when it is alleged that the cat stole the cream, you blandly say—'Pussy, you surely did *not* steal that cream?' The virtual indignation of that *felis domesticus* may be conceived. I said that (unless when thieves fall out) the service and race bias is so strong that you never get the truth. The race bias makes the ordinary Magistrate let off the ravisher or the murderer; the service bias makes the whole official series, more or less, uphold the erring Magistrate. The whole tone of administration is growing rotten. I listen to men talk—Alas! in too many cases, the old desire to have right done, for the love of justice and of God, has melted into a determination to prove the service right, and uphold its dignity and impeccability—and woe to official . . . or outsider who tries persistently to lift the veil.
> The bureacracy is demoralised. You may laugh, but it is alas! too true, and there is no remedy but to break the traditions of the service to introduce a new and powerful element into the administration.[1]

In 1885 the Indian National Congress had measured support from the new Viceroy, himself slightly uneasy about the autocratic nature of British rule. The second and third meetings of the Congress were welcomed by official social receptions. An

[1] Glover, *British Policy Towards Indian Nationalism*, p. 128–9.

Indian national organisation which asked for change but remained moderate and loyal in tone would actually assist government. Extremists would be isolated, liberal criticism, Indian and British, which complained that the administration was indifferent to native wishes would be assuaged, while at the same time the broader political education of Indians towards participation in affairs would occur. The danger was, as Lord Dufferin knew, whether an organisation established to advise could stop short of criticisms blatantly hostile to the ruler, whether it would not claim rights the Government was unable or unwilling to grant. An all-Indian party would assert a place of influence not yet agreed to by the highest officials in the administration. What would happen when the new party found the Government unyielding to the 'national' demands? Would there be an increase in hostility between the Congress and the officials, providing just the reason for not approving of the existence of the Congress? The inherently cautious Government would drive the inherently impatient Congress Party to become exclusively anti-British, 'like the Irish revolutionists'. In time Lord Dufferin's worst fears were to be realised, but only after many years when the Congress found a way to join with the masses to make them an asset, in order to contradict the Government's allegation that the small professional Congress Party did not represent the nation as a whole, and when events proved the British Government less liberal than generally believed.

But from 1885 to 1920 the Congress Party remained, as Dufferin expected, 'neither very dangerous nor very extravagant'.[1] The essential moderation of the party was assailed by militants like Tilak and crises like the partition of Bengal, but divisions among Hindus and disagreements between Hindus and Moslems weakened, by confusing India's aspirations as a whole. Congress resolutions often reflected the vested interests of the English-educated wealthy and professional classes who supported the Party. Their demands fell into three categories. (1) Indians should be able to participate in greater numbers and in positions of executive responsibility in government, the civil

[1] Lord Dufferin to Lord Kimberley, 26 April 1886, quoted in Glover, *Official Attitudes Towards the Congress*, p. 176.

service including the police, the judiciary and the army. With this claim began the interminable wrangling of rulers and ruled about numbers, proportions, and the specific authority of Indians. Issues like simultaneous examinations in England and India for entering the civil service and equal pay for native and European teachers were essentially middle-class requests for fair opportunity within the existing framework of British rule. (2) The removal of laws and regulations effective in India which contravened English legal principles and political traditions. A large percentage of Congress leaders were English-trained lawyers who could point to the discrepancy between the assumptions and precedents in English law and legal practice in India. Press censorship, taxation without adequate representation, lack of Indian representation in government, deportation without trial, and the magistrates' right to impose punishment by whipping for a wide range of crimes indicated a double standard at work in British rule. (3) Congress asserted their right to criticise the Indian Government and the official bureaucracy as if it were a legal review body. From this grew the protest that Congress should be consulted before policy was decided and that Congress opinion should influence the decision-making process. Many Congress resolutions simply wanted government to look at matters from an Indian perspective; they called for financial independence in the provinces, reductions in military expenditure, and inquiries into the economic conditions of the people.

What prevented Congress resolutions from being anything other than principles *potentially* dangerous to British authority was the general meekness of the Party's leaders and the fact that no tactics could be devised which coupled fulfilling the intentions of the resolutions and keeping the respect of the British Government. Too much depended on the willingness of the Government to grant requests. G. K. Gokhale, the greatest leader in this phase of history of the Congress Party, also founded the Servants of India in 1905 which believed in the divine purpose of British rule; though self-government was on the horizon it had to be 'earned by Indian assimilation of the British way'. The early period of the history of the Congress revealed that, until Indians believed they were ready for self-government, there was insufficient militancy to challenge British rule.

Militancy blossomed with the discovery and lauding of the traditions of Indian life. Traditional India was preferred over anything associated with British rule. At first it seemed, in the manner of Ram Mohan Roy, that nationalism would be a way to recharge a lethargic people with a new concept of themselves and their country founded on reforms derived from contact with the West. The turning point in the history of Indian nationalism occurred when India's new conception of itself followed the model of the culture already familiar to the masses of people. The past was thus used to condemn or question the present; the original character of Indian society was praised in order directly to cancel the value of present British rule. As Indian nationalism became clearer about its ends, it became more sympathetic and compatible with the older forms of Indian life.

Significantly, Nehru called one of his books *The Discovery of India.* The letters he wrote to his daughter while in prison continually assumed the relevance of the past for the nationalist revolutionary. Though he acknowledged how much better it is to make history than read it, and that there were sad and unhappy periods in the past in India, 'but on the whole it is a splendid past of which we may well be proud and think with pleasure'.[1] As Nehru wrote the letters, old India became personally more important to him than the intellectual's analysis of 'the burden of old traditions' in a backward country. Even the clinging, hampering customs which diluted all change were customs common to people, a unifying base with mysterious powers straddling centuries, drawing peasants, leaders, and countryside together.

One morning in 1931, Nehru had woken early to see the dawn when he heard voices and rumblings in the distance. 'The pilgrims were marching in their thousands for their morning dip at the [River] Sangam, where the Ganga meets the Jumna and the invisible Sarasvati is also supposed to join them. And as they marched they sang and sometimes cheered mother Ganga-Ganga Mai ki Jai—and their voices reached me over the walls on Maini Prison. As I listened to them I thought of the power of faith which drew vast numbers to the river and made them forget for a while their poverty and misery. And I

[1] J. Nehru, *Glimpses of World History,* 1942, p. 4.

thought how year after year, for how many hundreds or thousands of years, the pilgrims had marched to the Triveni. Men may come and men may go, and governments and empires may lord it awhile, and then disappear into the past; but the old tradition continues and generation after generation bows down to it.'[1]

The British could be categorised as foreigner and enemy, who neither cared for nor understood the uniqueness of India. British presence, reforms, attitudes could be readily interpreted as examples of the foreigner's inclination to rob their country of its essential character. Everyday incidents became a common proof of English misunderstanding, further evidence of the unnaturalness of millions of people perverting their own culture to suit the foreigner. Since the English were prone to make individual Indians the specific cause of their general discomfort at having to live in India, there was no shortage of scenes to show how insensitive the Raj could be. Colonel Drury in his *Reminiscences of Life and Sport in Southern India* tells the following charmless story about Indian fecklessness.

> Onwards I rode till about eight o'clock it began to wax very warm, and, alas I had no prospect of breakfast before me. When I started I wrapped up a cold fowl, a biscuit or two and a piece of cold mutton, and summoning a boy from the village, had ordered him under threat of immediate chastisement to run as far as his dirty feet could carry him to the next bungalow, only twelve miles, a mere step for the lad, who had moreover the promise of three pence held out to him as a douceur at the end of his journey . . . but of course, I over-took him before I had gone a mile.[2]

Indian nationalism also had the assistance of venerable institutions assisting their work of uniting the country, opposing British rule, and extending the belief in Indian self-sufficiency. The system of caste practised throughout India, even among some Muslims, taught the people of India to accept diversity and to have a special attachment to their local environment and community. Caste induced immobility, only more compellingly to integrate a person into his region, occupation, and social responsibility. The rewards of the caste system were consider-

---

[1] *Ibid.*, p. 21.
[2] Col. H. Drury, *Reminiscences of Life and Sport in Southern India*, 1890, p. 23.

able: pleasure in fulfilling one's duty, so important in Hinduism, assistance in all the phases of human development, birth, marriage, death, and burial. National pride in India began in simple local attachments, a fondness for one's own shrines, or holy river.

Much of the history of India militated against a nationalist idea becoming based upon central, abstract theories remote from everyday life. Villages were left untouched by centralising political authorities. Neither the Mogul nor the British Empire was powerful enough to subvert the structure of Indian society founded on caste and village. Hinduism, without a church or defined body of dogma, became in practice the performance of rites designated by caste. The local character of the system allowed for a multiplicity of cellular divisions and varieties, letting the basic idea adapt to change. Caste divisions, sub-divisions, contradictory stories, customs, and laws embellished the 'common cultural idiom' of caste. The caste system prized exclusiveness, aloofness, and self-reliance which in the context of the political struggle for independence became a national expression of a local truth.

Outstanding physiographical features are associated with Hindu deities and with incidents and characters in the epics and *puranas* [ancient poetical works in Sanskrit]. Every major shrine in India has a *sthala purana* describing the mythical associations of the place, and linking it up with divine and epic characters. Eventually, local myth finds it way to the sea of *puranas*, *upapuranas* (minor *puranas*) and epics. Indian intellectuals laugh at the inconsistencies in, and absurdities of, the *puranas* and epics, but they fail to perceive the function which the *puranas* form, viz. knitting together into one religious society the numerous heterogeneous groups in India, and giving them all the sense that their country is sacred. Patriotism is invested with a religious quality. The epics and *puranas* have also helped considerably in the great task of assimilating the many diverse groups which were marginal to, or completely outside, Hinduism. They have also given art forms to different parts of the country which beneath their diversity deal with incidents in the lives of the deities and epic characters which are familiar to Hindus every-where in India.[1]

[1] M. N. Srinivas, *Caste in Modern India*, Bombay, 1942, p. 106.

Like the institution of caste the Indian village gave to the majority of people a definitely organised community of ancient origins dependent on itself for government, justice, and means of living. Village life reinforced the commandments of caste by making the village public guardian over actions and observances and making these part of the daily routine. The village strove to produce all the goods and services it needed from money-lender to barber while at the same time it conditioned people to subsist on their own efforts. The socio-religious government of the village consisted of a headman who was the richest person in the settlement, who held his office, as he did his property, by hereditary right. In no sense had he absolute power. He ruled with the help of the *panchayat*, or 'council of five', which could in practice be made up of many more than that number. The *panchayat* had representatives from all the major communities living in the village including Muslims and the headmen of the different castes and families. It had responsibilities for organis-ing village rituals, arbitrated on minor disputes between villages, set taxes or other contributions from families for work necessary for the community as a whole. The British Govern-ment in the nineteenth century made the local *panchayat* respon-sible for maintaining roads and water supplies. The *panchayat* also carried on negotiations with communities outside the village and with the provincial government on issues of state. It is always wrong, however, to stress the formal nature of the village institutions. Institutions in India contort to human prac-tice. For example the head of a caste did not necessarily attend the village council meeting, and someone else, keener or more loquacious, might be sent in his stead. The size and nature of village life, therefore, taught the members of the community to live with one another, for people and places were permanent.

The Indian village became to the nationalists another model of Indian life to place against the intruding English foreigner. As one of the most ancient Indian institutions it stood in their minds for a special quality of endurance and order. Its anti-materialism and self-reliance were to become ideals for the nationalists, arguments to show how the people of India, the simplest ryots, could manage for themselves. When the Royal Commission Report on Agriculture in 1928 advised the break up of the small village to draw the villager into the factories and towns and cities as a means of raising his standard of living, the defence of the village as a way of life fitted neatly into the nationalist's contention that the British philosophy of improvement meant the destruction of the most significant Indian folkways. That philosophy of reform called 'pointing the way' or 'guidance is far more called for than anything in the nature of what, for want of a better word, we shall call charitable assistance' did nothing for the ordinary villager but advise his degradation, his transformation from a fixed place in Indian society to a rootless proletariat.

[ii]

Economic issues and the conditions of poverty have aided the growth of nationalism in Asia and Africa over the past hundred years. Colonial administrations took as one of their axioms that real responsibility for policy should rest with them, and thus indigenous peoples were consciously restricted from the higher reaches, the commanding heights, of power. The European ruler was clearly responsible for economic and social policy. This made high officials of colonial government easy targets for nationalist criticism because their powers and duties were extensive and noticeable. The psychology of nationalism demanded the apportioning of blame, with the leaders of the independence movement claiming for themselves the right to make judgements. The nationalists reasoned: Britain ruled India, but the country was poor and remained so. Good will, pious intentions, sympathy seemed ethereal measured against the conditions of poverty. They could ask guileless questions. Britain was the wealthiest country in the world, was this because she ruled India? If the justification for British rule was that it extended the material and moral improvement of the Indian masses, why did the masses remain poor and illiterate? When can government policy be judged; when can the rulers be found to fail in their duty? Who has the right to pronounce on government policy?

The structure and function of the Indian Government made it clear who had power. If rulers ruled they were responsible for what existed in the country. Indian nationalism acquired a degree of innocence in its own mind and among its diverse adherents when it frequently decided not to participate in constitutional reforms introduced by the British. By avoiding office they could not be blamed for the ills in the country.

British reforms became more and more British and therefore foreign when the major political leaders refused to work them. To join the enemy was to become like him and liable to the kind of blame the nationalist leaders reserved for the British. Thus the very nature of the nationalist position created added strain in Anglo-Indian relations. Whereas the British saw constitutional reforms as 'tests and trials', steps in progressive development towards responsible government, the Indian national leaders several times after 1919 rejected participation in the reforms lest the clarity of one of their essential distinctions be lost. With so much in India confused the matter of non-participation rendered the political struggle a fight between opposites. The idea of non-cooperation itself was to be enshrined as an ideal of revolt.

Indian nationalism has been frequently defined in moral terms, interpreted by Indian historians and others as a revolt inspired by rights and principles. The saintly figure of Gandhi has cast much of the nationalist movement in a silhouette of Indian moral philosophy. Participants in the movement liked the moral argument because it implicitly attacked the pragmatic style of British politics. Because of the great tradition of Eastern thought, peculiar Indian ideas touched the well-springs of culture. It was easy for freedom fighters in their books, articles and speeches to use the cultural idiom of thought as propaganda. In the excited climate of opinion in the 1920s the tentative, relative and obtuse arguments derived from economic trends were out of place. The statistics of Imperial and provincial administration were the facts of the foreigner; with right on their side there was less need to quibble over numbers.

Such points of view should not obscure how cunningly Gandhi drew on the dire conditions of the people in his mass civil disobedience campaigns in the 1920s. As he made clear many times, no government could be good that left millions 'soaked through and through in ignorance' and poor. The plight of India's masses, essential to the idealism of nationalism, was woven like the homespun cloth, into a spiritual and material form, the one reinforcing the other.

The call for national independence became a popular mass movement in a time when India as a whole experienced a period of relative prosperity. In the 1920s India maintained a favourable balance of trade for eight of the ten years. The average trade surplus was 66.08 crores of rupees. This was due to several different factors: the removal of wartime restrictions; the expansion of the world economy and thus demand for Indian raw materials which made up the bulk of the export trade; the rise of export prices.

India also showed signs of achieving economically what the Congress Party claimed politically, that the country should be self-sufficient. In the 1920s India purchased less manufactured goods than before while the government policy of 'Stores Purchase' meant that the country would try to purchase Indian goods as far as possible. The most important factor in India's decade of prosperity was the number of good monsoons after 1922; on this production and prosperity were based. The following table compares pre-war and post-war export production and export value in two of India's trading assets, tea and cotton, and shows the high increase in production in the 1920s.

TABLE II

	1909–14*	1919–24*	1924–29*
	(* Quinquennial average.)		
RAW COTTON			
Production (1,000 tons)	430	521	610
Export Value (lakhs of rupees)	3,327	6,473	7,160
TEA			
Production (1,000,000 lb.)	266	320	347
Export Value (lakhs of rupees)	1,306	2,692	2,972

Mining and industrial production also rose significantly in the 1920s. India's population grew by nearly thirty-three million in the decade. Thus at the same time that nationalists asked for independence, both the economy and the people expressed a new strength. These factors may partly explain the support nationalists gained from the population as a whole. A certain optimism and will to live manifested itself at the very time when Indian leaders claimed India's capacity to rule herself.

Yet these signs of economic self-sufficiency were only relatively better compared with the past. In absolute terms the decade did not witness anything like real prosperity or a fundamental improvement of life and work. The conditions of poverty could still be used as an example of the effects of British rule while India's economic ills were attributed to the policies of the Imperial Government.

Tables III and IV list the principal sources of revenue and expenditure for 1927–8, a year chosen because it is typical of the decade and because it preceded the turmoil created by the Simon Commission, the world economic slump, and civil disobedience.

TABLE III. PRINCIPLE SOURCES OF REVENUE (IMPERIAL AND PROVINCIAL)

Lakhs of Rupees (1 lakh = 7,000 rupees)

	1927–8
I. Land Revenue	31,44
II. Taxation	
Customs	47,37
Excise	17,26
Salt	537
Opium	307
Income Tax	14,81
Stamps and Registration	14,02
III. Commercial Services	
Railways	628
Posts and Telegraphs	47
Irrigation	146
Forests	229
Total	143,55

TABLE IV. EXPENDITURE

	1927–8
I. Debt Services	11,99
II. Military Services	54,79

Table IV—*cont.*

III.	Civil Works	12,68
IV.	Civil Administration	
	(i) General Administration	12,89
	(ii) Justice, Police, Jails	18,67
	(iii) Superannuation	573
	(iv) Education	11,88
	(v) Medical and public health	525
	(vi) Agriculture	207
	(vii) Scientific Departments	99
	(viii) Ports and Pilotage	23
V.	Famine Relief	7
	Total	137,91
	Revenue in **excess** of expenditure	564

For most of the years of British rule land revenue was the major source of income. It was a rent tax paid by the growers of crops either directly to the Imperial Government or indirectly through the villages and zemindars. What was unique about this tax system was that it was not uniform throughout India, the heaviest burden falling directly on the cultivator of the land, the poor ryot. The money due was a percentage of his annual crop, which in theory could be 50 per cent, but often was modulated according to annual production. In good years the rent was high, in poor ones low. Such a system allowed little surplus for fertilisers and new tools. In a subsistence economy with marginal profits, the system kept the peasant in debt by fixing a large portion of his crop as rent or tax.

The injustice to the poor farmers was obvious when compared with how the Government taxed other, more prosperous sections of the country. In 1793 the East India Company made a Permanent Settlement in Bengal and later in other places whereby former Mogul tax farmers were made proprietors over lands they had formerly administered. The zemindars, as they were called, agreed to pay then and forever a fixed amount annually, based upon the estimate and returns of the previous year. The amount assessed was high, 10/11ths, which no doubt attempted to take into account inadequate returns. By the 1920s this system saw wealthy zemindars paying tax on eighteenth-century scales, though the value of land and the yield had considerably increased. Land that produced no crops in 1793 but did so later owed no tax since they were in the area of the Permanent Settlement. Thus in the city of Calcutta in the 1920s land earning thousands of rupees per acre obliged the owner to pay in Land Revenue a quarter of a rupee per acre.

The greatest boon to wealth in India was the low rate of income tax. There was no income tax on agricultural income, by far the greatest source of wealth in India. 'Neither the zemindar himself, in respect of his zemindary, nor any of the immediate holders, in respect of their tenures, pays any contribution whatever to the state in the shape of income tax.'[1] While the poor peasant farmer had a permanent obligation to pay the state a proportion of his meagre produce, the wealthy land-owners paid tax neither according to their earnings nor their ability to pay. Income tax, a direct tax on wealth graded according to earnings, was unusually low in India compared with England and other countries. It was levied on non-agricultural incomes exceeding £150 at a rate of $2\frac{1}{2}$ per cent, rising to 10 per cent over £3,000. Supertax was 38 per cent on incomes over £3,750. This explains why the revenue raised from stamps and registration, a comparatively small item of revenue, nearly equalled the amount collected in income tax in 1927 (see Table III). Income tax in Indian finance was not the productive source of revenue it was elsewhere in the world at the same time. This system maintained the discrepancy between rich and poor. Insufficient money was raised for projects of welfare and improvement (see Table IV). Expenditure on justice, police, and jails exceeded the amount spent on education, medical and public health, scientific departments, and famine relief.

The other main items of taxation were all indirect taxes which fell heaviest on the poorest classes. Salt used as a condiment and preservative in the hot climate was an everyday item of necessity for the poor. The duty in the 1920s was Rs. 2·8a. per 82 pounds until 1925 after which it was Rs. 1·4a. The excise tax derived from duties on liquors made in India and the

[1] *Indian Statutory Commission*, 1930, Cmd. 3568, p. 339.

sale of drugs, opium, and hemp from Government-licensed shops. A large number of items were subject to customs duties in the 1920s including 25 per cent on sugar, 15 per cent on food and drink and household items, 11 per cent on cotton piece goods and 5 per cent on cotton yarns.[1] Such low incomes could not afford the incidence of indirect taxation on items of necessity like sugar and salt or even the rent in the form of land revenue. Money given to the Government meant that much less for other things.

Gandhi and the Congress campaign of non-violent opposition to British rule in the decade 1920–1930 confronted the laws of taxation. They attacked British rule at places and over items where the Government directly acted as administrator of the tax, and where the Imperial Government could be seen as the weight around the frail necks of the people. At his first trial in India for sedition in March 1922, Gandhi did not defend himself so much as claim his leadership over the masses of the people. He depicted 'the British lion shaking his gory claws'[2] with economic exploitation.

> Little do town-dwellers know how the semi-starved masses of India are slowly sinking to lifelessness. Little do they know that their miserable comfort represents the brokerage they get for the work they do for the foreign exploiter, that the profits and the brokerage are sucked from the masses. Little do they realise that the Government established by law in British India is carried on for this exploitation of the masses. No sophistication, no jugglery in figures can explain away the evidence that the skeletons in many villages present to the naked eye. I have no doubt whatsoever that both English and the town-dwellers of India will have to answer, if there is a God above, for this crime against humanity which is perhaps unequalled in history.[3]

Gandhi may have conceived civil resistance as 'a most powerful expression of a soul's anguish and an eloquent protest against the continuance of an evil state',[4] but in practice it

---

[1] There were also export duties on items of great demand abroad, raw and manufactured jute, raw hides, skins, rice and tea.

[2] *Young India*, 23 February 1922.

[3] Gandhi's statement at his trial in March 1922, quoted in H. Jack, *The Gandhi Reader*, p. 204.   [4] *Young India*, 10 November 1921.

interfered with government revenue obtained from peasants. He believed British rule would end when there was no money to maintain it. The idea of individuals refusing to pay taxes to a government of which they disapproved had a respectable heritage dating from Emerson and Thoreau in the nineteenth century. Gandhi and the Congress Party raised the stakes in a way appropriate to India by inducing masses of people to refuse to pay the land revenue, disobey the salt laws, picket Government-licensed liquor shops, and boycott the purchase of English cloth.

A major campaign against the payment of land revenue occurred in the *taluka* (tax district) of Bardoli, an area of 80,000 people and 100 villages in Surat, Bombay Presidency. The choice of Bardoli was no accident. Many of the people there had been with Gandhi in South Africa where the method of non-cooperation against government laws began. The region, near Gandhi's own place of birth, was peopled by the Gujeratis who had been influenced by the passive and non-violent ideas of the Jains, as had Gandhi. Yet there were also practical reasons to make the peasants of Bardoli particularly worthy of their task. The region had plentiful rainfall and large cotton crops; it was one of the richest areas in Bombay Presidency. The people were not crushed by poverty. On the contrary, many received a monthly income from relatives settled in South Africa. This income was estimated at £37,000 a month. The peasants had the means to resist government penalties for longer than most in India. When money was later raised to support the campaign the Congress Party used it for publicising itself because 'the Bardoli peasant is too proud to accept any relief'.

The campaign against land revenue began at the end of 1921 when taxes fell due. Not only was money withheld but children were withdrawn from government schools. Fifty-one of the sixty-five schools in the area were closed. Early in February 1922 Gandhi wrote to the Viceroy, Lord Reading, informing him of his commitment to the peasant's right of non-payment of taxes. A few days later in the middle of the campaign a mob at Chauri-Chaura overran a police station and set it on fire. Twenty-two constables were killed. Dismayed and remorseful, Gandhi called off the Bardoli campaign and began a five-day fast.

As if fate had forgiven him, four years later new opportunities arose in Bardoli to confront the Imperial Government over land revenue. In 1926 the area was due for its thirty-year review. The Assessment Officer recommended an increase of 25 per cent, to begin in February 1928. Eventually the Government asked 22 per cent, but the peasants refused to pay any increase. They remained firm for the next few months, though the Government confiscated moveable property and land. Yet by May 1928 only 1,600 acres had been forfeited and auctioned, mostly land owned by moneylenders. Vallabhbhai Patel, Mayor of Ahmedabad, led the Bardoli campaign and eventually convinced the Governor of Bombay and the Viceroy to establish an independent commission to examine the new assessment, release prisoners and return confiscated land and cattle. For their part the peasants agreed to pay their taxes at the old rates. In May 1929 the Maxwell-Broomfield Commission reported in favour of the peasants and suggested an increase of only 5·7 per cent. In finding justification for the cultivators' grievances the two commissioners criticised the method of land revenue assessment in phrases which tarnished the efficiency of the Raj on a matter of some importance, and should make all historians of British India wary. 'The rental and sale statistics have been carelessly compiled, are demonstrably incorrect in a large number of cases, and, in general, must be regarded as completely unreliable. Further, the established method of using statistics is, in our opinion, unsound in theory.'[1]

The single most spectacular campaign initiated by the non-violent movement was the protest against the salt revenue. 'Salt suddenly became a mysterious word, a word of power.' At the end of 1929 the Congress Party voted for complete independence within a year but left Gandhi to determine the way to achieve it. Gandhi chose to oppose the salt laws by a march from his ashram at Sabarmati to Dandi on the west coast. He informed the Viceroy, Lord Irwin, of his intention, making clear that the salt tax was part of the system of progressive exploitation of British rule. 'The whole revenue system has to be so revised as to make the peasant's good its primary

---

[1] *The Times*, 8 May 1929.

concern. But the British system seems to be designed to crush the very life out of him. Even the salt he must use to live is so taxed as to make the burden fall heaviest on him, if only because of the heartless impartiality of its incidence.'[1]

After prayers he and seventy-eight members of the ashram began their march down dirt roads and through scattered villages. As the band proceeded peasants applauded and threw leaves on the road to make their passage easier on the feet. It took twenty-four days to march the two hundred miles, time enough to melt 'the stoniest hearts' of the British Government and excite world interest. On 6 April Gandhi dipped into the sea and picked up some salt left by the waves. He had broken the law by obtaining salt from somewhere other than the government monopoly.[2] As he waited for arrest he called on the whole of India to defy the salt laws, explained how this should be done and how salt, in fact barely usable, could be made. On the day of his arrest Gandhi announced that the salt works at Dharasana, 150 miles north of Bombay, were to be raided. The strength of ideas is their capacity to inspire others even when the person who conceived them is absent. Thus the march against the salt works began on 21 May while Gandhi was in gaol, and precipitated scenes of awesome suffering, when the confrontation of police and protesters explained one of the meanings of *satyagraha*. 2,500 marchers, armed only with ropes to pull down the barbed wire stockade of the salt works and committed to using no violence, waded through ditches surrounding the stockade and advanced in silent columns. The police charged with steel laths to whack the unprotected skulls of the marchers. 'Not one of the marchers even raised an arm to fend off the blows.' While followers of Gandhi exhorted the crowds to retain self-control, waves of people advanced.

They marched steadily with heads up, without the encouragement of music or cheering or any possibility that they might escape serious injury or death. The police rushed out and methodically and mechanically beat down the second column. There was no fight, nor

[1] Gandhi's letter to Lord Irwin, 2 March 1930, quoted in L. Fischer (ed.), *The Essential Gandhi*, 1963, p. 260.

[2] This salt was later sold for 1,600 rupees. Gandhi also placed a few grains of this illegal salt in his cup when he took tea with Lord Irwin.

struggle; the marchers simply walked forward until struck down. There were no outcries, only groans after they fell.[1]

The leaders of the march were arrested and over three hundred were treated in a makeshift hospital. Two died.

The achievements of the civil disobedience movement of 1930 are difficult to measure. There was no practical effect. The salt tax was not changed, land revenue in general was not reduced, and India did not possess independence at the end of 1930. Yet Indians had publicly displayed what had been their fate for ages past: the capacity to accept suffering. World opinion, although very few British statesmen, saw something heroic and inspiring in India's struggle for independence.

In the same letter that Gandhi wrote to the Viceroy on 2 March he broadly criticised the whole of government expenditure with its 'expensive military and civil administration which the country can never afford'. The Imperial and Provincial expenditure, as seen in Table IV, gives some statistical justification to his claim. Over one third of all revenue was spent on military services, including an annual contribution to the British navy of £100,000. All defence costs, including pensions and allowances, were charged to Indian revenue though no Indian representative body could vote on the estimates. The Indian army appreciably added to Britain's world prestige and could be directed to support the civil administration during threats to law and order, but money for the army and civil administration was not approved by elected Indian representatives. British rule was also expensive. Gandhi showed that the Viceroy's salary was five thousand times greater than the average Indian's income, while the British prime minister earned only ninety times a Briton's average income. Certainly, specific items of civil administration were anomalous. More money was spent on justice, police, and jails in 1927, a period of relative calm, than on the whole of Indian education. More money was spent on pensions and superannuation in the Indian Civil Service than on medical and public health. It is significant that those constitutional reforms the British Government held out to India before 1945 gave neither full independence nor Indian

[1] W. Miller, *I Found No Peace*, 1936, p. 184.

control over the key items of revenue and expenditure. Both Indian and British statesmen saw that independence and absolute control over the Indian economy were inextricably linked.

[iii]

As religion became an element of nationality, indigenous traditions revived. The breadth of the culture sought included not just the passivity and gentleness expressed in the life of Gandhi but also tales of courage, violence, and war. There were many stories in Hindu literature where men found dignity and self-esteem on the battlefield. Some opponents of British rule acted to assert this virile strand of Indian culture. For them the fight for freedom was a literal war in which the Indian people regained their manhood.

Revolutionary nationalism, the adoption of an aggressive attitude towards the British in thought and deed, was intimately associated with the Hindu cultural renaissance. The life and thoughts of L. Tilak (1856–1920) were judged by the British Government, in its report on revolutionary conspiracies in 1918, to be responsible for the dangerous opinions which culminated in bomb throwing and murder. Tilak saw himself as defender of ancient Hindu traditions against the encroachments of a foreign ruler. Just as the cultural roots of the country established social and moral bonds between its people, so home rule became a right of birth since no nation with its own society and morality need be dependent on strangers for guidance. In a manner appropriate to Indian politics Tilak was a Sanskrit scholar, popular journalist and a radical in the Congress Party. Imprisoned for a total of ten years for writing seditious articles, he was able to pursue the scholarly side of his life and write a philosophical treatise on the Bhagavad Gita, and seminal essays attempting to date the Vedas and place their ancient home in the north polar regions.

Tilak had a mocking literary style which gave a sharp edge to his views. Unmoved by all vague professions of sympathy, he complained that the British were willing to share everything with Indians except power. The groans of the masses suffering under the foreigner's yoke were the primordial murmurs of

Indian independence. 'If you forget your grievances by hearing words of sympathy the cause is gone. You must make a permanent cause of grievance. Store up grievances till they are removed.'[1] He conceived the duty of a free press to show up the mistakes and injustices of an administration, though when he did this himself he was accused of sedition since hostile criticism worked to divide the country into opponents against the administration. Fearlessly, Tilak accepted that in British India journalism had the vocational risk of gaol, but he said: 'How can a diver work if he is afraid of water.'[2]

Tilak was also a skilful propagandist. He organised two religious festivals to gather the villagers into a celebration of a common national consciousness and social union. Thousands came to various centres throughout the country for several days to see art displays, hear poetry and music and the recitation of tales from the ancient epics. The contents of the poems and stories were often barely disguised parables to be applied to contemporary issues. The heroes of the two festivals, Ganesa and Shivaji, were carefully chosen to instruct the masses to acquire a new and independent attitude towards themselves and their country. Ganesa was one of the most popular Hindu gods, praised first before the worship of any other god. His elephant head and portly human body mounted on a rat, a former enemy subdued, offered an image of boyish fun, zest for life, and gentleness. He was the patron of literature because, according to one tale, he tore out his tusk in a paroxysm of enthusiasm to write down the *Mahabharata*.

Shivaji (1627–1680) was the founder of the Mahratta empire who as a boy became enamoured of the national epics and tried to emulate them. At the age of sixteen he formed a guerilla band of youths to maraud and pillage bastions of the Mogul ruler. He trained a ruthless corps of horsemen who won territory from the Mogul Empire, and even attacked the factory of the East Indian Company in Surat in the first fight between the English and natives. He founded an empire, reorganised civil institutions, and was a devout orthodox Hindu. He was an ideal example of bravery, orthodoxy and self-sufficiency who

---

[1] L. Tilak, *His Writings and Speeches*, Madras, 1919, p. 44.
[2] D. Tahmankar, *Lokamanya Tilak*, 1956, p. 83.

Tilak thought would stimulate national idealism. Accordingly, in 1895 a fund was begun to rebuild Shivaji's tomb at Raigarth and ceremonies were held there. Verses recited at the festival had particular meaning in the context of recent British efforts to interfere with the Hindu religion.

> We shall risk our lives on the battlefield in a national war; we shall shed upon the earth the life-blood of the enemies who destroy our religion.[1]

Like Shivaji's youth corps, societies for physical and military training were formed at the turn of the century, while in London India House became a haven of revolutionary activity. Lectures were given there on how to make and use bombs and special readings about the Indian Mutiny were intended to harden hearts. The language of nationalism became inflamed; death and violence became reverent words. 'Alas, you are not ashamed to remain in servitude; try therefore to commit suicide; alas, like butchers, the wicked in their monstrous atrocity kill calves and kine; free her [the cow] from her trouble; die but kill the English; do not remain idle or thereby burden the earth; this is called Hindustan, how is it that the English rule here?'[2] In 1907 a letter was published in a revolutionary paper:

> O Plunder I worship you today, be our helpmate. You so long hid yourself like a canker in a flower and ate away the country's substance. Come and do again here and there, resuscitate the old martial spirit behind the public eye.[3]

Deeds accompanied words. In 1897, on the occasion of Queen Victoria's Jubilee, the head of the plague committee, W. C. Rand, and an officer, Charles Ayerset, were shot while returning from a state banquet in Poona. Rand had been responsible for the employment of British soldiers to search and separate suspected cases of plague. Instances of molestation of women, disrespect to places of worship, wanton destruction of property, and general mistreatment, made the search parties of the Government as feared as the plague.

---

[1] *Report of the Committee on Revolutionary Conspiracies*, 1918, Cmd. 9190, viii, p. 10.
[2] *Ibid.*, p. 10.　　　　[3] *Ibid.*, p. 18.

Acts of violence in the decades that followed accompanied the national claim for freedom. In 1900 a mob killed five policemen in Kampur. In 1908 the wife and daughter of Pringle Kennedy were mistakenly killed during an attempt to assassinate a district judge who had punished a revolutionary. In 1909 Sir William Curzon Wyllie, political A.D.C. at the India Office, was murdered in London, and later in the same year the Chief Magistrate at Nasik was murdered after trying a revolutionary. There was an attempted assassination of Lord and Lady Minto in 1909, and of Lord Hardinge in 1912. The incidence of terrorist outrages was not lessened by the growth of Gandhi's movement; on the contrary the movement 'served to give it an odour of sanctity and blurred the distinction between lawful and unlawful activities'.[1]

The following is a special report to Cabinet by Samuel Hoare, Secretary of State for India in 1935, on Indian terrorism for 1930, the year of mass civil disobedience.

1930.	18 April	Chittagong raid, railway officer shot dead, set fire to buildings. Several wounded and a policeman murdered.
	22 April	Senior Police Inspector shot dead at Geni.
	25 August	Bomb thrown at Sir Charles Tegad, Calcutta Commissioner of Police in Dalhousie Square.
	29 August	Mr. Loman, Inspector General of Police died of wounds.
	30 August	Bombs thrown into homes of police inspector and excise sub-inspector in Mymensingh, by woman terrorist.
	8 Dec.	Lt.-Col. N. F. Simpson, Inspector General of Prisons, Bengal, shot dead in his office in Writer's Building, Calcutta.[2]

In practice violent and non-violent nationalism in India were intertwined. The British, looking at events from the practical and historical point of view, could reasonably interpret the non-violent campaign as a cover for violence. This view persisted to the very end of British rule. In 1942, at the time of the 'quit

---

[1] *Joint Committee on Constitutional Reform*, Vol. II, 1934, p. 337, quoted in the Templewood Papers, 'Revolutionary and Anarchical Crimes'. IOL.

[2] 'Terrorist Outrages in India: 1928–35', Vol. 77, Templewood Papers, IOL.

India' resolution, the British Government made no real distinction between a non-violent campaign and the outbreaks of violence; the two happened together. Thus Gandhi was seen as an inspiration for lawlessness or at least dependent on the 'hooligan element' for 'the execution of his schemes'.[1] Since the threat to British rule, no matter what its ideological basis, always resulted in dislocation of social stability and disruption of constitutive authority, Gandhi in the official mind became likened to a brutal dictator. Sir H. Twynam, Governor of Central Provinces and Berar, wrote: 'Since 1920 Gandhi has been the Hitler of Indian politics.'[2]

The persistence of violence in India contributed much to the firmness of British policy. To preserve the country from the break-up of law and order had long been a main reason for the continuance of British rule. Since the disintegration of the Mogul Empire, British statesmen had pointed to the need for British law and administration to maintain order. Violence among the natives also conformed to paternalistic ideas inherent in Empire: barbaric peoples need to be protected from themselves; the uneducated masses need the British Government to champion their basic wishes to have peace and security. By resorting to violence Indians were indicating how unprepared they still were for anything like self-government.

Though Gandhi was genuine in his hatred of violence, nevertheless he substantially contributed to the mood of lawlessness. The same logic that gave reason and justification to the non-violent, non-cooperation campaign was also applicable to the use of violence. The different means of opposition had a common basis of criticism. Nowhere is this more evidenced than in Gandhi's defence of those condemned for a variety of political crimes by the British authorities. The lack of justice in British rule, specifically and in general, made those who disobeyed the law hardly criminals. Gandhi in his defence in court in 1922 said:

> The law itself in this country has been used to serve the foreign exploiter. My unbiased examination of the Punjab Martial law cases has led me to believe that at least 95 per cent of convictions were wholly bad. My experience of political cases in India leads me to the

[1] *The Transfer of Power*, Vol. II, p. 848.
[2] *The Transfer of Power*, Vol. II, p. 196.

conviction that in nine cases out of ten the condemned men were totally innocent. Their crime consisted in the love of their country. In 99 cases out of 100 justice has been denied to Indians as against Europeans in the courts of India. This is not an exaggerated picture. It is the experience of almost every Indian who has had anything to do with such cases. In my opinion, the administration of the laws is thus prostituted or unconsciously for the benefit of the exploiter.[1]

Gandhi not only defended individual revolutionaries but also initiated his own campaigns to attack the existing laws. His actions against the salt tax and land revenue had the broad intention of showing British injustice and that the British Government should not have the right to demand obedience from people who in no way were represented in the existing political institutions.

Indian violence could be justified because the British used violence against Indians. There were notorious instances of brutality on the indigo and tea plantations, while the lathi charges of the police against demonstrators could not help but create excitement and anger. The Government of India Act (1909) authorised whipping as a punishment, which was later loosely extended to apply to political demonstrators, though the categories and offences were vaguely defined. Thus the Governor of Bombay, Sir R. Lumley, wrote: 'Usual sentence by Magistrates is 10 to 12 stripes against a maximum of 30, and penalty is inflicted under medical supervision and on tough, sturdy, bullying type of offender.'[2] The whole nationalist movement created a pitch of excitement which tended to raise life to a high plain where the present was filled with moral purpose and historic significance. Normal restraint and moderation traditionally reinforced by obedience to the law were frequently challenged.[3] The nationalist movement attracted youths and

[1] H. Jack, *The Gandhi Reader*, p. 204.
[2] *The Transfer of Power*, Vol. II, p. 700.
[3] 'Is it not remarkable that the British power which is soaked in violence, which is based on violence, which daily commits the most pitiless forms of violence, which grinds down millions of people and sucks their life-blood, should make so much about the violence others commit. . . . Whatever weapons we use the British have only bullets for us and looting and rape and arson.' B. Mitra and P. Chakraborty, *Rebel India*, Calcutta, 1946, p. 198.

adolescents; thus the normal period of hostility to authority
could be linked to the broader aspirations for independence, with
the British Government cast as the hated parental figure. Of the
convicted criminals in Bengal from 1907 to 1917, the largest
single category was made up of students.

Obedience to the law, a complex question for any society, is
usually possible because of a common tradition, history, and
law between ruler and ruled. To obey the laws is to conform to
the whole fabric of society as these have been modified but
inherited from the past. No society wishes regularly to have its
rules and laws reviewed lest the habit of obedience be upset.
Indian nationalism, the growth of Indian self-consciousness, did
much to assert the uniqueness of Indians and India and question
British authority. British law and rule aroused hostility after the
Indian renaissance; even their efforts at social reform were seen
as another example of interference; British expressions of
sympathy not only failed to be substantial enough but became
ethically redundant. Political independence was the practical
realisation of Indian moral self-sufficiency. The only changes
that could avert continual clashes between Indian subject and
British ruler were fundamental changes in the constitution
which made law an agreement achieved by the participation of
national representatives in the law-making process. If national
aspirations were represented in political institutions a major
degree of harmony would exist between the nation and government.

But what would be the place of the British Empire in such a
system of government? As every British statesman knew, Anglo-
Indian relations depended on constitutional reform. The acrimony
in these relations to the very end of British rule is a testament
to the failure of constitutions to achieve a classical model for
law and its obedience. The reason for this failure lies only
partially in the nature of the constitutions devised. Men make
constitutions. The clash of personalities among the men
responsible for the last and crucial phases of British rule in
India made its special contribution to the mutual distrust of
East and West.

FOUR

DRAMATIS PERSONAE

THE LAST PHASES before the transfer of power had many aspects of a dramatic play, a chivalric battle between irreconcilable moral ideas, life styles and concepts of praiseworthy deeds. An analysis of the period from 1920 to 1942 would lack its essential flavour if it concentrated exclusively on the political and constitutional arguments. There was a broader confrontation nurtured over the years, increasing with familiarity, which touched specific issues but was never wholly used up by them. Men took disagreements seriously, for the terms of reference and the setting reduced pettiness and self-seeking. The future of India was conceived in grandiose and patriotic terms; the patrimony of a magnificent tradition was being stolen by insensitive and barbaric enemies. Indian and British leaders took arguments personally if only because they accepted personal risks for their decisions. Assassination or imprisonment were real prospects.

The importance of India for Britain should not be measured in the quantity of actual knowledge. A month's or a decade's tour of duty was enough to create lasting impressions which could be remarkably similar. Visitors were satisfied to confirm the earlier descriptions and opinions of pundits like Kipling or Curzon. Even disasters, natural, political, economic, were engulfed in the traditional ideas of challenge and service associated with empire. Between the extremes of Indian needs and British suppositions spanned the British Government and the Government of India, explaining, encouraging, temporising. The permanent head of the India Office, A. Hirtzel, wrote to Harcourt Butler in 1925, 'If only we could go on doing nothing for a little longer.'[1] Butler, one of the most experienced administrators in

---

[1] A. Hirtzel to H. Butler, 2 December 1925, Butler Papers, IOL.

India, well appreciated the narrow lines on which Indian policy was made. Without a more thorough appreciation of Indian realities, discussion was curtailed by vague but traditional fears. He wrote to Geoffrey Dawson, editor of *The Times*: 'People at home are interested only when there is fear of a rebellion or a lost dominion. We shall have neither.'[1]

Reluctance to admit the possibility of a lost dominion in India had its roots in Britain's unwillingness to accept decline as a world power. The Indian Empire, particularly in the context of the 1920s and 1930s of decline in the stable export industries, labour troubles, and post-war disillusionment, seemed a symbol of past greatness almost miraculously surviving into the twentieth century. There was enough reality to the symbol to make it believable; the Indian army was an ultimate deterrent, India was still one of the largest single customers for British goods. Behind Stanley Baldwin's rhetoric there was a deep psychological need to trust in Britain because she had an empire. 'In a world still suffering from the shock of war, the British Empire stands firm as a great force for good. . . . It stands in the sweep of every wind, by the wash of every sea, a witness to that which the spirit of confidence and brotherhood can accomplish in the world.'[2]

In trying circumstances statesmen clung to themes that reassured. If Britain still had a positive role to play in India's development this was because history and political experience had trained the nation to rule, administer, educate, and extend its majestic legal system. So much in British domestic history, as well as selected moments in the history of British rule in India, demonstrated a political wisdom substantiated by wealth. Beneath the façade of pomp were pillars of national pride and self-confidence. The forces of disintegration and social revolution were to be denied in India. That Britain had weathered so many storms in India produced a suspicion that the British Empire in India would continue on terms not too dissimilar from those of the past, no matter what a number of public announcements about the future said. No doubt the fact that Churchill was prime minister during the Second World War,

[1] H. Butler to G. Dawson, 31 October 1925, Butler Papers, IOL.
[2] S. Baldwin, *Our Inheritance*, 1928, p. 71.

and well-known to oppose the end of British rule in India, contributed to government uncertainty and the view that anything might turn up. The Secretary of State for India wrote to the Viceroy in March 1942:

> The more I think of it the more probable it seems to me that in some form or other the Viceroy will have to remain, not merely as a constitutional Governor General, but as a representative of broader imperial aspects of government, for a long time to come, and to be equipped with the instruments of power required to carry out his functions.[1]

Without too much cant Viceroys and Secretaries of State for India acted to preserve a political heritage in a spirit of service and responsibility; they believed the Empire was a force for good in the world, especially in India where lawlessness, backwardness and division threatened what experience and knowledge had taught them to admire. This was trenchantly expressed by Lord Birkenhead, Secretary of State from 1924 to 1928: 'The history of India has always been a conflict of personality against numbers, of individuals against mobs; the mobs have always been beaten.'[2]

The classical theatre of India, like that of ancient Greece, gives a grand and religious dimension to plays by dramatising the story of men possessed by powerful life forces—the gods, fates, or destiny. Human action is compulsive as no one can act otherwise; conflicts are sustained by the existence of unseen forces. A little of this classical determinism seems to touch the last years of British rule when men drawn into the political issue of how long Britain should rule India, felt themselves swept up by different kinds of patriotism. The strident events of these years—war, depression, assassination, imprisonment, massive disorder—only raised the stakes of personal commitment and induced rigidity. In 1935, in response to an invitation from Lord Lothian, Nehru answered in words that indicate that he for one was aware of the nearly blind determinism at work.

> I do not think it is possible to charm away the conflicts merely by friendly contacts between well-intentioned persons. The conflicts are

---

[1] *The Transfer of Power*, Vol. I, p. 469.
[2] The First Earl of Birkenhead, *Turning Points in History*, n.d., p. 119.

obviously deeper and the best of individuals seem to me to play a relatively unimportant role when vast elemental forces are at play against each other.[1]

Hindu leaders, for their own part, wrapped the struggle for independence in terms of the heroic conflict as portrayed in their own classical theatre. Much in their experience lent itself to a story of a martyr's play where men submit to the 'higher' commands only to experience suffering and misfortune. The injunction to speak the moral truth, to fast or waste away in prison, became a *dharma*, in keeping with a passage in the Bhagavad Gita: 'And do thy duty, even if it humbles, rather than another's even if it be great. To die in one's duty is life: to live in another's is death.' Yet the will to defy others for the sake of a higher good became a source of inner strength as men saw themselves belonging to a cosmic destiny. Each new challenge was a new opportunity to affirm the universal significance of their cause. There were elements of folk-tale simplicity in the contrast between the rulers in their palaces meeting bare-foot saints. The luxury of the one heightened the penury of the other. There were few more dramatic encounters than Gandhi's meeting with the Viceroy, Lord Irwin, in March 1931 when the Gandhi-Irwin Pact ended the civil disobedience campaign and Gandhi agreed to attend the second Round Table Conference in London. Gandhi looked a pale sight to the Viceroy in his palace, 'small, wizened, rather emaciated, no front teeth, it is a personality poorly adorned with this world's trimmings'.[2] It was the physical and aesthetic incongruity which King George V commented on in his letter to Irwin. The King was 'only troubled by the comical situation of the religious fanatic with his very restricted covering being admitted to your beautiful new house for what,[3] His Majesty fears, must be rather interminable and irksome conversations'.

Just as a play needs an audience, the last two decades of British rule had world interest, expressly because of the striking contrasts between the intentions and personalities of the protagonists. International reaction to Indian events, especially

---

[1] J. Nehru, *A Bunch of Old Letters*, Bombay, 1958, p. 128.
[2] Lord Irwin to George V, 13 March 1931. Irwin Papers, IOL.
[3] Lord Stamfordham to Lord Irwin, 20 February 1931. Irwin Papers, IOL.

American opinion, raised the importance and heightened the tension of these years as tactics were formed with a mind towards their international acceptability. Periodically the British War Cabinet discussed 'India as a factor in Anglo-American relations'. The means of mass disobedience chosen by Gandhi and the Congress Party very much suited the conception of what was newsworthy throughout the world, while passive action produced gory scenes. The Indian drama had universal appeal.

Few Western visitors to India could help responding to the sense of 'history' fixed in buildings, monuments, and the many popular history books written about India and the Empire from 1929 to 1939. The latter, oddly perhaps, reflected in mood and language the opinions of ordinary government officials and the British public in general. Typical of this kind of history book was D. C. Somervell's *The British Empire*, written in 1930 and going through five editions by 1942. There was a British Empire, it explained, because the distinguishing characteristics of the European race, inherited from the Greeks and Romans, had been 'sweetened by the practice of the Christian religion'. Perseverance of the kind essential in government service, from district officer to governor-general, demanded a frontiersman's courage, 'a reckless devotion to great causes, an unflinching pursuit of untrodden paths'.[1]

Nor was the dramatic effect of government activity lost in the architecture of official buildings. A unique opportunity was offered from 1911 to 1931 when, after the King-Emperor's Durbar, the building of a new capital city in Delhi was started. The King wrote to the Viceroy, Lord Hardinge, 'I hope you will not allow anything to be done "on the cheap". For New Delhi will stand for all time as a monument of British art and workmanship and my name will always be identified with it.'[2] Two decades and ten and a half million pounds were spent in creating a suitable centre for government. The decision to make a city from the dusty and snake-ridden wasteland told of a determination to govern, sometimes hard to sustain in the circumstances of native opposition in the 1920s. The new city

---

[1] D. C. Somervell, *The British Empire*, 1942, p. 83.

[2] George V to Lord Hardinge, 22 January 1914, Royal Archives, Windsor Castle.

could not help becoming a symbol of British rule, expressing
boldly a European presence, and incidentally, as decoration, the
Asian world. 'The coloured and theatrical façade of Islam has
been annexed to a more intellectual, three-dimensional tradition
of solid form and exact proportion—the tradition of Europe.'[1]

Sir Edwin Lutyens, the designer of the Cenotaph and the
Municipal Cathedral of Liverpool, was commissioned for the
complex of buildings. The grandeur of his conception left no
place for arabesque frill and light detail. Rather, the ordered
arrangement of classical pillars supported by compact walls and
neat arches asserted rigid authority. Something of the starkness
of the building was reiterated in the inscription, modified by
Lord Irwin, Lutyens wrote for a column given by Maharaja
of Jaipur. Action and purpose were united because they advanced
Indian greatness. Without mention of cooperation the inscription was the ideal code for rulers.

> In thought faith
> In word wisdom
> In deed courage
> In life service
> So may India be great.[2]

No less symbolic was the placement of the Viceroy's House
in the very centre of the Secretariat and Government House.
'Never was so large, so well planned, so arrogant, yet so lovely
a palace—so fit a setting for the man who, if power be measured
by the number of those subject to it, is the most powerful man
that breathes.'[3] The Viceroy's Lodge stood at the end of a road
lined with trees; thirty-two white steps led to a pillared portico
which was the main entrance to the Durbar Hall, a circular
marble court with yellow pillars supporting a copper dome 177
feet above the roadway. The Hall was a room where the great
were meant to be seen but not heard as the 'acoustics were
abominable'. The house had 240 rooms; the *Times* correspondent, as he trekked through the rooms on a tour of inspec-

---

[1] R. Lutyens, *Sir Edwin Lutyens*, 1942, p. 47.

[2] Lord Halifax, *Fullness of Days*, 1957, p. 144.

[3] R. Lutyens, *Sir Edwin Lutyens*, p. 49. For a full description and pictures of
Viceroy's House, see Butler *et al.*, *The Architecture of Sir Edwin Lutyens*, Vol. II,
1950.

tion, felt as if he had walked 'through a marble city rather than
the corridors of a single building'.[1] Upstairs was the other
great room of the Viceroy's palace, the Ballroom, in white
with crystal chandeliers that hung in pairs in the middle. Two
fireplaces were crowned by coved arches where ten-feet-six
painted panels 'properly rococo in style' sentimentally reminded
the Raj of home. One panel freely interpreted the view from
St James's Park looking towards Horse Guards Parade and had
pelicans in the foreground. The other, tapestry-like, showed a
cluster of birds, bright with plumage and flowers. These decora-
tions, with their suggestion of a cooler and more familiar
world, gently contradicted the confidence in the architecturial
style of the exterior view. Here, political discourse was meant
to be formal and elevated.

It is impossible to include many of the people who strutted
across the stage of Indian history from 1920 onwards. Those
discussed in the following pages have been chosen because they
strikingly illustrate the deep-rooted contrast which existed
between those playing a major part in the course of events.
British and Indian leaders had a different time sense, not only
about how long was the future, but also over the amount of
involvement in Indian issues. Indians relentlessly pressed for
changes and reforms; they had few diverting concerns. British
leaders, with the exception of the Viceroys and Secretaries of
State, whose influence rarely lasted for more than five years,
relegated Indian problems to one among many. Their experience
of India, the attitudes acquired over a number of years, the
concepts about what the future should be, by their differences,
moulded mutually hostile personalities. Thus the confusions and
disputes of these years offered more than an argument over
what was feasible in the present, rather an expression of histor-
ically matured animosity.

*   *   *

George V (1865–1936) was the second son of Edward VII
and became heir to the throne in 1892 when his brother the
Duke of Clarence died. The Prince of Wales's personality bore
the influence of the years he served in the navy, first as a cadet

[1] *The Times*, 2 December 1929.

at Dartmouth as a boy of twelve through more than two decades of cruises and tours until he became a rear-admiral at thirty-six. Spared some of the tedium of bookish learning his father endured to satisfy Victoria and Albert, the Prince transferred the virtues of the senior service to his royal office—so much so that one biographer saw him as the 'Sailor King: there is a healthy tang of salt in the title'. Crowned in 1910 he performed his duties as might a benevolent captain: fastidious in dress without being modish, punctual and neat, his beard and posture conveyed the appearance of terse regularity. Without a very introspective nature, exactitude in the external world expressed for him correct values. He took inordinate concern that ceremonies were carefully enacted; protocol and dress were no absurd pomp but the outward manifestation of an inner commitment to what was fine and noble. He had 'the eyes of a falcon and could from a great distance detect the tiniest misplacement of a ribbon or a badge . . . any deviation from the norm of the previous decade [indicated] affectation, effeminacy, or potential decadence. His meticulousness in such matters can be partly ascribed to a sailor's passion for minute tidiness: but it also was due to a reasonable realisation that slovenliness or incongruity are as destructive of the magic of ceremony as two saucepans tied to the howdah of a state elephant'.[1]

The India the King visited first as Prince of Wales in 1905 and six years later to be crowned could not, as idea or reality, fail to confirm his views about decorum as the expression of decency. The pageantry of the royal tours, durbars, military parades, staid interviews (including in 1905 a meeting with the sole English survivor of the Sepoy Mutiny), and vast hunts,[2] created the definite belief, gleaned from 'reading the eyes of the people, that India was happy.[3] The royal eye did not pass over without criticism the low pay and poor conditions of Indian

[1] H. Nicolson, *King George V*, 1952, p. 391.

[2] In Nepal in 1906 the Prince had the most exciting sport of his life. Two camps fifty miles apart were connected by a specially built road that passed through jungle and forest. Fourteen thousand people were employed along with six hundred elephants. The first day's bag was full, with thirty-nine tigers, eighteen lions and four Himalayan bears. See J. Day, *King George V as a Sportsman*, 1935.

[3] Sir W. Lawrence, *The India We Served*, 1929, p. 264.

soldiers, nor how officers used the word 'native' as a term of abuse for a conquered and down-trodden race, but this only called for more generosity and sympathy, the theme of a much publicised speech he gave at the Guildhall in 1906. An imperial government could have no more effective spokesman for their sincerity and good intentions. Normal evidence and argument seemed superfluous against a prince's speech which called for 'wider sympathy, abundant and genuine respect, trust and confidence, [to] promote the well-being and further the best interests, break down prejudices, dispel misapprehension, better understanding, and loyalty'. The very desire of Indians to claim self-government offended these nearly sacred ideas. That individual Indians failed to appreciate the meaning and intentions of British rule and stand against the nationalist revolutions proved the fundamental unfitness of Indians for self-government.

> I suppose the real difficulty is an utter lack of courage, moral and political, among the natives, no individual dare take an independent line of his own, and this really shows how unfit they are for anything like self-government.[1]

No doubt the methods of the nationalist parties, the threatening behaviour of angry crowds, and the unseemly appearance of the leaders, the utter lack of formality at meetings of the Congress Party, conveyed a most uncongenial impression. During the Round Table Conference in 1931 delegates were invited to Buckingham Palace. With some trepidation the Secretary of State, Sir Samuel Hoare, approached the King to ask if Gandhi might have an audience. The King objected to the little man with no proper clothes on and bare knees. 'What! Have this rebel fakir in the Palace after he has been behind all these attacks on my loyal officers.' When reason of state prevailed the King could not resist warning Gandhi of the error of his ways. 'Towards the end of it the King told him that civil disobedience was a hopeless and stupid policy. To which Gandhi politely replied that he must on no account be drawn into an argument with his Majesty.'[2] On this inconclusive note

---

[1] King George V to Lord Irwin, 10 March 1928. Irwin Papers.
[2] Sir Samuel Hoare to Lord Willingdon, 6 November 1931, Templewood Papers.

two great and different heads of state asserted their differences.

The King-Emperor and the Mahatma were political symbols, the embodiment for millions of people of the highest aspirations of a time and place. The existence of such leaders touched the affairs of state with a 'mystic awe and wonder' and therefore they could completely command support. Both were the incarnations of a venerable and refined tradition, almost unique to their own country, to which masses of people responded with obedience, devotion, and filial affection. The striking difference between the two national symbols corresponded to the hiatus in the political outlook of the two countries: Britain had a noble charge to aid India's advance towards a stable and prosperous nation, and the outstanding problems especially between Hindus and Moslems made clear that the time was not yet near for any abandonment of guidance; Indians attributed all problems to the continuance of British rule—when that ended the conditions which enflamed politics would end and so would the problems, since Indians would be forced to settle their own fate. Both Gandhi and George V represented pre-industrial and pre-technological ideals when pride, duty and honour could still motivate people to believe in a higher mission in politics.

Men who are great national symbols, even of different countries, can share characteristics in common: they appear selfless, use elevated language, while their presence at an event charges it with excitement. Nor can the public have enough information about them. Gandhi and George V shared something of this functional similarity, just as each man, out of professional duty, tried to be tolerant of the other. But decorum and good manners could not long disguise how the one was the very opposite of the other.

*   *   *

M. K. Gandhi (1869–1948) was the last child of the prime minister of the small, independent state of Porbandar on the west coast of India. The family belonged to the sub-caste of merchants and moneylenders, the surname itself meaning grocer. Like many other people whose life has attracted wide interest, Gandhi made experiences in childhood, London, South Africa, and India episodes of struggle. The 'experiments with truth' were stories about and reflections on a number of critical events in his life with the personal and political mixed together.

Nor was he without skill at precipitating events which would test and purify him. The challenges to British authority which he led were lesser and periodic phases in this purification. Several times after 1920 he simply withdrew from politics. When active involvement landed him in prison this was not punishment. 'Jail for us is no jail at all,' particularly when 'the whole of India is a prison!'[1] He rightly called it his temple, where he fasted, meditated, simplified the routine of his life, and attracted world attention. To those not familiar or interested in Gandhi's inner struggles—and they included nearly all his British opponents—these were confusing and malevolent antics parading as holiness. Attlee once remarked about Gandhi: 'I neither approve of the tyranny of dictators or saints.'[2]

Gandhi also integrated aspects of his childhood and youth into the work of later life; the political career of his father was moderated by the religious gentleness of his mother who was a Jain; the ashrams he founded in South Africa and in India were extensions of the family household he grew up in; even militant non-violence with its self-suffering is not unlike a child's vindictive sulk to punish the seemingly unjust parent. The origin of the sit-down protest may be traced to a childhood event.

'He would remove the image of the ruling Prince [of Porbandar] from its customary stool and put himself in its place, a habit of pretending to be his father's master. . . . He also used to scatter the utensils of worship and to "write" on the floor. When his mother tried to forbid this, he . . . "stoutly dissented", in what may have been the ontogenetic origin of the sit-down.'[3]

Two events early in Gandhi's life caused him to feel irrevocably guilty; the depth of these feelings made him look for punishment. 'I must reduce myself to zero.'[4] In 1932 he said, 'The word "criminal" should be taboo from our dictionary. Or we are all criminals.'[5]

[1] *Young India*, 15 June 1921.   [2] Lord Attlee in conversation with the author.
[3] E. Erikson, *Gandhi's Truth*, 1970, p. 108.
[4] M. K. Gandhi, *An Autobiography*, 1949, p. 420.
[5] M. K. Gandhi, *Bapu's Letter to Mira, Allahabad,* 1949, p. 124.

This self-abnegation, running through much of Gandhi's writings, originated when he failed to administer comforting massage to his sick father. He left the sick room to make love to his pregnant wife. After only a few moments of accepting the 'shackles of lust' a servant knocked at the door to tell him his father was dead. No less heart-rending were the circumstances of his mother's death. He had promised her, before he left to study law in England, to keep a Hindu diet—a vow he subsequently broke. When he returned to India in 1891 he was told that his mother had died while he was in passage. That Gandhi was made an outcaste by the Indian community because he defied them to go to England to study must also have contributed to his sense of being an unworthy Indian. Indeed, it is tempting to see the essential Mahatma, with his abstention from food and sex and his championing of Indian self-respect by becoming a nurse to the British Empire, as a compensation for personal failings.

> The theme of nursing a stricken (and ambivalently loved) superior adversary reappears in Gandhi's later life both literally and symbolically. We shall meet it in the role of one who twice, although an adversary of British policy, recruits for an ambulance corps in support of British war efforts when the Empire was in danger. And we shall find it in the conviction of the *Satyagrahi* that in fighting nonviolently he is really taking care of his adversary's soul and its latent 'truth'.[1]

In 1893 Gandhi went to South Africa to start a legal career by defending the business interests of an Indian merchant. The case drew him to Pretoria whither he had to travel from Durban. As the only coloured man in the first-class carriage, he was insulted, beaten and removed. Obliged to wait in the cold railway station at Maritzburg he shivered and contemplated how to redress the wrong of racial prejudice. In Pretoria he started a campaign to teach Indians to expect their legal rights in a country where they were British subjects as well as to improve their sanitary habits, be truthful and to make friends with Moslems and Christians.

When the South African Government proposed to deprive

---

[1] Erikson, *Gandhi's Truth*, p. 130.

Indians of the right to elect members to the legislature, Gandhi found a specific grievance to defend the general interests of the 50,000 Indians in the country. He took it upon himself to inform the world about this injustice and the plight of Indians in South Africa, especially the system of indentured service, the poor wages and living conditions, and the high annual tax Indians had to pay if they wished to remain in the country after five years' indentured labour. His weekly journal *Indian Opinion* disseminated information about the wrongs meted out to Indians and had the effect of tightening the identity of the immigrants.

The climax of Gandhi's career in South Africa occurred in 1907 when the Transvaal Government passed a bill demanding that Indians register and show their registration cards to the police upon request. Gandhi argued this conferred an implied criminal status on Asiatics and demeaned their honour. He invented a mass passive disobedience plan to prevent registration—*satyagraha*. Registration offices were picketed, Indians were persuaded not to register, and some burned their cards. Gandhi was arrested but released by the prime minister, General Smuts. The two men talked and it was agreed that Indians should 'voluntarily' register and the odious aspects of the bill should be rescinded. But Gandhi was not satisfied with the new provisions the South African Government applied to Indians and in 1913 led another mass civil disobedience movement in the form of a 'great march' of thirty-six miles into the Transvaal where Indians were not allowed. All the marchers were arrested, but eventually public reaction in India and Britain forced the South African Government to modify its anti-Indian policy. *Satyagraha* was shown to work.

In the spirit of trusting one's opponents, Gandhi returned to India in 1914. He raised an ambulance unit and encouraged Indians to volunteer for service in the British Indian Army. However, the introduction of the Rowlatt Acts and the notorious massacre at Amritsar in 1919 turned him into an uncompromising opponent of British rule. In 1931 he outlined to Lord Irwin what independence meant. Though an explanation of his idea of self-government, it shows the malleable substance from which his ideas were made.

I want to see India established in her own self-respect and in respect of the world. I therefore want to see India able to discuss with Great Britain on terms of equality, and Great Britain willing to discuss with India on such terms. I know perfectly well that we want British help in many things for a long time to come yet—defence, administration and so on—and I am quite prepared to have safeguards or, as I prefer to call them, adjustments provided these are really in the interest of India and you will allow us to discuss them with you on equal terms. If we can be satisfied that I have got *Purna Swaraj* or *complete independence,* and India will have got it in what to me is the highest form in which it can be attained, namely, in association with Great Britain. But if Great Britain will not help me in this way, and if this achievement in partnership cannot be brought about, then I must pursue my end of *Purna Swaraj* or *complete independence* in isolation from Great Britain, and this I definitely regard as second best.[1]

After the Round Table Conference in 1931 Gandhi was less interested in the constitutional discussion with the British Government than in a reconciliation of communities within India itself. Well might he and others take his acceptance as an Indian into the spacious corridors of the Imperial Conference as enough of an achievement, recognising that the many specific issues could not be readily solved by logical formulae. But there was still no basis for continued discussion or cooperation. The publication of a fake interview which purported to quote Gandhi as saying he planned to renew the boycott of British goods in order to accentuate Britain's economic problems, and the upsurge of civil disobedience in the United Provinces and terrorism on the North-West Frontier and in Bengal, eventually led to Gandhi's re-arrest in January 1932. When Ramsay MacDonald made his communal award to the depressed classes in the form of separate electorates, Gandhi began a fast unto death which lasted six days. Self-purification and the admission of untouchables into temples, not political independence, were his concerns when he began to fast in May 1933. Released but again arrested in July 1933, as he set out on another march of civil disobedience, he was given a year's imprisonment. Two weeks later Gandhi began another fast because he was prevented

[1] Lord Irwin to His Majesty—The King-Emperor, 3 March 1931, quoting Gandhi. Irwin Papers, IOL.

from helping the untouchables, and was again released. However, within a year, the civil obedience movement was suspended and he left the Congress Party. This only made more confusing Gandhi's position in Indian affairs. The reform and integration of Indian society superseded direct opposition to British rule. Indeed when the 1935 Constitution gave provincial autonomy, Gandhi advised the Congress to work the reforms by accepting office, a move opposed by Nehru. Gandhi gave himself to social welfare and even devised a plan for universal primary education throughout India.

Gandhi did not need to be a member of the Congress Party to be its leader; by detaching himself from day-to-day events he became a purer force of 'divine' and disinterested judgement. Non-violence and distrust of British war aims led Gandhi to start a new campaign against both the war and British imperialism: first in the form of 'single non-cooperation' when individual members of the Congress Committees conducted anti-war propaganda so as to get themselves arrested in 1940; and in 1942 by a massive civil disobedience movement calling on the British to 'quit India'. Arrested in 1942 and detained in the Aga Khan's palace, in the following year Gandhi began a fast which nearly killed him, and in 1944 he was released because of ill-health. A confirmed believer in a united India and Hindu-Moslem cooperation, he tried unsuccessfully to mediate between the Congress Party and the Moslem League in direct talks with Jinnah in 1946. He was assassinated in 1948 because his views were judged too moderate by a Hindu sect. In 1968 his statue was erected in Delhi in the place where King George V's had previously stood.

*　　　*　　　*

Winston Churchill (1874–1965) went to India in 1896 in search of personal recognition, to add 'merit and glory to his already famous name'. As a lowly lieutenant in the 4th Hussars he was chagrined by the limited opportunities in a country he described as 'a 3rd rate watering place, out of season, without the sea'.[1] Polo and a skirmish on the North-West Frontier

[1] R. Churchill, *Winston S. Churchill, Youth*, Vol. I, p. 298. W.S.C. to Lady Randolph, 14 April [1897].

brought him a little of the excitement he longed for; the latter
was the subject of his first newspaper articles and his book *The
Story of the Malakand Field Force.*

While little in his political career remained constant, about
India Churchill kept a belief in the glorious sahib ruling in the interests of backward millions, though these interests were naturally
subservient to the greater British and Imperial needs. Indian
events and realities[1] were very much submerged beneath an
heroic conception of Britain, an imperial people who, raised on
the exertions of previous generations, had the experienced saga-
city to contribute to world affairs. Imaginatively caught up in
the great deeds of the past, as a biographer of his own ancestors,
Churchill had the self-educated man's unspoiled enthusiasm for
seeing in time past, clear patterns. India became a figment of
the English historical continuum, giving size and weight to the
English experience. 'Who touches India touches history.'[2] The
throbbing purpose behind English history was to show, by
example, truths useful to mankind; the language of didacticism
was ever-present in both Churchill's historical writing and his
more eloquent speeches.

Lord Randolph Churchill had been Secretary of State for
India in 1885 and was responsible for the armed annexation of
Burma. In his biography of his father Winston quoted the
peroration of a speech in which his father enjoined members of
Parliament to free themselves from the lassitude, carelessness
and apathy which too often prevailed in Indian debates. This
peroration expressed to a remarkable degree the credo of the
son learned from the father, including the mellifluous vocabulary
and the practical necessity for 'this small island' to measure its
greatness because Britain ruled Hindustan.

I would appeal to them [members of Parliament] to watch with the
most sedulous attention, to develop with the most anxious care, to
guard with the most united and undying resolution, the land and the

---

[1] When Lord Irwin suggested to Churchill that he should talk to some Indians
at the Round Table Conference so as to bring his ideas up to date, he replied, 'I am
quite satisfied with my views on India. I don't want them disturbed by any bloody
Indians.' H. Dalton, Diaries, 29 May 1930. Dalton Papers, LSE.

[2] 296, *Parl. Debates,* House of Commons, Fifth Series, col. 443 (12 December
1934).

people of Hindustan, that most truly bright and precious gem in the crown of the Queen, the possession of which, more than that of all your Colonial dominions, has raised in power, in resource, in wealth and in authority this small island home of ours far above the level of the majority of nations and of States—has placed it on an equality with, perhaps even in a position of superiority over, every other Empire either of ancient or of modern times.[1]

In 1906 Churchill went to the Colonial Office as Under-Secretary. With the Colonial Secretary, Lord Elgin, in the House of Lords, Churchill played a leading role in the conciliation of South Africa, and led an attack on Lord Milner's proconsulship in South Africa and that arrogant imperialism which turned a blind eye on the treatment of Chinese labour the more fervently to gaze on protective tariffs and imperial preference. But from Lord Morley, whom he greatly admired and whose adroitness he overrated, Churchill had confirmed his belief that India was different: principles applied in white colonies or in other parts of the colonial Empire must not of rights be valid in India. India had to be governed on old principles: a firm, judicious, and impartial administration caring for the diversified needs of the masses of people ruled without recourse to democratic reforms which pretend to give responsibility to native politicians; the emphasis given to constitutional questions as opposed to administrative ones had behind it the assumption that an Indian government run by Indians would be superior to that administered by Englishmen. The patriotism, so eloquent and admired during his war-premiership, denied as foolish such an assumption. Constitutional reform was a 'starting point for some great new lurch, some downward slurge'.[2] Churchill was at his most pugnacious when he described native politicians: they were unworthy replacements. Gandhi was 'that half-naked fakir', Nehru and the Congress Party as a whole 'Brahmins who mouth and patter principles of Western liberalism and pose as philosophical and democratic politicians'.[3]

Churchill had been a member of the Cabinet at the time of the

---

[1] W. S. Churchill, *Lord Randolph Churchill*, 1951, p. 379.

[2] 299, *Parl. Debates*, House of Commons, Fifth Series, col. 1267 (20 March 1935).

[3] *Joint Committee on Indian Constitutional Reform*, IIc, viii, 1933, p. 1797.

Morley-Minto (1909) and Montagu-Chelmsford (1917)
Reforms. The latter, for all their use of the term 'dominion
status', never 'meant, contemplated, or wished to suggest the
establishment of a Dominion Constitution for India in any
period which human beings ought to take into practical account'.[1]
It was this point of view he sought to make clear between 1930
and 1935.

In the early 1930s India's future constitution almost dominated
British politics, as Europe and the dictators did in the latter
half of the decade. Churchill opposed both the bribing of Indian
nationalists with necessarily partial responsibility in the
provinces and the placating of the aspiration of dictators by
appeasement. Indeed, the men associated with Indian reform,
Sir John Simon, Lord Irwin (later Lord Halifax), and Samuel
Hoare, became Foreign Secretaries in the 1930s who drifted
and compromised in the gathering storms. Though Churchill
may have been regarded as 'die-hard' turned 'war-monger' in
the 1930s as a whole, he was cast free of the leadership of the
Conservative party 'which had lost confidence in itself'. The
Indian debate was a kind of maiden voyage over troubled seas
which showed Churchill, if not an omniscient captain, at least
definite and self-assured. By 1940, when the men and policies
of the Conservative party were discredited by the outbreak of
war in Europe and the resignation of Congress provincial
ministers in India, Churchill was vindicated. He was the
appropriate war leader.

Churchill's onslaught against Indian reforms sought to
prevent the weakening of British authority and Indian loyalty.
'Everywhere the waves of so-called popular and democratic
movement will be lapping against the foundations of your
institutions and pressing upon the structure of your power.'[2]
Reforms gave responsibility to native politicians before any
real situations had arisen which made them necessary. In 1933
he wrote a memorandum for the Joint Committee on Indian
Constitutional Reform, 'obliquely improv[ing] upon' the
Simon Commission's proposal for provincial autonomy. While

[1] *Ibid.*, p. 1776.
[2] 296, *Parl. Debates*, House of Commons, Fifth Series, 1934–5, col. 451 (12
December 1934).

prepared to support provincial home rule, in other words responsible government by elected Indian ministers, he set out conditions which still indicated that Britain ruled. His main theme was that the present reforms once instigated should not have attached to them the vague suggestion of larger and greater changes to follow. The provinces could become autonomous if the power of the central government, the Government of India under British direction, were strengthened by retaining control over the police and judiciary. An inspectorate should also emanate from the central government to scrutinise regularly the practices of the provincial governments; and Parliament would retain the ultimate right to revoke any of the powers delegated to the provinces. Churchill, in an outspoken way, merely asserted that there were limits to Indian self-government—what many Conservative politicians believed but recognised as imprudent to admit in such tempestuous times. As Prime Minister from 1940 to 1945, Churchill restrained ministers from making definite commitments about India's future, confounding the numerous official pronouncements about Britain's intentions. In August 1942 when Churchill heard on the B.B.C. Leo Amery's broadcast pledging the Government 'to give India her independence after the war', Churchill wrote from Cairo: 'Surely this goes beyond the declarations approved by the War Cabinet.'[1] Amery quickly explained that he was misquoted.

* * *

Jawaharlal Nehru (1889–1964) belonged to the patrician class of natural leaders which any government would hope to draw into its confidence. If India would be governed in ways compatible with British political traditions—modified appropriately because of the unique requirements in India or the Empire—then English-educated and trained Indians, who by wealth and status had a responsible stake in society, could assist in more than daily administration. Here were leaders able enough to inculcate Western science, technology, and practical reason. If these same people could become important officials in government, fusing the oriental-intellectual-cum-politician, a

[1] *The Transfer of Power*, Vol. II, p. 643.

form of partnership could flourish, hinting at a modicum of popular support officials too often had to pretend existed. Just as the rulers of Indian States generally relied on and believed in British rule, so lesser nobles within British India proper would indicate their approval of the existing form of government and become a nucleus for popular acceptance.

Nehru's father, Motilal (1861–1931), was one of the richest men in Allahabad where he had a successful legal practice. Descended from Kashmiri Brahmins and nobles of the Mogul period, the family had an extensive practice at the High Court Bar. The Nehrus adopted English ways in clothes and life style; the father played tennis, drank wine, bought a splendid motor car, the first in the city, and was fond of trips to Europe. Distrusting politics and politicians, Motilal possessed the temperament of the most imperialist Raj-combative, hedonistic, easily angered, practical, and proud of his own success. His son was given English tutors and at fifteen sent to Harrow. Two years later he went to Cambridge where he read chemistry, geology and botany. With a second class degree he joined the Inner Temple for two years and returned to India in 1912 to work in his father's practice at the High Court. The years in England had taught him how to 'ape the somewhat empty-headed Englishman' but not how to penetrate serious questions with any clarity.

The India to which he returned seemed, as it had to innumerable Englishmen, insipid and boring. The weakness of British rule was that it could offer no more exciting political opportunities than government administration, with its hierarchy of advancement and tedious files. The *status quo* was imbued with dreariness. The Congress Party, moderate as it was, at least had one of the prerequisites of political awareness, argument. He joined it in 1913, and with the impetuosity of youth, drifted towards a policy of action, but remained unclear about what this meant. He felt ill-equipped to speak in public since his English, the language of authority, was better than his Hindustani.

In 1919 the country, expecting reform as one of the spoils of loyalty during the Great War, saw passed the Rowlatt Acts, asserting the continuance of the Defence of India Act, 1915, which suspended normal legal procedure by denying revolutionary suspects the usual defence or appeal and allowing internment without specific charges. *Hartals* or national days of mourning were set throughout India in protest; there was violence in some places, but not initially in Amritsar, a town of 150,000. Officials of the city, however, took precautions with a defence scheme to protect European areas. Murder and rioting did break out on April 12 and General Dyer was called on to restore law and order. This he did by proclaiming a ban on all public meetings. When an unarmed crowd of 5,000 gathered in the garden of Jallianwala Bagh he ordered the crowd to be fired upon without warning. 'I fired and continued to fire until the crowd dispersed.' Between two hundred and five hundred were killed and another thousand wounded; the shooting stopped when ammunition ran low. Swelling with confidence after a letter of approval from his superior officer and from the Lieutenant-Governor of the Punjab, Dyer, a man of duty, believed the moment demanded a show of fearless authority. On the filth-strewn street where a Miss Sherwood had been attacked, her *alleged* molesters were whipped and for nearly a week Indians passing down the street were forced to crawl on their bellies.

To such scenes Nehru rushed, gathering material for a Congress Committee Report. The 'lacerated heart of the Punjab' throbbed in his memory. By chance, on a train journey, Jawaharlal heard General Dyer himself say 'he felt like reducing the rebellious city to a heap of ashes.' This and the callousness at Amritsar went beyond the categories of right or wrong; it dramatised long-suspected truths. In the following year Nehru discovered on a visit to a poor village a further challenge to the moderation of the Congress Party and a broader condemnation of British rule; anger no longer had to wait on isolated massacres. The tales of permanent sorrow lived by peasants, 'their sense of ever-impending tragedy', vitalised and humanised politics by making the everyday needs of people the reason for freedom.

> Looking at them and their misery and overflowing gratitude, I was filled with shame and sorrow, shame at my own easy-going and comfortable life and our petting politics of the city which ignored this vast multitude of semi-naked sons and daughters of India. A new picture of India seemed to rise before me naked, starving, crushed

and utterly miserable. And their faith in us, casual visitors from the
distant city, embarrassed me and filled me with a new responsibility
that frightened me.[1]

As Gandhi's non-violent methods won popular support, a
success Indians could claim as of their own making, Nehru felt
a near-mystical exhilaration at mixing with vast crowds and
becoming accepted.

With leadership came imprisonment. He was arrested at each
wave of the Government of India's reaction to Congress
initiatives: in 1921 during the boycott of the Prince of Wales's
visit, in 1922 for picketing the shops of a merchant who
surreptitiously bought foreign cloth, in 1930, 1932, 1940 and
1942. In total he spent nine years behind bars.

Incarceration did not teach repentance. In prison he produced
an autobiography and two large books on the history of the
world, putting into words feelings denied action. Purpose
became firmer under challenge, as the denial of personal freedom
could be generalised to apply to the whole country. In this way
the patrician earned the right to be tribune. He wrote to
Gandhi after being released from prison in 1934: '[I feel] a
bubble of conceit thrown about hither and thither on an ocean
which spurned me. But vanity and conceit triumphed and the
intellectual apparatus that functions within me refused to admit
defeat. If the ideas that have spurred me to action and kept me
buoyed up through stormy weather were right—and the
conviction of their rightness ever grew within me—they were
bound to triumph though my generation might not live to
witness that triumph.'[2]

As this extract shows, Nehru's reluctance to compromise
produced a haughty confidence which assimilated the considerable nervous strain he felt. He frequently threatened to resign
his place of leadership in the Congress Party because of the
prevailing shyness, even in Gandhi, to concentrate on economic
reforms and complete independence. He often complained of
feeling estranged and ill-at-ease. Imprisonment, the death of
his father in 1931, and the early death of his wife reinforced a

[1] J. Nehru, *Autobiography*, 1936, p. 52.
[2] J. Nehru, *A Bunch of Old Letters*, Bombay, 1958, pp. 113–14.

sense of loneliness, which Gandhi's close friendship was able to soothe. Nehru had a fastidious sensitivity, capable of more emotion than his dignified appearance showed, which required fixed purposes and precise aims. When elected president of the Indian National Congress in 1929, a friend, Mrs S. Naidu, wrote perceptively to Nehru that she thought she was 'envisaging both the Coronation and the Crucifixion'.

Under Nehru's influence Congress asserted demands: the right to secede from the British Empire, complete independence, an impartial international tribunal to adjust financial debts, a united India. Where most politicians learn to adjust their demands for the practical benefits derived from agreement, Nehru distrusted all agreements which fell short of his demands. Perhaps the too-fine awareness of the injustice, unhappiness and brutality of the world darkened his mind to anything less than history readjusted according to his own wishes.

*   *   *

In 1896, C. R. Attlee (1883–1967) entered Haileybury College, the school founded by the East India Company earlier in the century to qualify students for public business and the higher departments of commercial life with the Company in India. When the Company was dissolved in 1858 the College had no formal connection with Indian affairs, though it was proud of its origins as shown by the fact that it was renamed in 1862 Haileybury and Imperial College. Here young Attlee, for whom 'conservatism was synonymous with patriotism',[1] developed a romantic and imaginative view of politics in the heady imperialism of the late nineteenth century; he was 'intoxicated by the vision of large portions of the school map coloured in red with people ruled for their own good by strong, silent men, civil servants, and soldiers as portrayed by Kipling'.[2] By 1909, however, the knowledge he gained of working-class poverty in Limehouse—'The grey and cruel city, Though streets that have no pity, The streets where men

---

[1] 'Conversion', Attlee Papers, Great Missenden.
[2] Lord Attlee, *Empire into Commonwealth*, 1961, p. 6.

decay'[1]—caused him to rebel against the values of the public school man: 'All he has are a few prejudices.'[2]

He gave up an insubstantial legal career to be manager of the Haileybury Boys' Club. The Club made up a company of the 1st Battalion of the Queen's London Regiment. At the outbreak of war in 1914 he volunteered along with the boys he lived among and trained. Major Attlee became Under-Secretary of State for War in the first Labour Government and three years later was chosen by Ramsay MacDonald to represent the Party on the Indian Statutory Commission, an all-party committee sent out to India by Parliament to review the effects of the constitutional changes introduced by the India Act of 1919. Attlee had no particular qualifications for his selection except that the importance of defence and the Indian army required some members of the commission to have enough military experience to understand and advise on strategic questions.[3] Indeed, before 1927 he had never spoken on Indian affairs, but this kind of negative asset, as so often in his political career, worked to his advantage. Never an exciting choice for new responsibilities, he was always the appropriate one: this was true in 1919 when he became Mayor of Stepney, leader of the Parliamentary Labour Party in 1935, and Prime Minister in 1945. He could be seen to be uncommitted, though of course MacDonald knew he had in Attlee a cooperative and moderate representative of the kind of Labour Party he hoped to present to the country. Without preconceptions about India's future he coasted down the gentle slopes of sensible and well-meaning platitudes; 'I accepted the general party line that India was on the way to self-government, but that the way would be long.'[4]

Not surprisingly the Indian popular press did not receive their future liberator with any enthusiasm when he and the Commission arrived in 1928, though one journalist's report touched on that personal insecurity which was perhaps the source of his later style of political leadership: the fixed awareness

---

[1] C. R. Attlee, 'In Limehouse, In Limehouse', *Socialist Review*, September 1910.

[2] 'India,' Attlee Papers, Great Missenden.

[3] Stephen Walsh, Secretary of State for War in the same Government, was first chosen to accompany Attlee, but had to refuse because of ill-health.

[4] 'India,' Attlee Papers, Great Missenden.

of party interests, well-mannered but impersonal relations with colleagues, and a preference for displaying the nature of his political party in deeds rather than words.

> Major Attlee cut a very sorry figure when tackled by the press people. . . . He was asked what was the significance of the Labour War Lords being chosen to represent Labour on the Commission? Major Attlee was so hopelessly flabbergasted by the volley of questions that his hand began to shiver as he tried to light his pipe. The pressmen thought it cruel to bully him any more and as they were taking leave of him, the Major said, 'Thank you.'[1]

The whole Commission was boycotted by the Congress Party and crowds 'greeted' them with black flags and the cry of 'Simon, go back', because no Indian was included on the Commission supposedly sent to decide India's future. Increasingly, Attlee became aware, as he travelled throughout India, of the incongruity of British rule with indigenous traditions. 'The truth is that over here they have been trying to put an Anglo-Saxon façade on to a Mogul building and the two pieces are not structurally connected. The Anglo-Saxon Mogul building was an effective piece of work in the classical style, no freedom but balance and grace.'[2] Was balance and grace enough to make a constitution effective, particularly if it still curtailed the freedom of those for whom the constitution was made? Britain could only make a ready-made constitutional garment cut from her own political and historical experiences. Could some patchwork pattern be made acceptable to Indians? So Atlee mused after his work on the Commission. Privately he began to doubt the wisdom of a policy which proposed concessions to India's wish for responsibility subject to a few reservations which turned out to be very substantial. 'The real difficulty in dealing with the Central Government is that there is no feasible transitional stage between a government responsible to Great Britain and a government responsible to the Indian people.'[3]

The turning point in Attlee's political career occurred after

---

[1] *Indian National Herald*, 5 February 1928.
[2] C. R. Attlee to Tom Attlee, 14 November 1928. T. Attlee Papers.
[3] C. R. Attlee to Tom Attlee, 27 June 1930. T. Attlee Papers.

the 1931 crisis and MacDonald left the party. Disowned and dishonoured were the vague proffers of reform. The gloom of the depression, the miniscule Parliamentary Labour Party, the blurred intentions of the National Government, justified a more radical approach to issues. The reforms of the next Socialist Government, the determination to legislate a new kind of society, revived the Labour Party's belief in itself. India was also affected by the radical turn of the Party. Attlee became the Party's leading spokesman on India; he tried to find a distinctly 'socialist' approach to the issues. With a boycotted Commissioner's disdain for the Congress Party he had the ordinary man's suspicion of foreigners; he conceived of the Indian bureaucrat as sitting at his desk with a variety of coloured pencils drawing designs of heaven, but within the imperatives of the 1930s he had to have socialist reasons for disliking them. Accordingly, they were not sufficiently devoted to social reform to warrant support; Congress had less a love of mankind than a very shrewd awareness of its own interests. In his draft proposals as a member of the Joint Committee on Indian Constitutional Reform, Attlee was explicit that any new constitution should 'state beyond all cavil that it is the intention of this country to grant full Dominion Status to India within a measurable period of years'.[1] 'Safeguards' retained by the British authority should be those 'mainly with a view to protecting the poorer sections of the community from exploitation'.[2] For the first time, in 1933, Attlee said that the only workable constitution for India was one acceptable to the nationalist. No intricate mesh of balances and delicately delineated authority could replace popular consent. British rule was alien rule and thus incapable of introducing enough measures of social and economic improvement which are the reasons for any government. 'The evils from which India is suffering today can only be remedied by Indian action.'[3]

The 'will and the way' to socialism as conceived in the 1930s extended to Attlee's post-war Government. The determination

[1] The Labour Members Draft Report, 'Mr. Attlee's Draft' for the Joint Committee on Indian Constitutional Reform. Lansbury Papers.
[2] *Joint Committee on Indian Constitutional Reform*, Vol. I, Part II (1934), p. 258.
[3] 276 *H. of C. Debs.*, 5th Series, 723 (27 March 1933).

to model the welfare state carried with it the departure from India. Social and economic reform were given the highest priority in the Government's thinking; Britain's world-power status was no longer to be sustained by a vast overseas empire but in its experiments in state intervention and control of society. The glory heretofore vested in far distant lands was now to be found at home.

*   *   *

One genre of theatre conceives of the play as an educational process: people discover or reveal truths after a series of errors. Last scenes end confusion. Misunderstandings, upon which so much in the play thrived, have been shown to be unconstructive and therefore eventually must be disregarded. Life goes on. The climax has a simplicity about it, for earlier scenes of contretemps, alliances, unexpected events with only a hint of the eventual dénouement, portrayed a world too unfixed and unlimited for ordinary people to trust.

Like a character in such a play, M. A. Jinnah (1876–1948) adjusted to changed situations; past failures instructed him. Rational, objective, argumentative, in the course of the Indian drama he learned the most. The idea of an independent state for Muslims he broached in 1940, only after less radical solutions were attempted. He understood the awkward position Muslims were in but showed remarkable skill at devising a middle and sensible policy that was complicated but plausible for the times. He once described the plight of the Mussalman in India as 'a dweller in no man's land'. This was his own plight. Caught in the cross-fire of British intentions and the effects of Hindu nationalism, friends and enemies were indistinguishable for the Muslim leader. Could 'no man's land' become an autonomous position?

Jinnah in background and temperament was favoured to have a middle orientation in a country of extremes. Much in his political development showed the capacity to make the middle viable. His family had been Hindu converts to the Khoja sect of the Aga Khan; like its spiritual head, religious devotion did not interfere with the family's practical interests and appreciation of the European world. Jinnah's father was a hide merchant and exporter. He had no qualms about sending his son to the Christian Missionary Society School in Karachi. Jinnah's mother came from Kathiawar—where Gandhi had lived. He was taught Gujerathi at an early age. Thus Gandhi and Jinnah literally spoke the same language.

Also like Gandhi, Jinnah became a law student in London. Though he adopted Joseph Chamberlain's monocle, it was Gladstone's liberalism of principled self-determination and the style of well-argued reasonableness which made the most sense to him. No student studying in a foreign country can help but feel an expatriated ambassador, if only because people in his host country so regard him. A unique opportunity arose in 1892 for Jinnah to participate in British politics and yet keep an Indian perspective. Dadabhai Naoroji, the grand old man of India, stood as a Liberal candidate for Central Finsbury to demonstrate the spirit of cooperation, justice and generosity, in which he and the Indian National Congress believed.

In 1906 Jinnah became Naoroji's private secretary at the conference of the Indian National Congress which protested against the partition of Bengal and demanded a greater amount of self-government. The partition split the large province of Bengal into two, giving Muslims a majority in one half where before they had been a large minority. The Muslim League was formed in 1906 to watch over Muslim interests, particularly those so recently established by the British Government. Jinnah stayed clear of the League and attended the conferences of the Congress. But it was as a Muslim that he secured a place on the new Imperial Legislative Council instituted in 1909, becoming one of the thirty-five elected members of the Council, the representative of the Bombay Muslims. He soon argued with the Viceroy (interestingly in the content of the treatment of Indians in South Africa) over his choice of the word 'cruel'. When the Viceroy suggested he adapt his language to the circumstances, the advocate, not wishing to 'trespass for one single moment' on constitutional decorum, relented with: 'The treatment meted out to Indians is the harshest which can possibly be imagined.'[1]

In 1912 Jinnah attended the session of the Muslim League

[1] H. Bolitho, *Jinnah*, Lahore, 1966, p. 48.

presided over by the Aga Khan, which far from asserting
sectarian aims began to amend its constitution to comply with
the Congress Party's call for self-rule and social and economic
reforms which fostered national unity and cooperation. In 1914
he worked to have the annual conference of the Muslim League
and the National Congress occur in Bombay at the same time.
Committees bridging the two parties agreed on joint proposals
for political reforms. These in turn were submitted to the
Imperial Legislative Council, signed by nineteen members. In
1916 Jinnah became President of the Conference of the Muslim
League at Lucknow where a pact was signed with the Congress
agreeing on separate electorates for Muslims and, in provinces
where Muslims were in a minority, guaranteeing them a
number of seats. Jinnah had become an ambassador of unity by
finding a way to placate Muslim worries about their rights as a
minority, and proving that the Congress Party was less Hindu
than Indian.

Sensible solutions proved tenuous in but a few years. A
Hindu-Muslim, Congress-League accord could only flourish in
orderly circumstances where agreements began to fit into a
larger structure of trust and responsibility. When the British
Government, by its constitutional reforms of 1917 and after,
did not provide enough of a basis for political growth, no habit
of cooperation developed. Indian politics became inorganic.
Instead, the rational approach to politics which would set a pace
for progress and harmony was undermined. By 1920 Jinnah saw
the real basis of Hindu-Muslim cooperation dissolve when
Gandhi took over the leadership of the Congress. He feared the
long-term effects of a non-violent non-cooperation campaign in
a volatile country with desperate conditions, illiteracy and
superstitions. He thought Gandhi's methods would prove
disastrous, for splits and divisions must develop as a concomitant to the encompassing disorder and chaos. In practice, how
could there be political advance without cooperation with
Britain? The absolute boycott of Britain and the Empire would
only reduce the area of responsibility available to Indians.
Gandhi's spirituality would charge the Congress Party with a
religious enthusiasm, Hindu in content, which would arouse
Muslim distrust. Disillusioned, in 1920 Jinnah resigned from

the Congress Party and the Imperial Legislative Council. Unlike other Muslim leaders, he did not see in the Khilafat Movement, which attracted Congress support, any basis for permanent cooperation.

While Congress leaders adopted methods of protest which landed them in prison, Jinnah joined the Central Legislative Council in 1923. More and more he represented Muslim interests. He served on important government committees for political reform and Indianisation of the army. He still spoke in generalities about Hindu-Muslim unity, but no basis for permanent cooperation arose. Jinnah believed Gandhi's methods made the country restless and impatient, which in turn forced him, Gandhi, to promise a near-immediate end to British rule— a promise belied by events. These methods and their notoriety inevitably made the Congress leaders feel that they were the only party representing the nationalist or independence cause.

Jinnah, having rejected Congress methods, turned to the British Government in the hope that, when self-government was given to India, it would be on terms which left the Muslim minority a guaranteed political status. Changes in the constitution had to have Muslim approval. In 1930 he joined the Aga Khan in presenting the Muslim case at the Round Table Conference. They argued that Muslims should have one third of the seats set aside for them in any future legislature, and provincial autonomy must leave the Muslim provinces free from a central government dominated by Hindus. At the conference Jinnah was depressed by what he saw as the intransigence in the Hindu mentality. He decided to reside in London. 'The centre of gravity is here and in the next two or three years London will be the most important scene of the Indian drama of constitutional reforms.'

He returned to India in 1935 to prepare for the elections established by the new constitution. In the next few years, unity and cooperation with the Congress Party gave way to a new direction of thought. The coming of elections and the tendency of the Congress and sometimes the British to disregard Muslim interests led Jinnah to believe that Muslims could only assert their political status if they had sufficient mass support throughout the country. A minority is a minority, but a minority of eighty million firm supporters would command respect. The All-India Muslim League and the All-India Muslim Conference, hitherto rival organisations, joined to organise a common platform. Jinnah played a major role in the unification and organisation of Muslims. He became President of the Central Election Board of the Muslim League and began touring the country. In the 1937 elections the League did poorly, winning only 108 out of the 1,585 seats. Congress on the other hand gained a working majority in seven provinces. When Congress refused to share power with Muslims, or only if Muslims joined the Congress party, Jinnah virtually declared war. In 1938 the Pirpur Report of the All-India Muslim League found that in many Congress-run provinces Muslims were discriminated against; it was alleged that Hindi replaced Urdu, children were taught anti-Muslim songs, and made to swear allegiance to the Congress flag. In 1940 Jinnah proposed Muslims should have an independent state of their own, Pakistan. He believed there could be no safeguards for a minority if the majority were the controlling power. In a unitary state there is no outside force to adjust wrongs. A minority would always remain a minority, struggling for recognition and eventually despised as obstructionist. The partition of India had to accompany the transfer of power. After 1940 Jinnah never changed his mind.

*   *   *

Edward Wood, Lord Irwin (later Lord Halifax) (1881–1959) had a natural and hereditary interest in India. Like other Viceroys before him—Lord Minto, Lord Hardinge, and Lord Chelmsford—family associations with India's more halcyon days in the previous century conferred an element of tradition and distinction on the highest office in the Government of India. Those with names enshrined in the annals of the history of British India were sought after to perpetuate in the eyes of the nation the 'service' of their ancestors. Irwin's grandfather, Sir John Lawrence, had been the first Secretary of State after the Crown replaced the East India Company and the Governor-General.

An M.P. since 1910, Edward Wood became Under-Secretary of State at the Colonial Office under Churchill in 1921. His main task was to visit the West Indies to report on conditions there and advise on the matter of extending direct representation in the legislatures. This was the first of those diplomatic missions in which he showed exceptional skill at creating the right impression by dignified charm and 'sensible' conciliation while also winning for himself some modest acclaim. Later in India and in Nazi Germany he found *terra firma* with adversaries others had deemed implacable.

In a letter written to Churchill published in the *Report of the Parliamentary Under-Secretary of State for the Colonies On a Visit to the West Indies and British Guiana* (1922), he recommended that elected members should be admitted to the different legislatures of the islands, eventually to the extent that the official majority would be lost. The African population in the West Indies owed all they were to the British and therefore it was not surprising they should look for political maturation from 'the only source and pattern they knew' and thus want to try 'the peculiar British gift of representative institutions'.[1] In the context of the profound loyalty of the people to the Crown, representative legislatures were no part of the demand for responsible government, 'nor within the measurable distance of time could such a demand be rightly conceded'.[2] His constitutional plan for advancement was generous without real expense. Indeed, even when there was no longer an official majority in the legislatures, ultimate control was retained by the Secretary of State while the Governor could carry any vote or measure he thought essential for the good government of the colony. Yet this real control by the British authority did not preclude *proposing* some remission of insignificant but wished-for authority. Advancement in the West Indies as later in India meant avoiding the mistake of 'endeavouring to withhold a concession ultimately inevitable until it has been robbed by delay of most of its usefulness and all its grace.'[3]

Irwin too humbly claimed that he had no special training or acquired knowledge[4] when he reached India in 1926. What he

[1] *Report of the Parliamentary Under-Secretary of State for the Colonies on a Visit to the West Indies and British Guiana*, Cmd. 1679, 1922, p. 6.
[2] *Ibid.*, p. 7.   [3] *Ibid.*, pp. 6, 7.
[4] The Earl of Halifax, *Fullness of Days*, 1957, p. 110.

lacked in detailed understanding—indeed ever since the contentious Viceroyalty of Lord Curzon such knowledge could have precluded his selection—he made up by personal qualities ever-essential in Eastern administration. With a high churchman's spirituality, he could take the broader view of human foibles; aloof but sincere, there was a deliberateness in his manner which impressed a variety of people that here was a man of consideration and reasonableness. Born with an atrophied left arm, without a hand, the Viceroy was an altogether more human emblem of authority to illness-ridden India, for like the country in his charge, he combined physical disability with a religious temperament.

His first year was spent in those social and ceremonial rounds, seeing and being seen, which formed the preliminary education of Viceroys. First impressions were: 'Our life here is very much of a routine, a good deal of entertaining, fairly regular lawn tennis or riding and a good deal of work, but work under pleasanter conditions than sitting up all night in the House of Commons.'[1] He detected little anti-British feeling among the masses of the population and devised a schedule of visits and tours to go over the heads of agitators by appealing directly to the people. 'That is why I try to lose no opportunity on these tours of doing something in the line of a little personal touch.'[2]

The effects of Irwin's personal touches palled into insignificance when, upon his advice, the Indian Statutory Commission was appointed without any Indian members. This 'Imperial insolence' threw the country into chaos: crowds protested and police patrolled the streets of the cities. The President of the Legislative Assembly obstructed government business.

In place of cheering crowds the Commission was usually welcomed by officials, petitioning minorities, the local Chamber of Commerce, and prominent Europeans. Because the Commission stayed in India for a long time, from February to March 1928 and from October 1928 to March 1929, the irritation it created was protracted. Commissions were meant to aid government administration not become a *causus belli*; this one became a greater obstacle to public tranquillity than the original problems

[1] Lord Irwin to Lord Halifax, 4 May 1926. Irwin Papers, IOL.
[2] Lord Irwin to Lord Halifax, 8 December 1926. Irwin Papers, IOL.

it was sent to adjudicate. The Viceroy feared an attitude of opposition would crystallise in the country, which could be exploited by Communist subversives. He thought the 'great problem for Great Britain was to keep a contented India within the Empire', which meant taking greater risks and approaching the 'whole thing with a good deal more imagination'.[1] To this end he announced in November 1929 that 'the natural issue of India's constitutional progress . . . is the attainment of Dominion Status'.

This should not be taken to mean that the Viceroy intended to launch a great scheme of immediate advance towards an independent India free of British control. Conditions which make democracy (by which he meant representative government) successful—education, responsibility, the faculty for forming judgements and 'a hundred other things'—were absent in India. British authority was the ballast necessary to keep the Government and the country on the rails. Confident while troops and police could contain all manifestations of the nationalist spirit, he could out-manoeuvre Indian leaders, 'tiresome people[2] . . . who have let loose the evil genii of disloyalty which they are incapable of controlling . . . and even genuinely frightened of the demon they have let out of the bottle, it is not physically within their power to cork him up again just when they want to'.[3] Using 'Dominion status' as an allurement, the Viceroy showed he had some of the wiles of Sinbad. Thus, Dominion status was nothing more than 'a long-term definition' of final purpose which cannot be 'held to queer the pitch of decision as to your immediate policy'.[4] When no longer in India's sunny climes he was clearer about the limited practical meaning of Dominion status. 'The special traditions of India today make it difficult, if not impossible, to apply full Dominion status in the sense of function.'[5]

But the Viceroy did not make it easy to understand what his offer meant. He had a circumlocutious manner of expression and a slight tendency to agree with his correspondent. The

[1] Lord Irwin to Sir S. Hoare, 10 June 1930. Templewood Papers, IOL.
[2] Lord Irwin to Lord Halifax, 5 June 1928. Irwin Papers.
[3] Lord Irwin to Lord Halifax, 12 August 1926. Irwin Papers.
[4] Lord Irwin to Lord Halifax, 6 November 1927, Irwin Papers.
[5] *Joint Committee on Indian Constitutional Reform*, IIc, 1933–4, p. 1793.

offer coming after the tumultuous year of 1928 could only be interpreted as an advance on the previous position. In this sense he wrote to his friend Lord Robert Cecil: 'The fundamental fact we have got to get into our minds is that we must be prepared to move from the theory of relationship of superior and subordinate to one of partnership.'[1] Yet in the middle of the crisis within the Conservative Party at the time of his announcement, he allayed suspicions by writing to Baldwin: 'You may be quite assured, that both I and my colleagues with you regard full Dominion status, in the sense in which you mean the words [as government free of British control] wholly impracticable whether now or in the near future.'[2]

*   *   *

The theatre of this century has explored the theme of the hero as failure, examining situations where a man cannot find in society or politics a way to realise the essential characteristics of his personality. The different stages of life remain unintegrated, good intentions are wasted, proven impractical. Human institutions seem to be at fault because, lacking moral purpose, they doom to failure any who try to make them moral. Authority is heartless. The protagonist reflects on a life of bits and pieces and the non-functional nature of his own suffering; he feels a victim of an ignoble system which nonetheless has time and again been able to defeat him.

Such was the state of consciousness of Lala Lajpat Rai (1865–1928) when, submitting to 'the lava of pessimism', he reflected on his life-time of public work and political agitation. 'I am sick of life—both mentally and physically . . . I have no zest left in me, no go, no desire. Whenever anyone asks me to do anything or whenever I think of doing something the invariable question that comes out from the depth of my mind is—"Oh! what is the good?" Is there any good in this world? Is it worth all the trouble one takes over it. . . . The sense of impatience, humiliation and misery overwhelms me. . . . [The world] is no place for justice or mercy or kindness or benevolence.'[3]

---

[1] Lord Irwin to Lord Cecil of Chelwood, 1 October 1930. B.M.
[2] Lord Irwin to Stanley Baldwin, 6 July 1930. MacDonald Papers.
[3] Lala Lajpat Rai to G. D. Birla, in *Writing and Speeches of Lala Lajpat Rai*, Delhi, 1966, Vol. II, pp. 417–19.

Lajpat Rai was the son of a poor Urdu and Persian teacher in Delhi; he belonged to the first generation of English-educated Punjabis. In 1881 he joined Government College, Lahore, but had to give up his studies after two years because his family was too poor to maintain him. Through self-study he was eventually able in 1886 to pass the Pleader's Examination, which enabled him in a few years to become one of the leading and most successful lawyers of Hissar and then a Pleader of the Punjab Chief Court. The boyhood years of poverty made it natural for him to identify with the needs and suffering in the country. 'I have deeply felt the degradation of my country and the humiliations of my countrymen have sunk deep into my soul.' He threw himself into charitable works: he founded in 1897 the Hindu Orphan Relief Movement for the young victims of the raging famine, and established industrial projects for them to earn a living. By 1908 the Movement was expanded to encompass general relief to anyone in need. He travelled throughout the country collecting money and guiding volunteers. He started the Hindu Elementary Education League to extend education to all classes.

Without the status of a free people, no passionate Indian who believed in independence for his country—and there were many—could avoid government suspicion and investigation. A leader, by his very elevation to prominence, posed a threat, especially if he was not employed by the Government. In circumstances where the distinction between opposition and sedition was difficult to draw because one or the other might ignite a riot, there were few innocent activities in British India. Was not a street row a potential insurrection? Without the functional representation of popular interests heroes of the people were easiest to detect and seize. Lajpat Rai was a hero made martyr by events he disliked as much as he did martyrdom, for it was his wish to play some practical part in the improvement of the life of the people ('milk for babies, food for adults, education for all'). Instead he was caught in one storm and then another.

As the friend of L. Tilak, Lajpat Rai's guilt was implicit in the association, according to government officials. In 1896 Lajpat Rai published popular biographies of Mazzini, Garibaldi and Shivaji, which, in keeping with Tilak's method of avoiding censorship, used men of the past to supply a contemporary message. Books about men who fought to tear the yoke of oppression and unify their country had particular relevance for a people who could be moved by an inspiring story. Moved to do what? This was the worry of the Home Department. A confidential file on Lajpat Rai was opened and his books were labelled seditious. Even his Orphan Relief Movement was put under surveillance lest money raised for relief were used for political purposes.

In 1907 disorder swept the Punjab. Riots broke out in Lahore and Rawalpindi. The causes of unrest were many: bubonic plague was still rife in the province, killing more than half a million people; government officials were notorious in the area for their corruption, supplementing their income with the fines they levied; charges on land revenue and water had just been increased causing economic hardship; and the proposed Punjab Colonisation Bill which empowered the local authorities to sell the newly claimed, through irrigation, agricultural land only to 'agricultural tribes' was seen by Hindus as a way of obstructing them from buying the new land. The keen new Governor, Sir Denzil Ibbertson, decided to act with firmness and arrest Lajpat Rai, the most popular leader in the province. He was duly arrested and deported to Mandalay under Regulation III of 1818 which precluded trial or legal defence. After six months in gaol and some conscience-searching by the Secretary of State, Lord Morley, he was released. Morley irritably commented on the Governor's deportation: 'Nothing could be *thinner* than what they call evidence.'

During the Great War, fear of arrest forced Lajpat Rai to exile himself and live in the United States in 1915. But exile, 'the most cursed word in the dictionary of man', was no comfort to someone looking to direct the course of change in his own country; 'it shuts the doors of heaven and makes life a continued agony.'[1] In New York he founded the Indian Home Rule League of America and edited a newspaper called *Young India* to explain British rule and Indian nationalism. He wrote an open letter, banned in India, to Lloyd George in 1917 with the bitter-

[1] *Ibid.*, Vol. I, p. 256.

ness of an outcaste: 'Just as a lion may die of sheer exhaustion when attacked by an enemy rather than willingly loosen his grip on his prey so long as there is breath in his body, so a nation holding another in subjection might endanger her own existence without loosening her grip on her victim.'[1]

The India Lajpat Rai returned to in 1920 saw the Congress Party, committed to Gandhi's non-cooperation, soon declared illegal and its leaders including himself arrested in December 1921. Released in January 1922 he was immediately re-arrested on another charge and confined until August 1923. The political creed which so ran counter to the authorities intermingled socialism and nationalism, relating the destructive features of industrialism and imperialism 'like twin sisters'. The Government of India, as employer, in the railways, post office and administration, exploited labour and entrenched its own position. But Lajpat Rai took a practical view of India's problems and stressed the need for the economic uplift of the masses. Though a leader of the Congress Party, he joined the Swarajist Party to try to work the new constitution. He was soon disappointed over how little he could actually do for the people of the country; he felt like one 'who ploughs the sands'.

Lajpat Rai was unable throughout a rich and varied career to find a permanent and constructive profession. He lamented that, in India, politics were synonymous with agitation. Nothing tells of the futility which pervaded his life more cogently than its end.

When the Simon Commission arrived in Lahore at the end of October 1928, the police banned protest meetings. In defiance of the law a crowd of a thousand people gathered at the railway station where wire barracades were placed. The crowd surged forward in a gap of four or five feet. The police alleged stones were thrown and retaliated with a lathi charge. Lajpat Rai, at the front of the crowd, was struck twice on the chest. When he died a few weeks later two doctors said the blows hastened his death for he had tubercular pleurisy. The Punjab Government set up a committee to investigate the incident at the railway station, but as so often in his life, findings were uncertain. But

---

[1] Lala Lajpat Rai, 'Open Letter to Lloyd George', 13 June 1917 in *Writings and Speeches*, Vol. I, pp. 256–62.

this made no difference. News of his death 'made a dull anger spread over the country'.[1]

Could some means be found to assuage the animosity that cast its shadow over nearly half a century? Could men with such different experiences and attitudes devise some structure or institution mutually acceptable? Could the disastrous episodes of the past be erased, helpfully forgotten, or were they irremovable scenes of the Indian drama? Could a noble constitution, crystalline and precious, begin a dialogue in Anglo-Indian relations hitherto filled with soliloquies?

[1] J. Nehru, *Autobiography*, p. 174.

FIVE

CONSTITUTION-MAKING

[i]

WHAT IS A CONSTITUTION? The question assumes
an advanced, sophisticated society able to refine governing into consistent and fundamental principles.
Personal whim, arbitrary power, and random policy, familiar images of monarchs and court intrigue, are supplanted by consistent,
reasoned, and more popularly acceptable ideas about how affairs
should be managed. The existence of a constitution becomes a
sign of political advancement; the laws and customs belonging
to an obscure and irrelevant past are either brought into
harmony with the principles of the constitution or they are
superseded. A constitution, no matter how complex in itself,
whether written or unwritten, is a practical formula which
explains the relationship of government and community.
Procedures become regular, authority is limited, obligations
are specified, and the institutions in use become indications of
government intentions. Abstract words like freedom, rights,
and liberty become clearer because they function in a context;
here is the fount of law and justice. The classical constitutions of
the eighteenth century were able to cleanse the soiled nature of
ordinary language. Thomas Paine wrote in *The Rights of Man*[1]
'The American constitutions were to liberty what a grammar is
to language: they define its parts of speech, and practically
construct them into syntax.' At times, constitutionalists revel
in the logical and almost mathematical aspects of their work, as
if thereby to suggest the physical and mechanistic origins of
their ideas.

Every constitution describes the components in the machinery
of government and states or implies the principles which inspire

[1] T. Paine, *Rights of Man*, 1921, p. 77.

it. Constitutions are concerned with designating or apportioning sovereignty 'with propriety and exactness'. The sources for the principles of sovereignty are derived, often by a process of careful selection, from long-established statutes, legal precedents, and the history of the society which made them. The classical constitution thus articulates in current institutions changes in society, the growth of new and powerful classes, and new ideas which re-interpret the past. Ideally, for social harmony, constitutional changes, as in much of English history, should occur slowly so as to make popular acceptance' of them easier.

Just as the word constitution refers to the physical nature of the body, its political meaning reflects the character of the nation, remaining for the period in which it works the collective political wisdom of the community, in short the best way devised to run affairs. The concern of constitutions with justice leads them to penetrate deeply into beliefs and ideas. A religious sense of right and wrong, the genealogy of a country's morals, contribute to the solidity of the constitution which helps make it fit into the larger pattern of obedience, propriety and civility upon which everyday life depends.

Since a constitution touches on so many vital aspects of consciousness, it is not surprising that constitution-making has been associated with political revolution. To write a formal document acceptable to the various orders of society, or their representatives, in a single moment in time, can precipitate a crisis in confidence in the *status quo*. Cahiers and petitions, a necessary preliminary phase for constitutional reform, elucidate discontent and create expectations for their resolution. Fashionable ideas are employed to confront the established authority and to show how principles of government exist outside current practice. The constitution, when made a prime object of argument and reform, can provoke vitriolic disagreements.

No less disputable than the principles upon which a constitution should be based is the question of who has the right to make one. In those countries where a constitution was written, the members of the constituent assembly claimed for themselves the *vox populi*. With new world common-sense the founding fathers of American Constitution ordained and established a new constitution because they saw themselves as 'we, the people'. On the eighteenth-century model, which influenced all later thinking, the new constitution represented as many interests in the society as had sufficient power to exert pressure during the time when the constitution was written. These constitutions extended the right of influence to a number of sections in the commonwealth. Political alignments became firmer. The founding of a new constitution coincided with the origination of political parties. In order to have the new constitution gain as much support as possible, elections, as a mechanism of consent, were extended. The constitution thus contributed to a rise in national sentiment through a legal bond of unity, and an oath to common ideals. The idea of a national, democratic government responsible to the governed developed alongside the new constitutions, for everyone now accepted to live under the same rules, and it remained open to others to effect changes by similar means.

Any penetrating analysis of the Indian constitution had to reveal what was unconventional about British rule. Frequent and periodic adjustment to the form of government discredited the established Government, which therefore found it necessary to review again and again fundamental political institutions. The regular tides of constitution-making gathered every complaint in its swirl. From the depths of India special interests, select minorities, power élites, pleaded for special treatment in memorials, memoranda, and petitions. For example, the Indian Statutory Commission of 1927 had to consider the views of such special interests as the Catholic Aborigines of Chota Nagpur. An already divided country was further sub-divided by having the right to stake a claim widely available.

As trained lawyers like Gandhi, Jinnah, and Nehru scrutinised the government of India, they saw the legal and historical traditions of the constitutional state abrogated. Indigenous laws and customs were not sufficiently integrated into the constitution. Justice and right had been construed according to the laws of England; as early as 1726 English common and statute law were introduced into the presidency towns.[1] Parliament could not use native laws and customs as a basis for government since

[1] M. Setalvad, *The Role of the English Law in India*, Jerusalem, 1966, p. 12.

they were strewn throughout the sub-continent.[1] Ambiguity pervaded political language. It was unclear how the long-term intentions of government—the education of a dependent people to political self-sufficiency and material advancement of the poor—were realised in practice. The system of government could not disguise some uncomplimentary—to Indians—reasons for British rule; British responsibility was ultimately justifiable because Indians were not yet ready or able to manage themselves. When, in the twentieth century, not only was the constitution brought under increased observation but made the object of reform, constitution-making raised Indian expectations British ministers found themselves unable to satisfy. Constitution-making also brought into question the right of Englishmen to construct a form of government for Indians and gave an opportunity for all national parties to claim that the new form of government had to have the consent of the people or their representatives. Constitution-making inevitably led Indians to wish for direct responsibility over affairs of state. Through the decades of discussion it became a source of irritation that British rule was based on unusual precedents and exceptional circumstances, an aberrant government established by historical accident, the whims of fortune, and police power.

[1] As later events showed these laws and customs were sources of disloyalty since they owed nothing to British authority. With the growth of Hindu and Moslem cultural nationalism what was Indian or preceded British rule was valued for its own sake. To defend an ancient tradition against the encroachments of a government dominated by British officials was a means of dividing a foreign administration from society and the community which they, the nationalists, purported to represent. Thus in 1891 the government bill to regulate child marriage by making it a penal offence for married children under twelve to cohabit and allow a child wife on attaining majority to dissolve the marriage contract provoked a major campaign by L. Tilak to oppose the bill. For the first time mass meetings of protest were assembled, with Tilak arguing that the government had no right to interfere with ancient Hindu customs. When raising the age of consent was again debated in the Legislative Assembly in 1925 similar arguments were used: 'You may lay your unholy hands on our ancient ideals and traditions, but we will not follow you.' (Quoted in K. Mayo, *Mother India*, 1945, p. 22). What was here asserted was the pre-eminence of native habits over British authority—the essence of nationalism. Jinnah in a similar way launched his political career by defending a Moslem law. In 1913 he introduced the Wakf Validating Bill in the Legislative Council, a 'Muhammadan Law to the Mussalmans', to guarantee a family's inheritance against a frivolous relative who might squander it.

Some experienced administrators soon acknowledged how misguided was the exercise of reform, how the effects of the discussion about change were more harmful than the old system. Better, it was thought, to leave undefended and unexplained a government ruling a country too vast for its resources.[1] Human ingenuity and the spirit of service could more than make up for the deficiencies in revenue, communication, transport, practical experience, staff, and legal niceties.

> Our policy hitherto has been based . . . on a wrong diagnosis of the situation. We have assumed the problem to be that of a people with a sense of responsibility wishing to be allowed to exercise it, but that was not in fact the case; the problem has rather been that of a people with no sense of responsibility and no experience of it, wanting to possess it, and dreading any situation which would cause them to reveal their deficiency. Having started from a faulty diagnosis, our prescriptions seem to me to have been progressively faulty. We have done nothing to cultivate the defective sense of responsibility, we have set Indians tasks in which they were bound to fail, we have asked them to advise men more competent and experienced than themselves, we have encouraged them to criticise everyone in a responsible position, we have allowed them to impede the policies and actions of others, and to think and say that they would do better themselves without giving them the opportunity to test their capacity.
>
> In such circumstances it was impossible for anyone to do any good. Parliament had given to public opinion in India an unlimited power of obstruction, and public opinion in England constituted an equal obstacle to the teaching of lessons at the cost of efficiency. The result was that Bengal, while I was there [as Governor], was probably the worst governed country in the world, in the sense that it was one in which it was the hardest to get any work of public utility carried out.[2]

Why, if government reform was inherently fraught with so many pitfalls, did Britain pursue it? Men experienced in Indian administration had no confidence that any good would come from these reforms; on the contrary, efficiency would be harmed by bringing to responsibility an irreconciled opposition. For a

---

[1] 'The English in India are, for the most part, to busy to think. They have their day's work; the vineyard is too large and the labourers are few.' S. Low, *A Vision of India*, 1911, p. 354.

[2] The Earl of Lytton, *Pundits and Elephants*, 1942, pp. 180–1.

coalition between different interests to be viable, must bring within its ranks the main political parties. While the major reforms of the twentieth century were attempts to form limited coalitions, on the Viceroy's Council, the Legislative Council, or in the provinces, the frequent unwillingness of Indians and particularly the Congress Party, the most powerful political party in the country, to cooperate in the reforms meant that the prospect of reform would exacerbate an already hostile or at least critical India. Better to do nothing. 'I am pleased to find that your view conforms to mine, viz. that our policy ought to be masterly inactivity.'[1]

One of the significant achievements of the Indian nationalist parties during the period of government reforms was the way in which it was able to force a system of administration, designed primarily for management, to explain and justify itself. The popular press generated political discussion, though as an odd dialogue, between government statements and itself. How sensitive the Indian Government was to press criticism is indicated by the Press Acts which sought to prevent articles being published which might lead to incitement and sedition, both of which the Government of India defined widely. But the impetus for government reform came not exclusively from proud Indians wanting first a share and then all power in running their country. Britain, in the face of weighty expert advice, launched the reforms. Why?

A simple explanation is that Britain was caught in the echo of its own promises. From the very early regulating acts, the Government of India was conceived in terms of guardianship with the implication that some day the backward nation under kind tutelage would attain maturity and its birthright. When 'adolescent' Indians claimed their birthright, the Government had to make efforts to show sincerity and good faith. Reform was such a sign.

Britain had inherited from the nineteenth century a pride in its administration. It was natural, therefore, for her to conceive of integrating a few trusted Indians, trained in an English manner, to participate in the Government as a kind of native Anglo-Indian. Since the vast Indian Civil Service, as well

[1] A. Hirtzel to H. Butler, 4 September 1924. Butler Papers, IOL.

as the Indian army, had to rely on Indian employment to fill its ranks, a form of cooperation already existed which logically could be moderately expanded to give Indians more staff authority.

Finally, what else could Britain do? The alternatives to political and constitutional reform might involve the mother country in expenses for social and economic reforms she was unwilling to undertake. Constitution-making was cheaper than any other kind of change. The vastness of Indian problems, the intractable realities of a backward, ill, and poor country would have demanded a corresponding concept of the welfare state organising the nation's resources for the general good inconceivable in the period of British rule. The proximity of constitutional reform and cost was ever-present in British thinking. For example, when the 1935 Constitution initiated provincial autonomy a financial inquiry was made by Sir O. Niemeyer, a former Secretary at the Treasury and keen advocate of financial orthodoxy. Analysing the Central Government, which remained essentially under British control, he wrote: 'From the central point of view . . . it is clear that the financial stability and credit of India as a whole must remain the paramount consideration.'[1] Provincial autonomy, the major concession of the constitution-making process, he suggested, was dependent on the income from the railways!

The British Government entered an era of constitution-making for India in the spirit of bringing Indians into a political association with established English principles of Indian administration. Never having made a constitution of their own at one single moment in time, it was as if they overlooked how the very anticipation of making a new Indian constitution would undermine Britain's right to rule, and cause to form an opposition party which wanted to act as a traditional opposition: to criticise, have a direct influence on policy, and eventually become a government.

As long as Britain was reluctant to admit the termination of her Empire, it was inconsistent to believe that popular, democratic, and responsible government was right for India. British rule superseded Indian political rights because responsible

[1] *Financial Inquiry, Report by Sir O. Niemeyer*, 1935, p. 4.

administration served the inarticulate masses of people. This was a static notion of government which allowed little alteration in fundamental relationships. The people had to remain dependent and inarticulate, and no spokesmen could be admitted into the bureaucracy who did not formally or informally belong to it. Government policy, after sensible consultation, should only be accepted by the masses of people but not judged by them.

How to introduce change? Successive British administrations held out the carrot of government reform by which Parliament determined the cadence of progress. Yet such reform had, by degrees, to weaken British control and give Indians greater responsibility. The confusion of nearly a century, from the foundation of direct rule in 1858 until 1945, originated in this dilemma: Britain accepted the justice of governmental and constitutional reform without rejecting an ultimate right to govern.

[ii]

The modern Indian constitution originated, not as a natural development of Indian society or as an application of indigenous legal principles, but as an effect of the Indian Mutiny of 1857. In 1858 Queen Victoria in her Royal Proclamation referred obliquely to the Mutiny; it was the 'divers and weighty reasons' which necessitated the transfer of the East India Company's administration to the Crown. The system of government devised and subsequently reformed never completely lost the taint of the early context which produced it. Government was deployed as a counter to Indian rebelliousness; it was a front-line force capable of pacifying opponents with firmness and clemency. Just as the Mutiny verified British distrust of Indians, so Parliament was justified in devising a system of government with echelons which isolated disloyal factions in society, so that the hierarchy of command left English officials or accommodating Indians with definitive residual powers. Institutionalised distrust thus took the form of restraining the amount and extent of Indian participation.

As a counterpoise to the disregard of Indian customs and traditions, the British Government disclaimed the 'Right and

Desire to impose Our Convictions on any of Our Subjects'. Indian society was thus doubly ignored; it was neither consulted for the establishment of government nor reformed. Instead government stood aloof from the world in its charge, with an administrative 'reason of state' with limited immediate objectives to govern as cheaply and as simply as possible. From the inception of Parliament's taking command of India, an important general purpose of a modern constitution was not applied: to draw society and government into an ambit of cooperation.

The Government of India Act, 1858, modified by the Councils Act, 1861, erred only on the side of caution in assuring a most complete and effective control by the Governor-General, by making him the central authority on which every section of administration depended. His assent was necessary to validate any law or regulation passed by provincial governments. He could promulgate ordinances which had the force of law for six months, if necessary for peace or good government. Over special areas—the army, customs, debt, among others—his prior consent had to be given before proposals could be put forward. The 1861 act fixed the composition of the Council of the Governor-General to between six and twelve. Members were appointed by the Governor-General for two years. Less than half of the Council were to be non-officials, i.e. not directly in the employ of the civil or military authority. Those nominated to sit on the Council, whether official or non-official, by the fact that both were chosen by the Governor-General, assured a unity in outlook and loyalty to British rule. The Council, though having legislative functions, in practice consulted and advised the Governor-General.

Such an administration made it obvious that reform would take place mainly by lessening the powers of the Governor-General. Since executive control of legislation gave law-making power to those obliged to administer government, increasing the responsibility and representative character of the Council or any other institution designed to have legislative functions would make the government of India less autocratic. All Indian constitutions tried to adjust the executive and legislative branches of government.

The Indian Councils Act, 1892, altered the Governor-

General's and provincial Governors' legislative councils by increasing the number of additional members. Nothing shows better how scrupulously guarded were institutional changes than the 'reform' which led to the selection of new members. They were not elected, for this might suggest that government needed an element of acceptance from those outside itself in order to function. Rather, non-officials in the Governor-General's Council were still appointed by the Governor-General but on the recommendation of the Bengal Chamber of Commerce. Non-official members of the provincial legislatures were in turn chosen by bodies like the association of merchants and manu-facturers, large landowners, and the universities. The right to influence affairs of state by presence was thus granted to those sections of Indian society and individual Indians who had a stake in the country's prosperity and were benefiting from British rule. That the Governor-General and provincial governors did not reject the nominations of these bodies indicates the harmony of interests between the two. Nor did the executive share any of its prerogatives. No member of the Council could submit or propose anything, nor call for a vote on financial matters, ask a supplementary question, or move an adjournment to allow for a debate on urgent questions of the hour. To listen, and by implication to learn and accept, were the privileges of membership in the legislative councils. Dissent and opposition found little favour. Sir A. Godley, Permanent Secretary at the India Office, wrote: 'In my personal opinion, [about publishing dissent in the debates in Council] which is founded upon a somewhat lengthy experience of the traditions and spirit of this office, any member of Council who directly or indirectly took steps to get his reasons published would be acting—I will not say disloyally—but in a manner calculated to impair the working of our official machine.'

Nineteenth-century principles of government did not remain unchallenged in the twentieth. Anglo-Indian affairs were channelled through the Scylla and Charybdis of constitution reform, though helmsmen serving in India appreciated the dangers. To them the prospect of reform, rather than the *status quo*, was more likely to create focal points of dissent; the dangers from the latter exceeded any advantage from the former. Lord

Minto mused over the prickly aspects of reforming anything in British India.

> Those who left India a few years ago can know little of it [the political movements spreading throughout India], and the tendency of the official still serving in India is generally to set his force against it or cast it from him as an unclean thing. He seems incapable of judging between absolute disloyalty of which there is more than enough and the legitimate ambition of educated men to possess a bigger share in the government of their country. He does not see the danger of ignoring the claims of these men. The question is whether it is more dangerous to break down the wall of prejudice which confronts one or to let it stand and face another danger which may eventually wipe the wall and all of us away together.[1]

To avoid the vortex was the job of the bureaucracy: this it did by becoming a *vis inertiae*, an autonomous machine with complex parts, enmeshed gears functioning with the simple principles of the early looms. The moving parts had been 'run-in' with the years, oiled by the traditions of the Indian Civil Service, while generations of Englishmen supplied the human source of power.

> I am becoming familiar with the system of government by 'files'. It strikes one as being a little cumbrous. The file, like the shuttle on the loom, shoots backwards and forwards from one person to another, and equally like the shuttle, the more it flies, the longer the material which it weaves. I am disposed to think, however, that in the case of a machine like ours in India . . . where the personnel of the staff corresponds to that of the permanent official in England by constantly changing, an elaborate system of records is necessary. The chief disadvantage of this particular type of machine appears to me to be an inherent tendency on the part of the different wheels of which it is composed, to slow down and finally stop, unless perpetually given fresh momentum. One of my chief duties appears to be that of winding up the strings as they show signs of running down. This can be done by making inquiries at frequent intervals as to the progress being made with any particular matter, and if necessary, by sending for the file.[2]

No file about past procedures could inform officials about the large historical waves which rippled through the country. The

[1] Lord Minto to A. Godley, 19 March 1907. Godley Papers, IOL.
[2] Lord Ronaldshay to Austen Chamberlain, 21 April 1917. Ronaldshay Papers, IOL.

growth of national consciousness, the surging patriotism and self-confidence, the application in Europe and at Versailles in 1919 of the principle of self-determination of peoples, the popularity of English education and with this the language of political debate, home rule in Ireland, the rise of Japan and her defeat of Russia in 1905 lashed against the old bureaucratic dykes. After 1905 government reform was no longer the exclusive preserve of officials, because forms of public opinion—press criticism, petitions, mob protests—encroached upon the decisions of the autocracy.

[iii]

Education was the hallmark of British rule. By invitation, selected Indians were to be shown the ways of political leadership and responsibility so that they could some day far in the future govern themselves. There was no guarantee that the same people who began this political training would be the ones in command, but somehow the level political experience would permeate the whole of Indian life. Political education was not meant to cause intrusions in the existing system; pupils are taught what is or was and rarely what may be. Reform of government was thus superfluous to political education. For most of the nineteenth century Indians believed their advancement would come under this kind of British tutelage.

The Indian National Congress, even with its patient and sensible resolutions, could not help but accuse the existing Government. To desire to secure 'the modification of such conditions as may be unjust or injurious', assumed the need for changes, and some inadequacies in the *status quo*. Could a party which took a critical view towards the Government have legitimate status? A disagreement over policy, if pursued with tenacious logic, would lead to the question of by what right did the official view prevail? What was the basis of sovereignty? In order to avoid such philosophical and impractical arguments, the Government looked to keep Congressmen on the periphery of affairs by giving them no *locus standi*. When the Congress held its annual meeting in Madras in 1903, Curzon advised the Governor, Lord Ampthill, of his and the Government's views of Congress: 'In so far as it is innocent, it is superfluous: and in so far as it is hostile to Government or seditious, it is a national danger. My policy ever since I came to India has been to reduce the Congress to impotence, (a) by never taking notice of it, (b) by carrying out such reasonable reforms as to deprive it of reasonable ground of complaint, (c) by showing such sympathy with and tolerance towards the Natives as to give no excuse to the Congress to revive racial issues, but (d) by never in the smallest degree truckling to its leaders or holding any communion with the unclean thing.'[1]

The only way in which Congress or any Indians critical of government policy could become anything other than supernumerary was for them to have a share of executive authority. Constitutional reform could make Indian opinions legitimate; for this reason the discussion about systems of government gathered within it so many contentious issues. Only by becoming necessary to the institutions of government would Indians achieve dignity, influence, and authority.

While nineteenth-century reforms tended to weaken the official autocracy by bringing in non-official members to the Viceroy's and Governors' councils, essential powers still resided with these executives. As we shall see, in the two major constitutions inaugurated by the British Government in 1919 and 1935 the powers of the Viceroy and Governor were preserved. Twentieth-century events and personalities fomented such an air of distrust that anything less than a shared executive could not satisfy Indian leaders. Indians were placed in the position of working reforms they judged to be inadequate because they did not have unlimited exercise of authority. For them government responsibility was not a training or apprenticeship for self-government, it was not a means to some future end, but an end in itself, that is, the immediate opportunity to rule and make long-term policy decisions affecting their country.

Over the different purposes of constitutional reform Anglo-Indian relations diverged. To Britain the reforms were rewards earned by Indian cooperation with the previous 'advance'. Each advance showed increasing Indian political understanding. It must never be thought, however, that constitutional reform was

[1] B. L. Grover, *British Policy Towards Indian Nationalism*, p. 213.

intended to be the step by step means by which the British Government disengaged from India. Only in the most general sense was this true, for few Britains believed it was possible to rule India forever. Constitution-making in British India was a stutter, a hesitation between long-term and immediate policies which fulfilled the practical needs of: (1) remaining in India; (2) appearing responsive to public opinion in India, England and the world by showing British rule as progressive; (3) diverting criticisms of past and present policies of the Indian Government by implying an altered political context—'the reforms' might satisfy former grievances; (4) challenging Indian politicians to be practical and cooperative which they were often loath to do; and (5) controlling the pace of Indian political advancement to suit broader imperial needs.

The Partition of Bengal (1905) introduced by Lord Curzon was the first of those twentieth-century reforms of government which tried to use reform as a means to satisfy British interests.

Bengal, the most populous province in India (78 million at the turn of the century), had a primacy over other provinces. Calcutta until 1911 was the country's capital, the Supreme Court and Bar of Calcutta had pre-eminence over others, the area was the centre of the jute industry, while racially and linguistically Bengal was more homogeneous than any other large area of India. Reducing the size and numbers the Lieutenant-Governor had under his control had been deemed a practical necessity if close knowledge and mutual understanding between ruler and people were to create that intimate familiarity upon which good government was thought to depend. In 1874 Assam, which included three Bengali-speaking districts, was separated from Eastern Bengal, and for the next thirty years proposals were made to fortify the sparsely populated and backward Assam by adding to it the more developed areas of Bengal.

In 1902 Berar was acquired on perpetual lease from the Nizam. This inspired further reconsideration of the territorial boundaries. In 1903 the province of Assam and Eastern Bengal, it was proposed, was to be enlarged by including Chittagong, Dacca, and Rajshahi divisions, the district of Malda and the hill state of Tipperah, to make a population of thirty-one millions and 106,000 square miles. Early in 1904 Curzon himself made an official tour of the areas of the partition to add his august presence to the explanations and defence of his proposal. The protests and popular demonstrations to his plans he dismissed as denunciations not arguments. In the district of Mymensingh he found only one English executive officer in charge of a population of four million, which confirmed his worse fears about the impossible burden placed on officials. Such a burden would cause officials to become callous in their work, unmindful to 'vigilantly safeguard the welfare of people'. Bengal was an area which produced young anarchists along with river pirates, it was explained, because government was negligent due to over-work.[1]

The tour of Bengal convinced Curzon, if not his numerous opponents, that the idea of partition was right and should be boldly realised. Bengal was to be reduced to fifty-four millions while Assam and Eastern Bengal were to become a Muslim province of eighteen million Muslims and twelve million Hindus. In the extensive correspondence about the partition there were no specific indications of how the reduced population of Bengal would be better administered. Fifty-four million people were still a considerable number. By creating a new Muslim province the partition scheme had the appearance of gerrymandering. Was the partition scheme a slap at the political agitators and youthful revolutionary conspirators who had grown up in the province?

Lord Curzon, a man of theatrical poses, who revelled in and believed his own stage thunder, conceived partition as a fitting riposte to the torrents of mud thrown at him and thus staining the majesty of his Indian years.

> The Bengalis, who like to think themselves a nation, and who dream of a future when the English will have been turned out, and a Bengali Bapu will be installed in Government House, Calcutta, of course bitterly resent any disruption that will be likely to interfere with the realisation of this dream. If we are weak enough to yield to their

---

[1] Some officials of the Bengal Government, including James Bourdillon, Acting Lieutenant-Governor in 1903, did not judge the work beyond their capacity. Henry Cotton, who had served under seven Lieutenant-Governors, asserted the people of Bengal were the easiest to administer in India.

clamour now, we shall not be able to dismember or reduce Bengal again; and you will be cementing and solidifying, on the eastern flank of India, a force already formidable and certain to be of increasing trouble in the future.[1]

Clearly, partition was a means of counteracting future trouble and preventing the realisation of Bengali dreams of Indian self-government. The Viceroy could dismiss clamour because it came from people demanding rights they did not in fact have. The impatience of the nationalists was antithetical to the moderate methods long traditional in a country administered by civil servants. Wrote Lord Curzon: 'You can scarcely have any idea of the utter want of proportion, moderation, or sanity that characterises native agitation in this country. Starting with some preposterous fiction or exaggeration the Bengalis, after repeating it for a few times, end by firmly believing its truth. He lashes himself into a fury over the most insignificantisms.'[2]

The redistribution of areas within Bengal was soon interpreted as much more than a geographical alteration for administrative convenience. What drew popular suspicion was not just the Government's indifference to popular sentiment but that the decision itself was made without effective prior consultation with Bengali leaders or representatives. The scheme was a government *diktat*, the effect of discussion within officialdom, and only desultory reference to native opinion. When, in 1903 Mr H. H. Risely, Secretary to the Government of India, wrote a minute setting out initial plans, it was the Secretary himself who presented other and contrary points of view, albeit meekly. No doubt keen to give the impression that a solution was not made in haste or alternatives not fully considered, and the superiority of his plan was conclusively established, he did, nonetheless, show the standards by which the Imperial Government judged matters. That Government, like an impressive monument, stood above the flotsam and jetsam of petty squabbles to discern the general good, not from those nearest the pedestal but according to the lights of far distant stars, ideas of service and duty.

---

[1] Lord Curzon to St John Brodrick, 17 February 1904. Brodrick Papers, IOL.
[2] Lord Curzon to St John Brodrick, 3 March 1905. Brodrick Papers, IOL.

The Government that is called upon to decide such cases must regard
them from a wider standpoint than that of purely local, and in all
probability transient considerations. They are bound to keep in view
the interests of the governed and the people as a whole. If they are
convinced that owing to arrangements, devised for a different state
of affairs and now obsolete, the administration suffers, if they see one
Government, weighed down with a burden which it cannot properly
discharge, and another Government shut out from development that
ought naturally to await it, they cannot permanently remain indifferent to the situation thus produced. Either a remedy must be sought,
or the responsibility for a conscious neglect of duty is incurred.[1]

The legislative councils were too frail to voice the volume of
dissatisfaction over partition, for they were not designed to
amplify public opinion, nor were the Viceroy, Governors, and
civil servants accustomed to accept the principle that either the
councils or public opinion should command administrative policy.
Bepin Chandra Pal, editor of the popular *New India*, nearly won
himself deportation for a speech he gave in Madras in which he
suggested Indian representation in a system of government
based on British principles was fundamentally irrelevant.

The whole Civil Service might be Indian, but the Civil Servants have
to carry out orders—they cannot direct, they cannot dictate policy.
. . . There are traditions, there are laws, there are policies to which
every civilisation, be he black or brown or white, must submit, and
as long as these traditions have not been altered, as long as these
principles have not been amended, as long as that policy has not been
radically changed, the supplanting of Europeans by Indian agency
will not make for self-government in this country.[2]

The partition of Bengal became one of those issues which
gathered former grave but vague grievances into a cause. The
1905 Indian National Congress led by Gokhale objected to the
policy, but true to its spirit of moderation, directed its energy
towards the structure of government, resolving that the non-
official and elected members of the legislative councils should be
increased to give Indians some veto. Such a point of view, not
beyond the conception of British officials, could hardly shake

[1] *Reconstruction of the Provinces of Bengal and Assam*, Cd. 2568, lviii, 1905, p. 17.
[2] Quoted in Ram Gopal, *How India Struggled for Freedom*, pp. 164–5.

the foundations of British rule. Rather, it was the new methods of popular protest carried on on a massive scale which not only added to the burden of government but also touched the old official worries; they discerned the first signs of mutiny in a campaign of protest. British goods were boycotted, foreign cloth was ceremonially burned, and only native products were purchased.

The *swadeshi* movement, as it was called, became popular because it rested on a simple negation people could understand; boycotting foreign goods and purchasing home-manufactured ones also made economic common-sense since the degree of protection for infant businesses in an under-developed country would proportionally stimulate native production and increase native trade. A national day of mourning was established when the partition scheme began, on 16 October, 1905. Students refused to write their examinations on foreign paper, women refrained from buying foreign bangles, and children gave up foreign sweets. The massive support for the anti-partition campaign was unprecedented in British India.

Three changes in 1905 presaged new opportunities for India: Curzon left India, Balfour's Conservative Government fell, and John Morley arrived at the office of Secretary of State.

While Lord Curzon was too boisterous a politician and too persistent a correspondent to be pushed very far from decisions concerning India, the heated controversies over Bengal and with Lord Kitchener which singed his last years as Viceroy increased a sense of alarm about India. Such things the traditions of the Government of India were meant to avoid. For a time Curzon no doubt enjoyed his exceptional status. Wrote Sir A. Godley, 'I never for a moment forget that I am a small man writing to a great man.'[1] Yet his greatness, which made his term of office full of government activity, could be blamed for initiating too much that was contentious and thereby moving the Government of India away from its poised image of quiet efficiency. Whereas the partition of Bengal had enough official approval to support public dislike of the policy, Curzon's hyper-sensitivity to Kitchener's status as military member on the Viceroy's Council which led the Secretary of State, Brodrick, to support the

[1] Sir A. Godley to Lord Curzon, 8 January 1904, Godley Papers, IOL.

gallant soldier, brought discredit on the Curzonian approach to Indian questions.[1]

The belief that changes were warranted was reinforced by the change of government in Whitehall. Balfour's Government and the imperial ideal of tariff reform and Empire free trade preached by Joseph Chamberlain and Milner were roundly thrashed in the 1906 general election. The new Government headed by Campbell-Bannerman came to power after years in opposition with an almost doctrinaire belief in reform and a revulsion against restrictions. Liberalism was 'a movement for liberation, a clearance of obstructions, an opening of channels for the flow of free, spontaneous vital activity'.[2] What area of administration was more opportune for the application of such ideas than the autocratic, bureaucratic Government of India?

The appointment of John Morley (1838–1923), 'Honest John', brought to the India Office a man imbued with the liberal spirit, a personal friend of John Stuart Mill, essayist, historian, and politician. Though unfamiliar with Indian perplexities he was eager to learn about them. The author of *On Compromise* believed in the displacement of old conceptions by new ones, the removal of 'the old institutions and ways of living in favour of greater convenience and ampler capacity, at once multiplying and satisfying human requirements'.[3] He observed that rational men would at times have to acquiesce when the bulk of their contemporaries showed themselves not yet ready for change. In the narrows of the Indian problem his liberal conscience veered to counteract the villainy of the bombs and yet tried to fulfil his philosophical disposition to encourage progress. In his period of office the Press Bills were passed, which widened the definition of seditious publications, invested the local government with the right to judge what was seditious, and asked newspaper owners to give a surety upon demand by the magistrates if it was thought likely that the paper would print seditious matters. The Seditious Meetings Act, passed in

---

[1] Most people who knew Curzon believed he had some flaw which detracted from his worth. 'He has the mood of a god with influenza,' R. Child, *A Diplomat Looks at Europe*, 1926, p. 102.

[2] L. T. Hobhouse, *Liberalism*, 1911, p. 47.

[3] J. Morley, *On Compromise*, 1896, p. 207.

1907, limited public meetings. Morley did not reverse Curzon's partition of Bengal.

The Morley-Minto reforms, the Indian Councils Act, 1909, were not intended to alter the character of British rule, as Morley made abundantly clear. 'Nor does the scheme now put forward contemplate any surrender or weakening of paramount British power in India.'[1] The reforms were meant as an expression of the enlightened liberalism Morley trusted would permeate the activities of the Government. 'What I do see is a stage reached in the gradual and inevitable working out of Indian policy, which makes it wise and in the natural order of things . . . that we should advance with a firm, courageous, and intrepid step some paces farther on the path of continuous, rational improvement in the Indian system of government.'[2]

Compatible with the 'natural order of things' were measures which brought Indians closer to government by extending the opportunity Indians had to express themselves in the councils of state. A seat was virtually reserved for a native on the Viceroy's Executive Council, and two Indians were asked by Morley to join the Council of the Secretary of State. The Councils in the provinces and at the centre could discuss specified aspects of the budget, raise questions, introduce private members' bills, and move resolutions. Significant for the future, the reforms deemed it rational to reaffirm Curzon's policy of giving special concessions to the Muslims. Separate electorates were established for Muslims with reserved places on the councils for exclusively Muslim representatives. This was compatible with the general aim of the reforms: to grant some privileges to selected and loyal sections of the Indian community Landholders, Zemindars, chambers of commerce, traders' associations, planters, and members of universities, along with the Muslims, were given the right to be a 'constituency'.

The Indian Council Act expanded the Indian Legislative Council to include the seven members of the Viceroy's Executive Council and some sixty additional members of whom the majority

---

[1] *East India* (*Advisory and Legislative Council, etc.*), Cd. 3710, 1907, lviii, p. 12.
[2] 161, H. of C., *Parliamentary Debates*, Fourth Series, col. 585 (20 July 1906).

were officials. Thirteen members were chosen by the non-official members of the provincial council, one from each of the six provinces by the large landowners, and six from the Muslim community. The official majority was secured through the right of the Governor-General to nominate official and ex-officio members to the Council, or the Supreme Legislative Council as it was sometimes called. Candidates for the Council were disqualified if they had been tried and sentenced by a court to prison for six months or more, deported, or debarred from legal practice. Anyone could be banned from the council if he was judged by the Governor-General to be by 'reputation or antecedents' likely to harm the public interest. Clearly, notorious opponents of the Government could not enter official precincts.

The provincial legislative councils, sometimes called the local legislative councils as we have noted, drew their elected members from a variety of respectable institutions: the large landowners, the chambers of commerce, traders' and planters' associations, the universities, and local government, while special representation was given to the Muslims. In one province, Bengal, the number of elected members of the Council exceeded the number of nominated officials, though as Morley well appreciated non-officials would not as a matter of course oppose the Government.

The legislative councils had to function within specified limitations. Councillors could discuss questions of general interest and move resolutions, though these had to be of a kind which contained no attempt to rebuke or embarrass the Government. The president of the council could disallow any resolution without explanation, and his judgement was final. An amendment could be moved, but it must not be negative. Nothing concluded in the councils was mandatory; amendments and resolutions were recommendations. Questions had to seek elucidation of policy or ask for further information. The annual financial statement, not to be confused with the Budget, could be discussed in councils, but no one could move a resolution about it; nor were the councils asked to approve of the statement.

Though large claims were made for the reforms at the time, in the enthusiasm of the moment, and later by some historians who see in them the foundation 'for a new political structure',[1] the political changes introduced were at the most a predictable development of the previous system. The very explicitness with which Morley informed Parliament that he planned no alteration in executive superiority in the Government of India shows their limitation. Like other politicians having to face debates in Parliament about the Indian constitution, he tried to appear well-meaning and conciliatory by shrouding the reforms in progressive language. But the reforms show a host of formidable restrictions, which were all too apparent to the British Government when constitutional matters were again considered in 1918. The elected members of the council were chosen by tiny constituencies, if constituencies they can be called. The largest single electoral body was 650, but most were considerably smaller. The average number of non-officials in the various provincial legislatures electing members 'of the people' to the supreme legislative council was twenty-two. The class and special character of the electorates hampered the non-official members of the councils from consistently joining forces on agreed policies, and there was no meaningful relationship between the electing body and its representatives. The existence of a rigid official bloc, nominated by the executive, and chosen as men closely associated with government administration, made the debates primarily another formal means of communication for the Government. Answers to questions raised in council often simplified already known and printed government policy. Decisions were passed by 'the silent official phalanx'. Though it was always open for members of the councils to convince the Government, few matters were so open as to make the Government willing to be convinced, especially on policies nurtured by the civil service and decided by normal government methods, methods which did not include a prior taking of points and opinions from the councils. The majority of the laws passed in the Legislative Council received no discussion. From 1909 to 1917 there were only nine bills which provoked serious opposition, but these were hardly about subjects where the Government would feel its basis of power

[1] S. Wolpert, *Morley and India*, Los Angeles, 1967, p. 166.

threatened. The nine included the White Phosphorus Matches Bill, Life Assurance Companies Bill, and Indian (Bogus Degrees) Medical Bill. Only five private members' bills were passed in the same period.

The Morley-Minto reforms did, however, have several indirect effects on the trend of government policy. In the councils Indian representation was pushed near the limit of numerical minority; when reforms were again to be raised this numerical minority would naturally, in certain areas, become a superiority. Direct Indian association with government, no matter how partial, caused civil servants to prune some contentious aspects of bills discussed in the councils to avoid fuss and adverse publicity. The Morley-Minto reforms reasserted constitutional reform as the central issue in Anglo-Indian relations; the idea of reform once so lodged would lead to other schemes, particularly as circumstances changed.

The outbreak of war in 1914 enlisted the support of the people of India in ways which might be thought surprising considering the clashes of the previous decade. Yet, as in England, the war in its earlier stages suspended the bitterest arguments, momentarily dissolving them before the patriotic adventure of a war to oppose German might, militarism and atrocities. Former rigid ways of considering problems were discredited as the war enlightened everyone about people in society, organisational methods, the competency of leadership, the availability of resources, the possible levels of expenditure, and the need to take broader and more generous views. Before the war the Indian army was designed to be used exclusively for Indian needs. There was little idea that the army could be employed in wars outside India or should accept obligations of an imperial character. In 1913 the Government of India informed the Secretary of State that if all was well at home India might be able to send two or three divisions into the field. In the event, by the end of the war 1,300,000 men were dispatched from Indian ports, 172,000 animals and over three million tons of foodstuffs. Nearly a million Indians were sent to the various expeditionary forces, the largest contingents to Mesopotamia, and then France and Egypt. In 1917 the Government of India offered £100,000 towards the expense of the

war and subscriptions to war loans amounted to £75,000,000.[1]
Leaders of the Congress as well as the young Gandhi, recently
returned from South Africa, supported and aided the war effort.
In many ways the war was the most explicit vindication of
British rule. It provided a context, outside the sterile political
one, for loyalty and cooperation because the distance between
ruler and ruled was shortened. Global war turned everyone's
attentions to real objectives, hardships were accepted in common,
stringent government measures like the Defence of India Bill,
1915, which gave the Governor-General in Council extensive
emergency powers to secure public safety and defend the
country,[2] were more acceptable in the circumstances of war,
particularly since similar measures for the defence of the realm
were passed in Britain. Significantly, when the ageing Tilak was
released from prison in 1915, he called on Indians to support
and assist the Government.

> Such spontaneity and unity of action cannot be explained by any
> theory of political domination. It was a definite expression primarily
> of adherence to an altruistic ideal, and secondly of gratitude from the
> abiding benefits received from the British system of government.[3]

Reform and reconstruction were second only to winning the
war when, in 1917, Edwin Montagu (1879–1924) was appointed
by Lloyd George to be Secretary of State for India. As Under-
Secretary of State in 1912 he had visited India. He was probably
the most knowledgeable Secretary of State appointed this
century, the only minister to be directly linked to two phases
of constitution-making. He brought to office a genuine sympathy
for the 'oppressed people' of India and little racial antagonism
towards Indians; the plight of Indians had enough in common
with that of the Jews, the people of his ancestors, for him to
conceive the struggles of the one not unlike the struggles of
another. 'I am an Oriental.' He had an anxious desire to effect
changes. 'It will not be well for the reputations of the administrations with which you and I are connected if we do not leave

---

[1] See Government of India, *India's Contribution to the Great War*, Calcutta, 1923.

[2] The Bill created special tribunals to try revolutionaries without appeal; suspects could be interned.

[3] Earl of Carnwarth, *Loyal Rulers and Leaders of the East*, 1922, p. xiii.

behind us evidence that we have faced the facts and considered schemes.' In 1917 he again visited India to prepare himself for the introduction of new reforms based on the most up-to-date knowledge of opinion, official and unofficial. He committed himself to his task with enthusiasm, decisiveness, and passion. 'My visit to India means that we are going to do something big. I cannot go home and produce a little thing or nothing; it must be epoch-making, or it is a failure; it must be the keystone of the future history of India. . . .¹ Of course my colleagues are good fellows, but the responsibility rests with me. Chelmsford [the Viceroy] will do his best, but the responsibility rests with me. It is I that have got to do this thing, and I spend my whole time racking my brains as to how I am going to get something which India will accept and the House of Commons will allow me to do without whittling it down.'²

Conscious from the start of the rift between the waves of reasonable expectations in India and the tide of conservative opinion within the war-time coalition, the Montagu-Chelmsford Report gravitated towards a policy where 'a substantial step is to be taken at once'.³ The sheltered existence which Britain had given India, labelled not uncritically 'constitutional autocracy', was to be altered according to the logical application of past promises. 'Indians must be enabled in so far as they attain responsibility to determine for themselves what they want done. The process will begin in local affairs, which we have long since intended and promised to make over to them; the time has come for advance in some subjects of provincial concern; and it will proceed to the complete control of provincial matters, and thence, in the course of time and subject to the proper discharge of Imperial responsibilities, to the matters concerning all India.'⁴

This statement contained many of the ambivalent aspects of constitution-making: reform with qualifications, clear intentions muffled by vague reference to Imperial interests, the present made a hostage to the future. The phrase 'in so far as they attain responsibility' still made Indians free to determine policy

---

¹ E. Montagu, *An Indian Diary*, 1930, p. 8.   ² *Ibid.*, p. 10.
³ *Report on Indian Constitutional Reforms*, Cd. 9109, 1918, p. 154.
⁴ *Ibid.*, p. 148.

only after they had shown themselves able and had been given the right to do so by the British Government. 'Attain' suggested trying to reach but not yet accomplished, which left the British authorities arbiters of what was attained. 'In so far' implied a continuing limitation. In another part of the paper a parliamentary commission was to report on the working of the new constitution. The reference to *'some* subjects' meant that others, and these were significant, were kept from provincial control. This was subsequently known as dyarchy, a form of dual control and responsibility dividing government power between an elected and an official authority with transferred and reserved subjects respectively. 'In the course of time' held out the future promise of self-government for the whole of India, in a vague and uncharted way. 'Subject to the proper discharge of Imperial responsibilities' could be construed to mean that British and Imperial needs were still superior to any popular measure. The word 'subject' applied a condition which could alter or undermine any decision.

Though subtle in his wording there can be little doubt that the Secretary of State intended a definite relaxation of British authority and power. 'As the Local Governments are more and more responsible to the people through the Legislative Councils, we must give more and more responsibility to Indians and keep less here.' The main areas to which the reforms applied were the eight provinces. Devolution meant decentralisation. To the extent that British and official control was loosened it would be achieved by giving local areas local control; in this way the governing tasks would be relatively easier since Indians could be expected to have special knowledge and a vital interest in their own locality. As we shall see, the system of representation reinforced the principle that special, informed, and narrow sections of the society should be given a definite place in the legislative councils.

The Montagu-Chelmsford Report was not adopted holus-bolus into the Government of India Act, 1919. Intervening between the Report and the Act was the Joint Select Committee of both Houses of Parliament which whittled down some of the liberal aspects of the reforms; the changes gave Governors the power to certify bills they deemed essential without recourse to any other procedure; the transferred subjects were not to be financed from separate purses, which would have given the legislative councils considerable financial power. The end of the war and the existence of a predominately Conservative Cabinet and House headed by Lloyd George kept men of firmly conservative views about India's future near the levers of power. Milner (1916–19) and Churchill (1921–2) at the Colonial Office, Balfour (1916–19) and Curzon (1919–22) at the Foreign Office, Bonar Law (1916–19) and Austen Chamberlain (1921–2) as Lord Privy Seal, Lord Birkenhead (1919–22) as Lord Chancellor weighted the opposition against reform. Curzon in particular felt more and more uncomfortable with the successive steps of the reforms which 'cut away foot by foot the somewhat precarious ground upon which I stand'.[1]

The new constitution relinquished the official majority in the provincial legislatures. Seventy per cent of the councils were elected from an enlarged franchise which included about ten per cent of the male population. A whole section of government, the legislature, did not depend on executive appointment but on popular support. However, the principle of an elected majority in the legislature should not be taken to mean the existence of an elected opposition with a majority in the legislature; the specialised constituents and the small proportion of the population made the councillors more delegates of a special interest than democratic representatives with general responsibilities. Franchise qualifications included residency in the constituency, payment or land revenue and other forms of taxation, or membership or former membership in the armed services. Separate electorates were reserved for people, classes or interests. These included: the depressed classes, Anglo-Indians, Indian Christians, Labour, Mohammadans, Sikhs, Europeans, landlords, university members, commerce and industry. The elected representatives of such constituents, because they did not come to the councils as general representatives, would more likely than not defend and argue from the point of view of the vested interest which had elected them. Thus the structure of representation favoured enfranchising sections of society with vested interests which would tend to be loyal and cooperative

[1] Lord Ronaldshay, *The Life of Lord Curzon*, Vol. III, 1927, p. 172.

5. Sir E. Lutyens, Viceroy's House, The State Entrance, New Delhi, 1931. See pages 98–99

Photo : The Times

6. The Indian Statutory Commission departing from Victoria Station for their first trip to India, January 1928. They are being seen off by the Prime Minister, Stanley Baldwin and the Secretary of State for India, Lord Birkenhead. From left to right: Mr Edward Cadogan, M.P., Col. Lane-Fox, M.P., Mr Vernon Hartshorn, M.P., Lord Burnham, Sir John Simon, M.P., Lady Simon, Mr Baldwin, Lord Strathcona, Mr Attlee, M.P., and Lord Birkenhead

Photo: *Keystone Press Agency Ltd*

7a. National Congress riots in Bombay, March 30, 1931

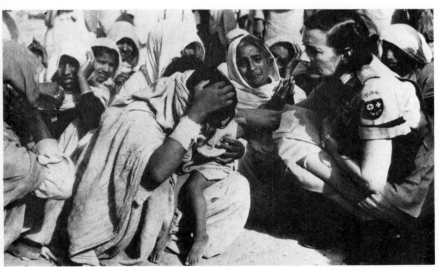

Photo: *Thames Television from the series The Life and Times of Lord Mountbatten*

7b. Lady Mountbatten visiting a refugee camp, 1947

8. The conference in New Delhi on June 7, 1947 during which Lord Mountbatten disclosed Britain's partition plan for India. From left to right Nehru, Ismay, Mountbatten and Jinnah

and to a degree reluctant to enter into cabals to form an opposition party critical of government.

Official and elected members of provincial India were given two somewhat separate spheres of activities. In general the transferred subjects in which elected Ministers had jurisdiction were concerned with welfare administration, subjects where there was a fixed and functioning policy and over which there was relatively little contention. At the same time the transferred subjects did not give real opportunity for raising money or deciding how money from the general fund should be spent. The reforms did give elected provincial members an opportunity to run public health, sanitation, medical administration, local government, education of Indians, public works, but not irrigation, agriculture and fisheries. On the other hand reserved subjects for the Governor and his council, the official Government, included the control of irrigation, canals, land revenue administration, famine relief, justice, police, control of newspapers, prisons, borrowing of money on the credit of the province, and factory inspection. It is quite apparent from a scrutiny of the lists that the two spheres of government divided lesser and more significant domains of authority into non-official and official respectively. Since there were many more portfolios than Ministers, no elected Minister could run one department alone.

As in the past, the position of the executive, the Governor, was crucial. He appointed both the Executive Council from officials, and also the Ministers, but from elected members. The Governor was still central to both official and unofficial government, with, as we have noted, overriding powers in any dispute. He was the instrument of cohesion in the dual structure of government. In the Executive Council he not only had the casting vote as President but the authority to overrule the majority. In the Governor's relation to his Ministers, those in the transferred subjects were to be allowed to have their own way, though subsequently he could veto a particular piece of legislation. Finally, if this was not enough, the Governor could allocate revenues between transferred and reserved subjects if there was disagreement between the two branches of government.

The 1919 Act established two houses of the central legislature, the Council of State and the Legislative Assembly. The

Council of State had a maximum number of sixty and consisted of men elected from a restricted upper stratum of Indian society. High property qualifications gave representation to the wealthiest landowners and merchants, and tests of probity—'personal stand and experience'—gave an aristocratic dimension to the Council. The electors were grouped according to communal constituencies. The Legislative Assembly also consisted of an elected majority, along with some officials, totalling at least 140. The franchise qualifications were similar to those for the provincial legislatures. While the Legislature had broad powers to make laws, the previous sanction of the Governor-General was necessary before the introduction of proposals relating to: public debt, religious customs, discipline in the armed forces, prerogatives of the provincial governments, or repealing or altering any act or ordinance established by the Governor-General. If the Legislature failed to pass essential bills, the Governor-General could certify them as passed. On occasions, there could be joint sittings of the two houses.

The Central Government remained relatively unchanged in the extent of executive control. There was division of subjects as in the provinces, between official and elected members, though none of the activities of the Legislature bound the Government. Government was still in theory dependent on the direction of the Secretary of State for India, and thus on Parliament. If there were disputes within the Governor-General's Council, the Governor-General could overrule any dissent; he could prorogue any legislature; he chose all members of his Council, and for six months if he deemed it necessary he could rule by ordinance, that is without recourse to sanction from other government institutions. Thus to simplify what is complex to describe, the degree of 'reform and freedom' extended to the provincial government was more than compensated for by the near absolutism of the Governor-General at the centre. Indians were challenged to work within the system, to be tempted by new responsibilities available in the provinces instead of uniting as a full-blooded opposition in New Delhi, however much it was the centre-ring of debate, controversy and public attention. If Montagu hoped to capture the imagination of India with his reforms the cumbersome arrangements militated against

comprehension or enthusiasm. The constitution palled next to
more dramatic events like the massacre at Amritsar, the arrival
of Gandhi and the non-violent campaign, and the uniting of the
Hindus and Moslems in the Khilafat movement to oppose
British pro-Greek and anti-Turkey policies.

The years which followed the introduction of the reforms
were indeed 'years of destiny'; the present tried to anticipate the
future by securing for Indians the progressive realisation of
their desires for self-government. The reforms endeavoured to
set in motion a logical though cautious policy of limited responsibility with democratic paraphernalia. Such a policy was
inherently capable of expansion at whatever pace thought suitable. However, when the massive civil disobedience campaign
broke out at the same time as the reforms began, the former
could be blamed on the latter. So wrote George V: 'The Montagu
reforms have no doubt produced the unrest which now exists.'

The danger, to which any compromise is vulnerable, that
one party would find the proposed solution too paltry or too
generous, weakened the progressive aspects of the reforms.
Indians after the disturbances in the Punjab questioned whether
these measures could wipe out the stain; the post-war Lloyd
George Coalition, increasingly under the influence of the
Conservatives, wished to rid the Government of its liberal
tendencies. When the reforms were shown not immediately to
satisfy many different shades of Indian opinion nor attract the
factious Congress, criticisms were ladled on the reforms themselves. The notion of relinquishing British control and eventually
the perpetrator, Sir Edwin Montagu, were blamed for the
failing policy. As the forces of reaction gathered strength in the
Coalition, Montagu, like Addison at the Ministry of Housing,
resigned, to the great satisfaction of the Unionist Party.
'A considerable band of Unionists had, for months, desired
his withdrawal from the Government.' The announcement
of Montagu's resignation was greeted in the House with the
wildest cheers of the session.[1]

----

[1] The 'resignation' of Edwin Montagu is laden with ironies and confusion. At
the time and later it was widely believed he was dismissed from office because he
authorised publication of a telegram from the Viceroy, Lord Reading, without the
knowledge or consent of the Cabinet. In the telegram Reading wanted to publish, in

the name of the Government of India, he expressed his disapproval of the Treaty of Sèvres; he called for the revision of the treaty: the evacuation of Constantinople, the right of the Sultan to maintain his suzerainty over the holy places of Islam, and the restoration to Turkey of Ottoman Thrace, Adrianople and Smyrna. Reading wanted, not to change or directly influence the Government's middle-east policy—for this a Viceroy had other means than publishing his views—but to placate Indian Muslims, who filled the ranks of the Indian army and were generally cooperative. He hoped to woo Muslims from their Hindu allies in the Khilafat movement, an alliance which had increased agitation and violence in the country.

Montagu took the unusual step after his resignation of making his case before his Cambridge constituents. He made it clear what were the reasons for his departure. 'The die-hards are the culprits . . . they represent the demand of foolish but honest people to crystallise against the march of time every anachronism in the world.'

There is much to suggest that the telegram was a pretext for discarding Montagu, a point made by *The Times* on 13 March 1922. (1) The Government of India's views on the subject of the treaty of Sèvres were well known. Reading in his replies to various Muslim deputations had already indicated his sympathy for their point of view. The telegram more formally restated them in order to reassure them. (2) The Cabinet was aware of the telegram. Montagu circulated its contents to members on 3 March. He had authorised its publication on 4 March, before the next meeting which was on the 6th. Before the meeting Curzon and Chamberlain (Lloyd George was absent because he was ill) had a brief word about it, expressed dislike, *but did not raise the matter in the Cabinet meeting itself*. Curzon, well known for his perennial martyred indignation, did not approve of the publication but wrote to Montagu on the 6th suggesting that in future he should be allowed to address the Cabinet before approval was given on matters affecting foreign policy. Though Montagu was dismissed because he supposedly broke the rule of Cabinet responsibility, what Curzon wrote complainingly about was not the right of the Cabinet to discuss the matter but his right to do so. The key sentence in the letter shows that Curzon knew about the publication, disliked it but accepted it; his warning clearly is meant for any future event. 'I hope this may be the last of these unfortunate pronouncements, but if any other is ever contemplated, I trust at least that you will give me an opportunity of expressing my opinion in Cabinet before the sanction is given.' Had Curzon or Chamberlain raised the question on the 6th, there was still enough time to prevent publication which occurred on the 8th. When Curzon was pressed to explain why he remained silent during the Cabinet on the 6th he said 'he was a sick man'. (3) Montagu could rightly believe that the publication of these views by the Government of India was consistent with his reforms which gave the Government the right to express opinions with some independence of the India Office and H.M.G., particularly since India was a separate signatory to the Treaty of Versailles and the Treaty of Sèvres. (4) Lloyd George's Coalition Government was notorious for the way in which the notion of Cabinet joint responsibility was broken, not least by the Prime Minister himself. ('The Cabinet is hardly ever called together and then only to register decisions. . . . I have not seen a single one of my colleagues this week and in all probability I shall not. . . .' Montagu to Reading, 30 November 1921, quoted in S. D. Waley, *Edwin Montagu*, p. 261.) In Lloyd George's letter to Montagu, quoted in *The Times*, the Prime Minister oddly did

The passing of Montagu near the time of the initiation of the new constitution, as well as the manner of it, ended the prospect, if it ever really existed, of amicable Anglo-Indian relations achieved by a constitutional formula. Receding further into the distance were the pillars of a constitutional structure which could attract the support of moderate men. The Montagu-Chelmsford Report was unique in the way it criticised old policies, expressed in tone an eagerness for change, and showed an expansive attitude towards problems. Hereafter, no report was written by a Secretary of State which was as probing and daring. In fact, the main constitutional reports until the end of the Second World War were written by specially apppointed men or committees, thus to some extent by-passing the regular institutions of Secretary of State and Government of India. The office of Secretary of State until 1945 was filled by men of firm conservative views or lesser political figures who found it too difficult to make any impression on the Indian political morass even if they wanted to. Some new crisis, parliamentary hostility or indifference, Cabinet uncertainty, other pressing problems, could at any moment extricate a Secretary of State from the difficulty of controlling the Indian problem. Samuel Hoare wrote to the Viceroy in 1932: 'The nearer we get to a Bill [for a new Indian constitution] the more apprehensive I am becoming of its possible fate. There is no doubt whatever that recent events in India have hardened opinion against many of the constitutional changes that we have been discussing. The result is that most people here are more strongly in favour than ever of an advance by two steps. If, therefore, we are to meet you over the comprehensive Bill, we must be more than ever careful not to create further difficulties in the two Houses.'[1]

not question the right of Montagu to sanction publication, the matter over which controversy raged, but the inopportune moment chosen for publication. 'The moment chosen was indefensible from the standpoint of broad Imperial interest and it had added considerably to the difficulties of an already difficult task.' (5) Considering the alleged offence and the career of the eminent Secretary of State, there was unnecessary haste to force his resignation. So thought Lord Reading: 'I find it very difficult to understand why he should be drummed out of the Cabinet post haste. Have our Ministers always been so strictly correct in their handling of situations?' (Marquess of Reading, *Rufus Isaacs*, Vol. II, 1945, p. 228).

[1] Sir S. Hoare to Lord Willingdon, 27 May 1932. Templewood Papers, IOL.

The reforms gave Gandhi's non-cooperation movement an ideal area in which to display their methods. The Indian National Congress showed their contempt for the new constitution by scorning the elections, leaving the moderate National Liberal Federation and the All-India Muslim League to swell the legislatures. That the oldest and most generally popular political party remained outside the new system of government made the reforms seem unreal. Just as unrealistically, the Central Legislative Assembly in the first few months of the first session passed a resolution calling for revision of the existing constitution in favour of an extension of authority to Indians. In this way the principle of reform stood in the way of developing a political tradition since the proximity of change, so explicit in the Montagu-Chelmsford Report, overshadowed the desire to work the present system. In the elections of 1923 members of the Congress offered themselves as candidates to the legislatures for the purpose of destroying the constitution from within. Called the Swarajist Party, led by C. R. Das and Motilal Nehru, they won forty-five seats in the Assembly. Nehru moved a resolution calling for a Round Table to establish full responsible government. The Government opposed the resolution but in the following year established a committee under the chairmanship of Sir Alexander Muddiman, Home Member in the Viceroy's Council. Predictably there was a majority and minority report published in 1925; the former believed the new constitution had a real contribution to make to India's political advance, the latter called dyarchy a failure and wanted a new constitution. An amendment approving of the minority report was passed in the Assembly, only to be defeated in the Council of State. While Swarajists refused to sit on committees or join the Government a group led by Mr Jayakar, Mr Kelkar and Dr Moonje formed a party of 'responsive cooperators' who would agree to do so. In the 1926 elections, amid considerable confusion within the Indian parties over who belonged to what, the Assembly divided into various groups without clear direction or resolve how to oppose the Government. In the provinces, where the reforms were intended to be most fully able to draw on Indian political support, the local nature of provincial preoccupations splintered the parties, while the official bloc voted with the Government on transferred as well as reserved subjects. The existence of the official bloc, and the Governor's exceptional powers, produced irresponsibility in some provincial legislatures. Indian politicians tried to make shouts reach where words could not.

[iv]

Lord Birkenhead, appointed Secretary of State for India in 1924, rarely chose the easy path of silence. He believed that if Britain lost India it would be 'a tragedy of inconceivable magnitude'.[1] Disturbed by the prospect of a Labour Government appointing a commission to review the working of the new constitution as stipulated in the 1919 Act he thought it 'elementary prudence' to appoint a commission two years early. Prudence also guided the choice of commissioners. The Indian Statutory Commission appointed in 1927 was headed by Sir John Simon, a man renowned for judicious indecision. Birkenhead noted his slow golf game and 'extraordinary suitability for this particular task'.[2] Attlee—along with Vernon Hartshorn, the Labour Party representative—wrote of Simon: 'He was at his best when a decision had not to be taken.'[3] The other four commissioners were staunchly conservative: Lord Burnham, editor of the *Daily Telegraph* was an unashamed imperialist, Edward Cadogan believed 'in the great imperial idea',[4] George Lane-Fox was related to both Baldwin and Lord Irwin, and Lord Strathcona was decidedly anti-black. Strathcona believed they were 'sent on the Commission to give it a certain elegant demeanour and make things socially easier for Lord Irwin; the main purpose of the Commission was for it to be a show of strength, Indians liking the aristocracy and being great snobs'.[5]

Because no Indian was included on the Commission, the 'simple seven' were abused by the popular press and boycotted by leading Indian politicians, when they arrived to tour India in February 1928. Birkenhead took Irwin's advice not to put

---

[1] Lord Birkenhead, *Last Essays*, 1930, p. 49.
[2] Lord Birkenhead, *F.E.*, 1936, p. 515.   [3] Lord Attlee, 'India', CRA.
[4] 160 *H. of C.* Debs., 5th Series, 149 (14 February 1923).
[5] Lady Strathcona in conversation with the author.

Indians on the Commission—'we shall have a good deal of screaming . . . but I hope and think this will not be very serious'[1]—but developed his own arguments for exclusion along rigid imperial lines of constitutional right which gave little importance to Indian politicians. No Indian was invited to join the Commission because Parliament alone reported and decided India's future. The Commission was thus a representative of the Imperial Parliament; no one other than a member of Parliament could belong to it. The Secretary of State also feared an 'unreal alliance' between Indian and Labour Party representatives. A strictly parliamentary commission asserted the sovereignty of Britain over India and might serve as a reprimand to hostile and non-cooperating Indian nationalists. 'The door of acceleration was not open to menace, still less would it be stormed by violence.'[2]

The dextrous chairman invited the legislative councils to choose from their non-official members a committee to *associate* with the parliamentary commission, assist in the interrogation of witnesses, and produce a separate report. This 'joint committee', without real equality of status, reiterated the perennial constitutional problem: 'agreement and cooperation' required Indians to submit to and comply with British rules. The joint committee was less necessary to the issue of constitutional advance than politically expedient. Lord Irwin realised the unbridgeable contradiction in the idea of two committees: 'The difficulty is that I can devise no means of meeting the demand for full equality of status between the Indian Committee and Simon's.'[3]

The Commission returned in October 1928 to consider the hundreds of petitions and memoranda submitted to its offices, and to cross-examine witnesses. There was a parched air to the commissioners' proceedings; as they travelled from place to place they explained procedure, and heard official witnesses duplicate one another's testimony. The dominating chairman interrupted, clarified and made points. Here is one sample of the truths uncovered by these methods of investigation:

---

[1] Lord Irwin to Lord Cecil of Chelwood, 7 April 1928, BM.
[2] Lord Birkenhead's speech quoted in *The Times*, 8 July 1925.
[3] Lord Irwin to Lord Cecil of Chelwood, 7 April 1928. Chelwood Papers, BM

ATTLEE: Did the supplying of meals to voters [in villages] amount to bribery?

SIR JOHN SIMON: Would the Commission be given hospitality in the villages?

NAWAB MUZAFFAR KHAN: (Director of Public Information, Punjab): You are welcome visitors, Sir, but even unwelcome visitors are given hospitality.[1]

It was obvious to Irwin that the Commission, instead of calming the Indian tempest, had embittered feeling and made the task of governing more difficult. Between the appointment of the Commission and its report, Government Ministers were abused and physically attacked. A bomb was thrown into the Legislative Assembly in 1929, and later the same year, an attempt was made to blow up the Viceroy's train outside Delhi. Not only had the Commission aroused anger by excluding Indians, but its primary task, assessing the previous constitution, was a desultory exercise since it was obvious the constitution had not been a success. But was this the same as condemning the reforms as unsatisfactory? Was it practical to blame the failure of reforms on the constitution itself or the attitude of Indians? Could the commissioners practically advise a step backwards though in many respects such a conclusion was justified? If the Commission was unsatisfactory could some other agency be made to serve similar ends without arousing an equal amount of rancour?

The coincidence of the formation of the second Labour Government and Lord Irwin's mid-term leave led to an ingenious solution. The Prime Minister, Ramsay MacDonald, and the Viceroy had identical goals: to propagate what seemed like a more liberal policy; both had a first duty 'to carry on the business of government'. On 16 October 1929 Sir John Simon wrote to the Prime Minister expressing a wish to extend the terms of reference of the Commission to include the Indian States. Subservient to this was the suggestion that 'some sort of conference', after the report of the Commission had been published and considered, should be convened. Simon assumed the conference would use the proposals of the report as a basis

[1] *Times of India*, 5 September 1928.

for discussion. MacDonald replied two weeks later, recommending that the conference should be composed of representatives of 'all points of view', implying the Commission's report would not be the basis of discussions. 'His Majesty's Government was to consider these [constitutional] matters in the light of all material then available.'[1] This meant, as later events proved, that the report was of no consequence to the discussions. On the same day that this correspondence was published, Lord Irwin made his famous speech of 'health and healing' that pledged the Imperial Government to the policy which envisaged the 'natural issue of India's constitutional progress . . . is the attainment of dominion status' and called for a Round Table Conference of interested parties.

This declaration, hailed as a solemn oath 'to Indian advance', was no more forthright than previous declarations. In a country inured to sincere words with substantial qualifications, Irwin's 'we cannot at present foresee on what lines this development may be shaped'[2] left undefined (1) what was being offered in the present, (2) the meaning of 'dominion status', (3) what part Indians had in the 'attainment', a word which had more future than present connotation.

This announcement, made when it was, created a crisis in the Conservative Party because it was widely interpreted as some new advance, or change of policy. MacDonald took the courteous step of writing to Baldwin. 'The answer to both parts of the question "whether the Viceroy's declaration implies any change in the policy hitherto declared or in the time when this status may be attained" is No.'[3]

The Indian Statutory Commission published its recommendations in June 1930, proposing the end of dyarchy, autonomy in the provinces, enlargement of the franchise and numbers in the legislature, and an all-India federation to include the Indian States. Such paper plans, however, were easily swept aside in but a few months when a constitutional pageant, the Round Table Conference, brought princes, maharajas, the Aga Khan, chiefs

---

[1] Both letters were published in *The Times*, 31 October 1929.

[2] *The Times*, 1 November 1929.

[3] J. Ramsay MacDonald to Stanley Baldwin, 11 November 1929. MacDonald Papers.

and representatives of every community and organisation in India, to 'historic assembly' to counsel representatives of the British Government. Only the Indian National Congress was absent.

The King-Emperor and Prime Minister inaugurated the meeting which soon divided itself into nine sub-committees to ruminate over India's constitutional future. Nothing could be finally settled by the reports of the sub-committee since there were no plenary sessions designed to reconcile different points of view. Instead, familiar general principles were hoisted: an all-India federation to include the Indian States, though the rulers were obliged to cede to the federation only those powers they wished to; statutory 'safeguards' to allow the Governor-General to carry on the task of governing; greater autonomy in the provinces.

Within the week of the close of the first conference Gandhi and other members of the Congress were released from gaol. The civil disobedience campaign was called off and Gandhi went reluctantly to London to a second Round Table Conference as the Congress's sole representative. The difference between the various communities and everyone's reluctance to settle future financial obligations caused the second conference to end without agreement. More sub-committees were assigned to report on franchise and financial arrangements, and a third conference without Congress or Labour Party participation discussed the reports of the sub-committees. The final conference terminated its session 'in the spirit of mutual understanding and goodwill'. The Secretary of State, Samuel Hoare, made modest claims in his concluding speech to the delegates. The conferences that had in truth expounded problems, difficulties, and questions 'delimited the spheres of activity of the various parts of the constitution . . . and created an *esprit de corps* amongst all of us that is determined to see the building that is going to be reared upon the field that we marked out both complete in itself and completed at the earliest possible date'.[1]

The Secretary of State had to pilot a new constitution for India if only to justify the effort of commissions, committees, officials, delegates who had mused over the Indian landscape

[1] *Indian Round Table Conference*, Third Session, Cmd. 4238, 1932, pp. 138–9.

since 1927. The financial crisis, the economic depression of the early 1930s, and the conservative predilection of the House of Commons 'not to surrender' were uppermost in his mind as he tried to make a policy broadly acceptable to the differing sections of the National Government. Hoare resolutely guided the new constitution along charted contours: 'There should be no rival government to our own in India, that terrorism must be stamped out, and that Congress must not be allowed to arrogate to itself the prerogative of negotiating Indian claims with the British Government. Do not let us blur the position by either appearing to give more than we can give, or by weakening the machine for political reasons.'[1] The new Viceroy, Lord Willingdon, could see no reason to fret over a perfect constitutional formula, for Indian politicians were frightened of independence and did not want control. 'They will depend on us in the future as they've done in the past, they hate responsibility and will be only too grateful to us to continue to look after their affairs.'[2]

In March 1933 the Government published a White Paper, *Proposals for Indian Constitutional Reform*, the first step according to the Secretary of State of a 'ceremonial exactitude which was not allowed to depart in any way from the accepted ritual of making Parliamentary constitutions'.[3] More like a ballet than a ceremony, the proposals recalled the fixed conventions of Indian constitution-making: agencies of government rhythmically joined together to make harmonious patterns of restraint and liberty, exquisite details and careful gestures difficult to interpret, familiar themes in a prominent position, while the whole throbbed with expectation.

There was no mention in the proposals of 'Dominion status' or any specific time when India would be free of British rule. An all-India federation with provincial autonomy was proposed, though the executive retained safeguards, called by the White Paper 'special responsibilities'. The special responsibilities of the Governor-General, later embodied in the Act, were all-

[1] Sir Samuel Hoare to Lord Willingdon, 17 December 1931. Templewood Papers, IOL.

[2] Lord Willingdon to H. Butler, 22 February 1933 Butler papers, IOL.

[3] Viscount Templewood, *Nine Troubled Years*, 1954, pp. 87–8.

embracing; (1) the prevention of grave menace to the peace or tranquillity of India or any part thereof; (2) the safeguarding of the financial stability and credit of the federation; (3) the safeguarding of the legitimate interests of minorities; (4) the securing to the members of the public services any right provided for them by the constitution and the safeguarding of their legitimate interests; (5) the protection of the rights of any Indian State; (6) the prevention of commercial discrimination; (7) any matter which affected the administration of the reserved departments.

After the Joint Select Committee of both Houses of Parliament set forth recommendations, the Government of India Act, 1935, was passed. Significantly, there was no new preamble of promises but the one of 1919 was reiterated. The Act did not establish a federation but provided for a federation *after* half the Indian States acceded to it, and Parliament approved. The federal legislature had two houses, a Council of State chosen from the provinces (150), six nominated by the Governor-General, and the Native States (104). The House of Assembly had 250 members elected from British India, on an extended but still-restricted electorate of about 14 per cent of the population, and 125 from the Native States. The latter could be dissolved at the Governor-General's discretion. A bill had to be passed by both Houses but the Governor-General could withhold his assent or return it to be reconsidered wholly or in part. Armed with special powers for emergency, or the breakdown of the existing constitutional machinery, or if he simply thought it necessary, the Governor-General dominated government to such an extent that it was thought necessary to stipulate that the Crown could disallow acts of the Governor-General as some check and balance to his power. Dyarchy was abolished in the provinces but introduced at the centre, though the Governor-General assigned the Ministers in charge of reserved and transferred subjects.

Five provinces had bicameral legislature, and five unicameral. Allocation of seats followed according to the principles of separate electorates or special groups and interests as in the past. Provinces with two houses had a permanent Legislative Council and Legislative Assembly, the others only a Legislative

Assembly. Bills passed in the Legislatures could be reserved for consideration or withheld from consent by the Governors, thus duplicating the powers of the Governor-General but applied in the provinces. The Legislatures could neither repeal nor amend Acts of Parliament extending to British India, which in effect again removed sovereign authority from India. Bills relating to the procedure under which Europeans were tried in court could not be changed by provincial legislation. Any finance bill had to have the consent of the Governor before it was introduced.

Though these were significant limitations to the opportunity for Indians to manage their own affairs in the provinces, the chance for Indians to form ministries in the provinces after elections was a progressive measure. If the political history of the previous two decades had been less confusing and stormy, such a devolution of authority from British to Indian hands would have seemed a clear indication of Britain's desire to share power and trust in Indian ability to undertake the responsibilities of leadership. The Act virtually forced cooperation between the Governor and the leading political party in his province. The Governor appointed his ministry after consultation with the leader of the majority party in the Legislature. The Governor could dismiss a ministry or it could fall because of a vote of no-confidence in the Legislature. But the past did cast a spell on the present. Suspicion of the kind prevalent in the minds of Congress leaders and even moderate Indian politicians always led to tortuous and protracted negotiations which inevitably rekindled the embers of former disputes. A constitution made up of compromise, restraints and balances, inherently offended Indian politicians who thought in final and absolute terms; nothing less than self-government was capable of justifying the years of suffering, imprisonment and indignity.

The 1935 constitution ended an era. No more reports by commissioners, or constitutions, were made. In the future, problems were negotiated in an *ad hoc* way; special arrangements had to be devised to bring different opinions and interests together. The inability of the constructed machinery of government consistently to aid communication by bringing order to political discussions—a necessary prelude to the resolution of India's many difficulties—remained the weakness of all British-made constitutions for India. Yet, as long as British politicians believed in Britain's role as a world power—and it should never be forgotten that events in the inter-war years forced British statesmen, if at times reluctantly, into such a role—it was impossible for them, when considering India, to lose the imperial perspective and a corresponding confidence in the value of British rule. The constitutions were logical attempts to reconcile all interests—from imperialist to nationalist—into a sensible if necessarily highly complicated system of government. When Indians continued to show their dissatisfaction with constitutions, there was no effective opportunity for long-term and amicable relations between Britain and India. Increasingly after 1935, British officials found it difficult to find any purpose to British rule save as a carrying-on task, devoid of any meaning beyond the honour of fulfilling an inherited responsibility. 'There is nothing for it in this business but to go on stone-walling and expressing our readiness to play. It is not an easy task.'[1]

[1] *The Transfer of Power*, Vol. III, pp. 262–3.

SIX

'GIVE US CHAOS'

[i]

BETWEEN THE ROYAL ASSENT to the India Act,1935, and its implementation in the provinces in April 1937, over a year intervened, time for Indian opinion to congeal. The whole issue of accepting or working the constitution, like milk standing in tepid air, had gone sour. Circumstances called for an incisive initiative which made clear Britain's sincerity in seeing India self-governing. Instead, the 1935 constitution had too many of the now familiar and odorous globules of safeguards, reservation, executive intervention, veto, and promulgation of legislation, for it to be wholly palatable to many Indian politicians. Responsibility to be meaningful had to be complete; anything less would fail to confer the status of political equality on Indians. Nor did the highest government officials regard the constitution as the fulfilment of past promises which hinted at self-government and independence. The Viceroy Lord Linlithgow wrote to Lord Zetland, the Secretary of State, 'You will, I think, agree with me that, having regard to the political situation as a whole, it will be very important, as far as possible, to give these Congress majorities and Ministries they will support, plenty of rope.'[1] The rope is not an instrument of freedom, except perhaps in existentialist thought, but a weapon to dispose of a criminal enemy, hopefully one this enemy would use against himself. The last decade of British rule did not begin with favourable omens.

The Indian National Congress held its conference at Faizpur, a small village in Bombay Presidency totally without adequate facilities for the delegates. Gandhi told the thousands gathered at a village industries exhibition, 'I am prepared to go back to

[1] Lord Linlithgow to Lord Zetland, 4 February 1937. Zetland Papers, IOL.

gaol again, and I am prepared to be hanged.' The Party, feeling that nothing in the past decade warranted their cooperation, called the reforms 'this new charter of bondage'. Since they were not necessary to any stage of the reforming process, they saw no reason to support the results of such a process. The conference, led by Nehru, agreed to fight the forthcoming provincial elections not in order to sanction the new Government but to end it. By drawing nearer to the institutions of authority they could penetrate and corrode the apparatus of domination by direct friction. The Party called for a constituent assembly where Indians would write their own constitution. As long as the Party had never proved its ideas by constitutional means— and this was highly unlikely to happen since it was the unacceptability of the British-made constitutions which was at the heart of all controversy—the Congress corroborated government criticisms of it as disloyal, negative, and impractical. However, the leaders of the party shrewdly understood that the new elections, with an electorate of over thirty million, would give them an opportunity to become representatives, legitimising opposition to government. By being outspokenly hostile to government they would, if successful, possess a unique mandate which would establish consent for their existence and a corresponding lack of it for their opponents. The key to the next decade of Indian politics was that the Congress Party crystallised, in trying and varied circumstances, its aims into a few unchanging, uncompromising policies. This helped to make the Party confident that it alone spoke for India.

> Every party and group that stands aloof from the Congress organisation tends, knowingly or unknowingly, to become a source of weakness to the nation and a source of strength to the forces ranged against it. . . . The Congress offers that joint front which comprises all classes and communities, bound together by their desire to free India, ends the exploitation of her people and builds up a strong and prosperous and united nation, resting on the well-being of the masses.

Yet the very extent to which the Congress believed in itself and was able to claim to represent the political aspirations of the country would make it an unsatisfactory spokesman for those sections of Indian society which, over the previous fifty years, had looked to the Government of India for special concessions and privileges in the form of reserved electorates and a political influence disproportionate to their numerical strength. Broadly based elections would, theoretically, alter the dispensatory base of privilege and authority. Would the more traditionally cooperative parties let the 'criminal' Congress Party become their spokesman if they could not receive substantial concessions or the right to influence party policy decisions? Could the very lengthy past experiences of failure to agree suddenly be forgotten—especially when the same leaders of the Congress exerted their old influence?

The Muslim League was clearly worried. They could feel some satisfaction over the course of past events. The Communal Award of 1932 had acknowledged the right of an exceptional form of representation of Muslim electorates, giving to Muslims a reserved number of seats in a number of provinces where they were a minority—Madras, Bombay, United Province, Central Provinces, Bihar and Orissa. The number of seats granted was greater than the Muslim percentage of population in those particular provinces. The Muslim parties, dishevelled through lack of money and organisation, and in most respects not yet ready for the independence they nevertheless wished, had secured considerable advantage from the disruption caused by Government-Congress hostility. They could feel relieved at the way their interests were guaranteed in the provinces, but naturally were suspicious of the proposed federation which would lessen their powers.

The Conference of the Muslim League at Bombay in April 1936 complained that the new constitution was unprogressive but agreed to cooperate with the provincial part of the act but not the proposed federation. The League later issued a manifesto which indicated, true to its past, that the Party wanted to keep as many options possible open at the same time. But it was still confused and uncertain about the extent to which it wanted to be a Party determined to initiate its own policies. To preserve its already secured political status, the Party was wary of obnoxiously asserting itself. 'The Muslim League in the various Legislatures will utilise the Legislatures in order to extract the maximum benefit out of the constitution for the uplift of the

people in the various spheres of national life. The Muslim
League Party must be formed as a corollary so long as separate
electorates exist, but there would be free cooperation with any
group or groups whose aims and ideas are approximately the
same as those of the League Party.'

Other political parties—Hindu Mahasabha, National Liberal
Federation, Madras Justice Party—were only moderately
critical of the new Act and agreed to work within the constitutional framework. The results of the provincial election of
January-February 1937 posed a number of paradoxes. The
party most hostile to the Act was the most successful. The
parties with a moderate willingness to cooperate, and therefore
able to give the provincial governments the best chance of
success, met with defeats at the polls in inverse proportion to
their professed cooperativeness. The communal award and the
elaborate system of special electorates which theoretically were
intended to divide but represent various Indian minorities, by
the results of the elections, gave one party an all-India pre-
eminence.

The Congress Party won an absolute majority in five provinces and was the single largest party in four others (Bombay
Bengal, Assam and North-West Frontier Province). Out
of a total of 1,585 seats the Congress won over 700, including constituencies reserved for Muslims, labour, land-holders,
commerce and industry. The political viability of the Party
was unmistakably proven. The combination of a mass-based
party, with a radical wing of social and economic reforms,
plus the allegiance of wealthy industrialists and land-owners,
gave the Party a mixture of assets unequalled in British India.
The success of the Party was all the more remarkable since those
who voted for it could expect little or no immediate benefits
from a Congress victory: neither the pacification of tempestuous
past decades nor the realisation of self-government, only a
continuation of the kind of combative politics which made India
an inordinately confusing country. Nehru sagaciously thought
that 'India must have a clean slate on which to write afresh', but
the triumph of his party at the polls transfixed the familiar
quandaries of mutual dislike between Congress and the Government of India and added new and equally bitter markings.

With votes to adorn its prestige the Congress put demands to the Government of India. The Party refused to accept ministerial office in provinces where they had a majority in the legislatures unless it received assurance from the Governors that the special reserved powers under section 93 of the Government of India Act would not be used. This was clearly an impossible demand. No Viceroy or Secretary of State could fundamentally alter sovereign rights 'to repudiate the special responsibilities with which they were specifically charged in the terms of the constitution'. The Government could not be seen to give in to such demands lest 'the risk of a landslide' among princes, the services, and silent Indians waiting to join the side with the best prospects, disturb the foundations of government. The new provincial governments could not begin with a major provision destroyed.

However, a number of well-meaning people believed a gesture on the Government's part, though not a concession but a clarification of the outstanding differences, would pay sufficient compliment to Congress's vanity to gain its acceptance. In Cabinet Lord Halifax suggested that another Viceroy's conference with the Congress leaders might be such a gesture. C. Rajagopalachari, the moderate Congress leader in Madras, devised a number of formulae to specify the Governor's responsibilities in the event of the fall of a ministry. When Gandhi in June 1937 said he was hopeful that Congress would take office if the Government showed itself conciliatory, the Viceroy sent out a broadcast which, though in fact slightly patronising, and intended 'not to give way on any single point', was widely accepted as sincere, and forward-looking.

> The British were proud of their own patriotism, love of liberty and liberal institutions of government, so it has seemed to me that my countrymen should regard the growth in India of those same qualities and aspirations, not as a matter for anxiety or disquiet, but as an occasion for pride and as a call upon them for their understanding and their ready help.[1]

On the following day the Viceroy published a statement

[1] P. Sitaramayya, *History of the Indian National Congress* Vol. I, Bombay, 1969, p. 63.

explaining how the special powers of the Governor worked, should a ministry resign or be dismissed. The Working Committee of the Congress and provincial leaders, as well as Gandhi, saw greater advantage in accepting office than in protracting the nebulous wrangle about future possibilities. The Congress by accepting office would show itself responsible, capable, and the functioning political party of India. For his part Lord Linlithgow saw vindicated all his methods of dealing with the Congress: delay, unwillingness to have direct talks with Congress leaders during a political storm, no concessions, maintaining the prestige of the ruling authority by showing no eagerness to win popular support at the expense of the fixed legal course, a keen awareness of the embarrassment which would befall the British Government if it pursued an overtly conciliatory policy that Indians might rebuff.

Whereas the new constitution designated the balance of power and the structure of government for the provinces, when it came to the federal scheme most important outstanding issues were left to be worked out after the native Princes had voluntarily joined a federated India by signing a legal and binding document called the Instrument of Accession. Without their accession federation could not occur. But the Princes were on the whole loath to relinquish the administration of their lands where it should fall within federal jurisdiction. They were Sovereign in their own domains, and a share in the control of a yet untried and widely criticised federal government, even though it was planned for the princely states to have a say in affairs disproportionate to their number, did not strike them as a reasonable exchange. Most of the Native States had no parliament, or institutions to diminish the absolute and feudal character of their regimes. Federation, mentioned at the time of the Montagu-Chelmsford reforms when the Chamber of Princes was established, suggested by the Simon Commission, and agreed to in principle at the Round Table Conference of 1930, was feasible in a politically stable country. As the princely rulers pondered the details and implications of federation they became unwilling to accept limitation of their powers in return for what seemed the dubious responsibility of a share in all-India affairs. Lord Linlithgow was anxious to launch the federation as it would draw into his orbit of government those loyal rulers of the states who could be relied upon to be generally helpful. In this way he would muffle the acrimonious Congress Party by bringing into existence a federation which functioned by the acceptance of a number of other Indian groups. In 1936–7 he sent three high government officials to tour the major states to expedite negotiations. Yet the States remained distrustful. The success of the Congress Party at the provincial elections, and that Party's declared identification with the masses within the States suggested to the rulers a threat from federation where social and economic reform could be directed against their interests. When the Congress also suggested that State elections be held instead of allowing the rulers to appoint representatives, the States devised methods of allowing the rulers to appoint representatives, to postpone the uncertain future. Meetings in London, at the India Office, and with the parliamentary council, dragged on, helped in no way by the princes' habit of changing their counsel and nego-tiators from time to time. The princes held conferences which raised so many questions, objections, and problems of financial detail that their accession loomed further and further into the future. Exasperated the Viceroy pressed for a definite answer within six months of January 1939. A conference of the rulers and their ministers in Bombay, while not wishing to alienate the British Government on whose support their authority legally rested, found the present terms of federation unsatisfactory. Like a ruined village, half standing, half in shambles, the newest Indian constitution was overgrown with the brambles of archaic and contorted issues which became more entwined as time passed. The most spiky aspect of the political situation after 1937 was not the failure of federation, but the sancrosanct provision of the new constitution which left responsibility for safeguarding the legitimate interests of minorities as a special executive responsibility, to be exercised at the Governor's will. The British Government and the Government of India found a solid justification for retaining reserved executive powers not only in the contention that they ruled in the interests of the illiterate masses, a claim equally and somewhat more convincingly made by Congress, but in the

convulsive hostility between Hindus and Moslems. The
communal award and special electorates tried to take into
account the interests of minorities that might otherwise be
swamped in a sub-continent predominantly Hindu. The unques-
tioned assumption at this time was that minorities needed
protection. A list of Indian languages and religions, as well as
reference back to the multifarious petitions and claims submitted
by classes and parties not in alliance with the Congress,
indubitably asserted a reason for the type of government in
India whereby British civil servants and administrators im-
partially umpired for the good of all, and directly for the
protection of minorities. More appropriate for the later stages
of British rule in India than the classic 'divide and rule' was the
concept that an India divided within itself necessitated an
imperious and transcendent ruler.

The central issue of Indian politics became whether in truth
communal, religious, social, economic, and linguistic divisions
within the country constituted a need for their special representation in a future government of India. Put another way, could
the Congress Party with its all-India perspective form the basis
of national unity which, in the demand for independence,
expressed the will of all? Did special groups and minorities want
self-government more than retaining the self-identity of their
unit? From whom did minorities need protection? Needless to
say, the Congress saw itself as the democratic all-India party
with a tolerant and magnanimous attitude towards every
section of India. For it the danger to minorities was an artificial
issue conjured by the British in order to attack Congress,
frighten would-be allies, and explain the need for the continuance of British rule. As ever, Congress was eager to make every
effort to secure communal harmony and protect by agreement
the rights of all recognised minorities, but it expected full
authority to be given to it as the majority party, an authority
synonymous to them with democracy. In reply, Jinnah daringly
said, 'I oppose democracy.'

Fortunately, events did not leave such problems suspended in
theory. The Congress victory in the 1937 elections and the
formation of ministries in the provinces gave an unprecedented
opportunity for all to see the intentions of the Congress. What

place Muslims were given in Congress-majority ministries, how Congress ruled over the different communities, proved the ultimate test for Indian Muslims.

With so many details unsettled in British India, the relations between Hindus and Muslims should have remained open to discussion. Both parties agreed that communal antagonism was an evil and that they should set an example of cooperativeness. In a few provinces during the 1937 elections the Congress and the League had the same platform, while afterwards a number of independent Muslims supported and thus made possible Congress ministries. For the first time in India's political history an opportunity existed for the formation of a broadly-based political party which cut across community and special interest, bound together by legislative responsibilities and the desire to support government policies and the minister who introduced them.

But this was not to be. The Congress believed the elections vindicated their assertion that there was only one political voice in India. Accordingly they felt no need to ally themselves with former opponents who neither wholeheartedly supported the Party's platform nor received popular approval at the elections. They argued that the more conservative Muslim League, firmly allied to the wealthy landowners and with little claim to represent the suffering Indian masses, would oppose the Congress programme of social and economic reform. If brought into the ministries they would destroy ministerial responsibility, since in a crisis—and one was expected—between the Governor and his ministers, the Muslims would, as they had often done in the past, side with the British and official viewpoint, and thereby weaken the effect of the resignations.

The United Provinces proved a test case. There, the two parties had worked together in the elections, and Muslims expected to be offered two ministerial offices. In the event they were only offered places if the Muslim League was virtually disbanded; the League was to run no candidates in by-elections and merge its organisations with the existing Congress one. The League was not offered an alliance, but a take-over by the majority party. Disgruntled at the off-hand methods of the Congress, Muslims in the province joined with the landowners to form an opposition party.

Just as an individual can experience 'reaction-formation', that is aquire self-identity and purpose as an effect of anxieties so the Muslim League in 1937 began a process of binding itself together out of fear of total domination of the Congress Party, which they labelled Hindu Raj. In rejecting the Congress the League asserted the 'two nations as a principle' which within a few years crystallised into the policy for the partition of India. The indifference of the Congress high command to Muslim sensibilities inspired the League to become an independent party with a complete and national programme of its own. At the annual conference of the party in October 1937, 'one of the most critical that has taken place in the last thirty years', Jinnah correlated the frightening aspects of the present Muslim position and the emergence of a Muslim nation.

> There are forces which may bully you, tyrannise over you and intimidate you and you may even have to suffer. But it is by going through this crucible of fire [and] persecution which may be levelled against you, tyranny that may be exercised, the threats and intimidations that may unnerve you, and it is by resisting, by overcoming, by facing these disadvantages, hardships, and by suffering and maintaining your true convictions and loyalty that a nation will emerge worthy of its past glory and history. . . .[1]

The conference passed a resolution calling on Muslims not to look for justice or good-will outside the League, and the Muslim premiers of Bengal, Assam, and the Punjab told their supporters in the provinces to commit themselves to the League and end all alliances with the Congress. By the time of the 1937 conference, disparate events and ideas which had in the past only fragmented the Muslim outlook, suddenly became meaningful. A variety of sources affirmed the more independent attitude of the Muslim League.

The 'vexed problem' of riots between Hindus and Muslims again inflamed feelings of distrust. In the first six months of 1937, a period surrounding the provincial elections, serious outbreaks of communal violence occurred in Behrar, Bombay, Danwaraja, Hardi, Madras, Perabore, Buddhi, Gubarga, Panipat, Tatnagirir, and Sangli. The frequency and intensity of these disturbances, frenetically reported in the vernacular press,

[1] G. Allana (ed.), *Pakistan Movement Historic Documents* Karachi, 1967, p. 150.

acted as a bellows to the smouldering Muslim idea that it was impossible for them to live among Hindus and remain devoted to their faith.

The recent election campaign had also led to sharp exchanges between the two communities. Nehru, in his nation-wide campaign, claimed there were two political parties in the country: Congress and the Government. There was no practical reason for a Muslim party to exist. As an exclusive communal party it was their inevitable fate to break apart when touched by any real problem 'because no common principle or policy binds them'. To suggest as he did that the Congress represented the whole of India, without first obtaining formal agreement from Muslims who were not members of the Congress, was fairly interpreted as a slight on the Muslim community. Muslims saw no reason to believe that the Congress would better represent their community than a party solely of their own people. Jinnah curtly replied: 'There is a third party in this country—the Muslims.'[1]

The defeat of League candidates in the elections made it imperative for the Party to adapt to the changed circumstances if it was to survive. Winning only around 109 seats of the 485 reserved for Muslims pushed the Party towards a nationalist policy which could attract the support of Muslim masses, crucial if they were to fare better at elections. The existence of a considerable number of reserved places in the provincial legislature and of three provinces where Muslims were in the majority—N.W.F.P., Punjab, Bengal—made it obvious that there was considerable opportunity in the future.

It was to the provinces that Muslims looked to expand their influence. The communal award and the special responsibility of the Governors for minorities reiterated the need for the single large minority to maintain a vigilant watch lest their secured position be eroded. Quite logically the League opposed a federation since in a larger political unit the absolute majority of Hindus and the absolute powers of the Congress would find a larger context in which to dominate. Thus, provincial autonomy became the constitutional basis for the creation of a Muslim state because a few provinces afforded Muslims the chance to

[1] *The Times*, 5 January 1937.

run their own affairs, not as a minority, but as the government of the largest single people of that area. The full honour and justice they associated with independence would be achieved by a separate Muslim state.

The League also reached deeply into its intellectual resources to vindicate its new approach to politics. The eminent Muslim poet-theologian-barrister, Muhammad Iqbal (1876–1938), inspired the people of his faith with ideas about man's striving for freedom and self-assertion which leads to a holy union of one with the many. A transcendent meaning is given to struggle when it becomes identified with the eternal Muslim religion and community. Only a reconstructed nation imbued with the ideals unique to Muslims could fulfil the poet's yearning.

> For me, every particle of my country's dust is a deity.
> Come, let us remove all that causes estrangement,
> Let us reconcile those that have turned away from each other,
>   remove all signs of division.[1]

As President of the All-India Muslim League in 1930 Iqbal proposed the formation of an autonomous, consolidated Muslim state which would give India an 'internal balance of power' and also bring the followers of the Prophet closer together in the spirit of their religion. More prosaically he wrote in 1937 to Jinnah: 'The enforcement and development of the Shariat of Islam is impossible in this country without a free Muslim state or states . . . the only other alternative is a civil war which as a matter of fact has been going on for some time in the shape of Hindu Muslim riots. . . . A separate federation of Muslim provinces . . . is the only course by which we can secure a peaceful India and save Muslims from the domination of non-Muslims.'[2]

A leaflet appeared in 1933, *Now or Never* by Rahmat Ali, which designated the areas of the Muslim state to be called Pakistan, the land of the Paks, 'the spiritually pure and clean'. 'It symbolises the beliefs and the ethical stocks of our people, and it stands for all the territorial constituents of our original fatherland.' Ali argued that the differences between the two 'nations' were too fundamental to reconcile. Religion, culture,

---

[1] M. Mujeeb, *The Indian Muslims*, 1967, p. 485.
[2] G. Allana, *Pakistan*, pp. 130–3.

history, tradition, literature, economic system, laws of inheritance, succession and marriage were such imposing barriers, 'the
Himalayas of the human heart', that goodwill or cooperation
was impossible. The separate nation theory now had a name and
places to rally support and become a focal point for nationalism.

Yet it was the changed circumstances after 1935 which made
the formerly vague ideal of a Muslim nation plausible. The new
constitution, by extending provincial autonomy, gave the
majority community new authority and proportionally withdrew
something of the full weight of British guarantees to the
Muslims; the League, along with the Congress, advocated
complete independence—which meant that they had to anticipate a very different future. Their opposition to the proposed
federation left the Muslim parties obliged to propose an
alternative. An independent state based on the Muslim majority
provinces eventually became that alternative.

Though politically shrewd, the claim for an independent
state could be substantiated in the deteriorating community
relations which, as we have noted, occurred at this time, and
by an analysis of the effects of Congress rule in the provinces
from 1937. Both confirmed the simple basic contention of the
League that the two communities could not live together
without the rights of the minority community being challenged.
A Congress Party in charge of a province without any need to
rely on Muslim support was inherently a threat to the status of
the Muslims.

The extent of the deterioration is most convincingly revealed
in the correspondence between Nehru and Jinnah in 1938. It
might be thought two politicians would have much to discuss at
that time. Federation, communal tension, policies of social and
economic value to people which the new provincial ministries
could implement, the significance for India of the growing
hostility between 'fascism and democracy' in Europe, these
were sufficiently practical and urgent to warrant a gargantuan
correspondence. Nehru wrote to Jinnah in January 1938 saying
that the Congress was eager to 'put an end to every misapprehension', though at first he was at a loss to understand the
points of dispute. The tone of his letter barely disguised his
patronising irritability; he often complained he could not under-

stand what Jinnah was saying or implied that the arguments
Jinnah raised were so insubstantial as to deserve not a reply but
a reprimand. He curtly dismissed the allegation that policies in
Congress majority provinces were inimical to Muslims: 'I have
come across various statements to the effect that the Congress
is trying to establish Hindu Raj. I am unaware of how this is
being done or who is doing it.' When Jinnah hinted that a
meeting was a better way to argue matter than letters, Nehru
replied: 'But when we meet what are we to discuss?' and later
reflected, 'I am afraid our letters to each other repeat themselves.' Jinnah then wrote a further letter which spelled out a
number of specific issues. Nehru 'was somewhat surprised to
see this [list of grievances] as I had no idea that you wanted to
discuss many of these matters with us. Some of these are wholly
covered by previous decisions of the Congress, some others are
hardly capable of discussion'. Between the poles of 'wholly
covered by previous decisions of the Congress' and 'others are
hardly capable of discussion' there was truly no room for
manoeuvre. Nehru had asserted in this sentence the basically
rigid attitude of the Congress to lead Muslims on terms which
required acceptance not cooperation. For 'previous decisions of
the Congress' had not been made with League participation;
the phrase 'covered' in this context implied a finality to the
Congress decision-making process which was inappropriate to
the fluid nature of Indian political arrangements. That Nehru
should think points of grievance Jinnah raised were 'hardly'
capable of discussion only reinforced the original Muslim
suspicions about Congress arrogance and the diminishing
ability of Muslims to influence Congress policies and leaders.
Jinnah was not at a loss to write a lawyer's letter with meanings
between as well as on the lines. 'I must say that it is very
difficult for me to understand it [your last letter]. I fail to see
what you are driving at. . . . You have now flung at me more
complaints and grievances of a trifling character. . . . If you
think that necessity [to talk together] has arisen and anyone
of you is willing, I shall be glad to see you and equally welcome
a talk. The thing is that you prefer talking at each other whereas
I prefer talking to each other.'[1]

[1] See the *Jinnah-Nehru Correspondence*, Allahabad, 1938.

When the League scrutinised the practices of the provincial governments controlled by the Congress they found nothing but encroachments on the integrity of the Muslim community. The annual conferences of the League during these years were dominated by a list of allegations of injustices perpetrated by Congress provincial governments. Communal antagonism at this time as in the past was tangled in rumour and fact, obscure incidents and hearsay testimony, suspicion which allowed any event to be interpreted as threatening. Certainly the Congress Party was indifferent to Muslim sensibilities. Local organisations were established in the provinces specifically to propagandise and win over poor Muslims to support the Congress; children were taught to regard Gandhi as a saint; there were incidents when police too quickly sided with their Hindu co-religionists. One of the most abrasive developments, such was the tender nature of the times, was the introduction at schools and public meetings of the song 'Bande Mataram' ('I Praise Mother') as a national anthem. The song had been written in a novel by B. C. Chottoapadhyay (1838–1894), a Bengali writer and deputy Magistrate, and became popular during Hindu protests against the partition of Bengal in 1905. It was blatantly Hindu in content and could hardly fail to irritate a religion which abhorred idol worship: India was likened to a Hindu goddess.

> It is you who are Durga the Protector, and you stand there, with your ten-weaponed arms stretched out in ten directions to keep off all enemies and evils. . . .

> Though the exterior of your body becomes hot in summer, your lap becomes comparatively cool for your children, with the south-west monsoon and being covered with green crops, you assume a beautiful appearance.[1]

In 1938 the Pirpur Report catalogued Muslim grievances which indirectly reaffirmed the need for a separate Muslim State.

By the end of 1939 nothing had happened to sweeten relations between the leaders of the two communities. Fazl-ul-Huq, the Muslim premier of Bengal, wrote to Nehru a detailed list of

[1] S. Dinda, *Interpretation of the Bondy Matarom*, Calcutta, 1970, p. 24.

Congress and Hindu 'outrages' against Muslims. The stories of brutal crime and suffering—arson, assault, murder, mass terrorism in Bihar, the United Provinces and Central Province—were forceful indictments against Congress rule, though the evidence fell short of that admissible in a court of law. Nehru was invited to visit the devastated areas, but did not accept, for he like other Congress leaders disregarded Muslim complaints. Since the machinery of government provided no impartial method for investigating the causes of the break-down in community relations, save the general proviso that the governor had special responsibility to safeguard the rights of minorities, Muslims felt they were an injured party unable to obtain justice. The Congress Party with its democratic majority was able to remain above fair comment and criticism. Jinnah and the Muslim League moved into a position of irresponsible hostility to the Congress. 'Congress had dashed every possible hope of arriving at a settlement of the Hindu-Muslim question on the rocks of Congress Fascism.'[1]

The concurrence of the deterioration of Hindu-Muslim relations and Congress's acceptance of ministerial office, and the interaction of these two events intensifying the deterioration, ended any opportunity for a simple resolution to the Indian political situation. The crux of that situation was the conflict between power and justice; the political equation had become so finely balanced that no addition to one side could fail to cause an intensive reaction by the other. The successes of the Congress, holding ministerial office and widening its mass appeal, by the momentum it created, threatened to make the Party a unique political authority in India. Not surprisingly, the Muslims realised that only the British Government stood between the absolute authority of the Congress and annihilation. But since the Muslim League also wanted self-government, in this context the removal of the last barrier to Congress domination, the ideology and programme of the Muslims in the course of a few years converged on the partition of India as the only practical solution. In March 1940 the annual session of the All-India Muslim League passed the Pakistan Resolution, 'that geographically contiguous units are demarcated into regions

[1] *All India Muslim League Conference* 1938, p. 344.

which should be so constituted with such territorial readjust-
ments as may be necessary, that areas in which the Muslims
are numerically in a majority as in the North-Western and
Eastern zones of India should be grouped to constitute "Independent States" in which the constituent units shall be
autonomous and sovereign'. The single largest minority group
in India had found a way to become its own guarantor of security;
from now on Jinnah and the League consistently argued that
no changes in the Indian constitution or diminution of British
authority should occur without their approval; no interim
changes should introduce a series of policies antithetical to the
principle of an independent Muslim state. Since the British
Government had long established the principle that agreement
between Indian groups was a prerequisite for the next constitution advance, the Muslim League, though only a representative
of one section of the country, had procured by the Pakistan
Resolution a powerful instrument to obstruct all subsequent
political discussion.

Except for the periodic exchange of letters between Congress
and Muslim leaders, the two groups had little contact with one
another in this crucial period before the outbreak of war. It was
of the utmost importance that the British Government at this
time did not conceive itself as an instrument of reconciliation,
that the good offices of the Government of India would be used
to bring the different parties together. 'The Governor-General
could not, after all, spend his time running round like a waiter
with propositions on a tray, only to have them met with demands
for something quite different.'[1] When Lord Linlithgow saw the
various leaders, he talked to them separately. Nor did the Viceroy see much practical benefit, from the British point of view, if
Indian political opinion became unified since such cohesion
would make Indians more implacable and restless. 'From our
point of view, desirable as agreement between all parties may
be in principle, I am not sure that such a consumation is entirely
to be welcomed. But the alternative—absorption of the Muslims
by Congress—would be equally undesirable.'[2] The Viceroy
well appreciated that the Government of India had to govern,

[1] Lord Linlithgow to Lord Zetland, 13 November 1939. Zetland Papers, IOL.
[2] Lord Linlithgow to Lord Zetland, 27 October 1937. Zetland Papers, IOL.

and as one long familiar with the frustrations and disappointments of recent years, he came to rely on the legitimate constitutional structure introduced by the 1935 Act as his brief. 'The constitutional position of India and the policy of His Majesty's Government are governed by the provisions of the Government of India Act, 1935.'

The ideology of the Congress Party made it indifferent to the Muslim League; in its own eyes Congress was a political not a communal party and as such it had a wide spectrum of ideas to attract the support of landowners and peasants, labourers and industrialists, because they saw in it a microcosm of India and thus an apt organisation to state the claims of the nation as a whole. Consistent within its own creed Congressmen threw themselves into the task of enacting policies which would verify the integrity of their Party by introducing a number of reforms promised at election time. Ministerial office, they thought, would increase the ability of the Party to attract support of the masses, including the Muslims, who in their minds were the only Muslims who mattered. Every section of the country would see in the measures of reform and in the legislative acts in the various provinces a responsible Congress Party.

To a considerable extent this happened. Given the financial stringency under which they worked and the general inexperience of the ministers, difficulties often overlooked by critics of a political party committed to reform, the energy of the new provincial governments was considerable. In Madras, the Debt Relief Act (1937) gave direct assistance to farmers in debt and provided committees to guide debtor and creditor to an agreed settlement. The Removal of Disabilities Act, Malabar Temple-Entry Act, and the Temple-Entry Authorisation and Indemnity Acts removed the civil and religious restrictions placed by custom on the lowest caste Hindus, known as Untouchables. The province also agreed to the principle that public utilities, water, gas and electricity, should be owned and run by the state. Bombay introduced prohibition, and the money lost from the liquor tax was made up from a direct tax on houses. The Bombay Trades Disputes Act (1938) restricted the right of labour to strike and provided an intermediate conciliation procedure. Bombay, Bihar and United Provinces founded a basic education scheme after Gandhi's Wardha plan which asserted the principles of free primary education, the linking of handi-craft and learning, and the use of the vernacular as the language of instruction. Eighty-seven such schools were started in Bombay and thirty-five in Bihar. Agrarian reform in United Provinces and Bihar provided security of tenure and fixed rents for the ryot, the reduction of rents to the 1911 level, and the reduction of debts in arrears. A tenant could not be evicted because of the non-payment of rent. In Bihar a campaign against illiteracy was launched which organised teachers and students in centres throughout the province. By April 1939 there were nearly four million students. In Central Provinces, experimental schools, Vidya Mandir, were started to provide education by money raised from the farming and handicrafts of the students.

The release of political prisoners, and the improvement of conditions within the prisons, were election pledges of the Congress Party. The Premiers of Bihar and United Provinces demanded the release of all political prisoners in their provinces, reversing the previous policy of considering each case for parole on its own merits. Because the release of political prisoners might cause grave menace to the peace and tranquillity of India, the matter was referred to the Viceroy who rejected the advice of the Premiers. A major crisis followed and the two ministers resigned, claiming 'no council of ministers can dis-charge its function satisfactorily if its considered opinion is disregarded arbitrarily'. The Viceroy's communiqué reminded the ministers of the discretionary powers of clemency applied to prisoners, and under advice from Gandhi and the Working Committee of the Congress, the ministers returned to office. Within two months nearly all the political prisoners were released.

In his letter of resignation, the Prime Minister of United Provinces complained of the 'unsubstantial character of auto-nomy which provinces are supposed to enjoy, when advice of council of ministers can be trampled upon by one entirely outside the province.'[1] G. B. Pant was of course referring to the ominous powers of the Viceroy, which stood as a warning

[1] *Resignation of the Ministries in Bihar and United Provinces*, 1937–8, Cmd. 5674, xxi p. 10.

shadow to any form of radicalism, especially in financial reform and government expenditure. As we have seen, the Viceroy took the 1935 Constitution as the strongest guideline for his thinking on how to deal with a fundamentally sensitive situation, since the Act was based on the greatest measure of common agreement which it was possible to obtain at the time when it was framed. Over financial policy, on which in theory provincial ministers had wide discretion, he called upon the provincial governors to guide the interests of their areas towards orthodox and conservative policies, even though the Viceroy appreciated that strictly speaking such guidance was not sanctioned by the Act. The following letter written to the Secretary of State in November 1937 shows the degree to which the powers of the Viceroy were only bound by his own assessment of what was best for India; so long as Indians put no strain on the sensitive financial tendons in the provinces, they possessed the freedoms established by the new constitution. The letter illustrates that the British Government had not recognised the right (indeed they still had duties) of the provincial ministries to propagate policies at odds with British interests, an essential concession if provincial autonomy was at all meaningful as a step towards self-government.

I have been endeavouring to bring home to Governors the extreme importance from the point of view of the Ministry, of whatever party, in those provinces of pursuing a conservative financial policy and I have not failed to impress upon them that the adoption of wild-cat schemes or the sacrifice of sources of revenue such as excise for purely political reasons cannot but be relevant to the decision which the Central Government will have to take as to the response it is to make to requests for financial assistance to the Provinces once it finds itself in a position to distribute monies to the Provinces. I quite recognise that the Act imposes no special responsibility on Governors for the maintenance of the financial stability of their Provinces but for all that it does seem to me to be of extreme importance to bring home to them that whether they have special responsibility or not, they have a very clear and direct personal and moral responsibility for leaving their Ministries in no uncertainty as the risks which the adoption of certain types of financial policy may involve, as to their duties as Ministers to the Province and its future.[1]

[1] Lord Linlithgow to Lord Zetland, 11 November 1937. Zetland Papers IOL.

The British Government in the two years before the outbreak of war reaped some of the rewards of conciliation; they
had purchased time for Indian politicians to acquire political
experience and the appetite for policy-making. Moderate
conciliation in India, unlike appeasement in Europe, did not
give way to threats or demands; the British Government
distrusted their Indian opponents and realised they had the
power to arrest and thus contain most forms of Indian protest.
The achievement of drawing the hitherto implacable Congress
Party into the sinews of administration warranted a cautious
policy. The Government did not recklessly press their point
of view. Thus on the major controversies of the period—the use
of the special powers of the governor, release of political
prisoners, federation and provincial expenditure—the British
Government avoided coercing their Indian opponents.

It was the misfortune of these years that the progress begun
had too little time to mature. The outbreak of war in September
1939 placed a heavy burden on Congress ministries. The
Viceroy had unquestionable responsibility for defence and
foreign affairs; but the provincial ministries tacitly assumed
that they decided on policies which mattered. As long as the
issues to be decided fell within the delegated responsibilities
specified in the 1935 constitution, they were not disillusioned.
But when the crucial issue before the country was not one they
had a right to decide, the very status and credibility of the
Congress minister was raised. The haunting issue returned in
the guise of whether India should support Britain and the
Allies in the war. When Lord Linlithgow passed amendments
and laws preparing the country for war, and simply declared
'the issues are clear', 'India would contribute to the allied war
effort as a worthy nation', without prior consultation or
approval from Indian politicians, political cooperation from the
Congress dissolved. 'This has been done without the consent of
the Indian people, whose declared wishes, in such matters, have
been deliberately ignored by the British Government.' In
October 1939 all the Congress Ministries resigned; the Party
declared its equal hostility to Fascism and Imperialism and that
India had to be given immediate independence.

When the Viceroy declared India a participant in the Second

World War, the newly instituted constitution became suspect
in the eyes of many leading Indian politicians. How practical
were the powers conferred on them when such a vital question
as war or peace was never openly debated and entry formally
accepted? Such a decision by the Viceroy, completely in accord-
ance with the 1935 Act, bluntly asserted the considerable
degree of Indian dependence on British interests. Whereas the
two years of Congress ministerial responsibility in the provinces
had involved the energy of the Party in the many practical issues
of government and reform, because these were judged to be
consistent with the principles of self-government and progress,
Indian entry into European war had all the connotations of the
old Imperial master commanding his minions to obey.

The Indian Princes, as in the past, stood by the British
Government, 'their motherland'. The Muslim ministries in
Punjab, Bengal and the Sind remained in office and a number of
individual Hindu politicians agreed to fill government posts.
However, the two major political organisations, the Muslim
League and the Congress, made the war a reason to sharpen
their demands. Jinnah and the Working Committee of the
Muslim League eventually gave passive acceptance to India's
involvement in the war only after they had received from the
Viceroy his, if not agreement, at least acknowledgement of the
principle that Muslims should be the final judge and arbitrator
of any constitutions in the future which affected them. Lord
Linlithgow wrote to Jinnah in December 1939, 'You need,
therefore, have no fear that the weight which your community's
position in India necessarily gives their views will be under-
rated.' After the resignation of the Congress ministries in 1939
the Party continually opposed the war and in the next few years
developed methods of confrontation to challenge again Britain's
continuing right to rule India.

Yet the Congress Party was not in the main pro-Fascist.
Only S. C. Bose among the Congress leadership saw the Axis
powers as liberators of India. Leading Congressmen in fact
opposed Fascism. Gandhi told the Viceroy on 5 September 1939,
that 'he contemplated the present struggle . . . with an English
heart'. During the Munich crisis Nehru wrote to the *Manchester
Guardian*, resenting the British Government's foreign policy,

and prophetically warned: 'The people of India have no intention of submitting to any foreign decision on war. They alone can decide and certainly they will not accept the dictation of the British Government, which they distrust utterly.'[1]

When war came and the British Government and the Government of India boldly committed the peoples of India to the struggle, the inherent weaknesses of the political structure as it had developed over the previous two years were manifest. Most historians have overlooked the fact that only one member of the Congress high command, C. Rajagopalachari in Madras, became a chief minister in the provinces. This left the real leaders of the party still unattached to the existing political system. They were free to criticise and oppose with the same irresponsibility they had known before the 1935 reforms. The new constitution did not attract the support of the major political leaders of the Congress Party, leaving those who took up ministerial posts vulnerable to the influence of their party chiefs outside their provinces. Secondly, the failure of federation and the growth of Muslim independence of Congress, especially in the Muslim majority provinces, events of the greatest importance for the viability of the 1935 Act, detached the British Government of India from the main developments of the period. This detachment was unrealistic because neither the Viceroy nor the British Government accepted a loss of their ultimate authority to govern. In the past two years it had simply been convenient to avoid asserting this. Given the relatively passive function required if provincial autonomy were to be given a fair chance, the Government of India's unilateral decision to support the war seemed an utter negation of the spirit of the previous two years.

The Viceroy, after meeting fifty-two leaders of every shade of opinion in India (there were that many who had distinct opinions), was left to instruct the governors to form ministries from those who would accept office. The experiment of cooperative government in the provinces was over. When asked by many of his visitors to explain what Britain's future policy towards India would be, he made it abundantly clear that the oncoming war, or Indian support or lack of support, would not

---

[1] *Manchester Guardian*, 8 September 1938.

influence the next stage in India's constitutional advance. He
told Gandhi in September 1939, before the All-India Congress
Committee issued its statement opposing India's entry: 'I felt
bound . . . to be categorical with him [Gandhi] that there was
not commitment of any sort which I could enter into as regards
the future.'[1] To anyone familiar with Indian constitutional
history, the Viceroy's statement of October 1939 (reiterated in
1940), in which he referred to pledges given in the preamble
of the 1919 Act and Lord Irwin's announcement of 1929, was
'clear and positive' only to the extent of affirming what had
already been reaffirmed. The following passage has the too-
familiar qualifications, cryptic references, and vague illusions to
uncertain aspects of the future which dilute any actual commitment. He said that, when the time came again to consider the
future constitution of India and the plan destined to give effect
to the assurances given, 'it will be necessary to consider *in the
light of the then circumstances to what extent* the details embodied
in the Act of 1935 *remain appropriate.* And I am authorised now
by His Majesty's Government to say that at the end of the war
they will be very willing to enter into *consultation* with representatives of the several communities, parties and interests of India
and within the Indian provinces, with a view to securing their
aid and cooperation in the framing of such *modification* as may
seem *desirable.*[2] As the Viceroy explained to the Secretary of
State in September 1939, no matter what public statements
hinted, the direction of his thinking was not towards a different
future but the safe past. To evoke again Sir Samuel Hoare's
statement in the House of Commons in 1935 'gives us a first-
class opportunity to employ the magic words without entering
any new commitment.' He saw 'the extreme desirability of
leaving our hands as free as practical and to as late a stage as
we can achieve, in the present conflict'.[3]

[ii]

At the beginning of this century Lord Kitchener, as Commander-
in-Chief of the Indian Army, was puzzled to know what military

[1] Lord Linlithgow to Lord Zetland, 5 September 1939. Zetland Papers, IOL.
[2] Author's italics to indicate words which could be construed in many ways.
[3] Lord Linlithgow to Lord Zetland, 25 September 1939. Zetland Papers, IOL.

obligations Britain assumed in India. 'What after all is our policy? . . . We have got to realise we have promised more than we are able to perform. . . . We are in the position of a firm which has written cheques against a non-existent balance.'[1] His secret memorandum written to the Secretary of State for India in 1906 warned of the bankrupt state of British Imperial defence policy. He appreciated that Britain's reputation in Asia and position as a world power depended on its military organisation in a period of history when the vortex of world politics made war likely. The future Secretary of State for War sensed the weakness inherent in a loose and woolly Imperialism which might need to call on non-existent fighting resources. Military efficiency depended on what was blatantly lacking in British Imperial defence: developed strategic plans, an assessment of future needs, continuing investment in modernisation, coordination of human and material resources within the Empire as a whole, and a spirit of cooperativeness.

After the Great War, enthusiasm for defence expenditure and Imperial solidarity declined. In Britain the services squabbled for the limited money available from the Government. Cabinets avoided making defence policy; there was no Ministry of Defence until 1936 to push through unified plans. Rather, the defence budget was subjected to money-saving scrutiny to lighten the burden of the nation's taxation. From 1919 until 1932 the 'ten-year rule', which assumed there would be no war within the next decade, contributed to the lack of urgency in defence. The need to economise led to the formation of special committees to investigate or supervise the services budget. As a result, total defence expenditure from 1921 to 1935 was kept at a steady twelve to fifteen per cent of Government spending. By keeping the proportion of government expenditure on defence relatively fixed, there was little money for expensive new modernisation and mechanisation. For example, the Air Ministry could have small amounts of money for defensive but nothing for offensive operational research, though the advanced development of the Air Force depended upon offensive weaponry. The Dominions, with the memory of British bungling in the

[1] H. E. Lord Kitchener, 'A Note on the Military Policy of India', Simla, 1906. Morley Papers, IOL.

Dardanelles, on the Somme, and in Mesopotamia gnawing in their minds, took pride in that national spirit which owed nothing to the mother country. After the war the self-governing areas achieved greater national identity. They made their own tariff policy and kept independent diplomatic establishments. Britain's support of the Greeks at Chanak in 1922 was sharply repudiated by the Dominions when they were called upon by the Colonial Secretary, Winston Churchill, for military assistance. Meetings of the Prime Ministers of Britain and the Dominions, first begun in 1902, led not to centralised control, consultation or new institutions for the management of Imperial defence, but to the growing realisation of the independence of each Dominion. The view expressed by the Australian Prime Minister, W. M. Hughes, that wars are hatched by foreign policy, stressed how reluctant the Dominions were to be a party to British foreign policy. The separate Dominions were responsible for the defence of their local area but gave no one overall responsibility for Imperial defence. The Committee of Imperial Defence continued to advise on special areas and problems through sub-committees, but it remained a discussion seminar where no policy decisions were taken. Baldwin's defeat in the 1923 election over tariff reform, Lord Irwin's promise of 'Dominion status' to India in 1929, and the Statute of Westminster of 1931, indicate that the main trend in the period was disengaging Imperial economic, military, and political cooperation.

Similarly, British foreign policy in the inter-war years made efforts to lessen the need for Imperial defence by making agreements to fix and, indirectly, to restrict the ratio of armed forces, especially the navies, of the great powers. The Washington Naval Agreement (1922), the Four Power Treaty (1921), the Nine Power Pact (1922), the London Naval Agreement (1930) and the Anglo-German Naval Agreement (1935) were monuments to this passive defence policy. An elaborate, expensive, Imperial defence policy was proven to be unnecessary during much of the two decades between the wars because the *status quo* was judged to be harmless, or at least irrelevant, since the wishes of other nations could be satisfied by diplomatic concessions.

Such a cursory survey of British foreign and Imperial policy suggests the reasons why Britain preferred a languorous defence policy. It was against the character of the times for government in peacetime to conceive of its role as extensive, interventionist and permanent. Britain did not commit herself to evolving a closely linked defence system which efficiently gathered together the resource of Dominions and dependencies. Nor was there thoughtful preparation of defence needs gleaned from an assessment of the strength of potential opponents. The British Government, sensitive to the country's unprepared and vulnerable position, was tempted into appeasing the dictators in the 1930s in order to retain the advantages of unpreparedness, which were low government expenditure and taxation, a friendly but relatively uncomplicated relationship with the Dominions and dependencies, and a sense of security based on blind faith in the duration of peace. The general lack of purpose in defence proved disastrous in the early years of the Second World War.

The Second World War alone did not destroy the old British Empire, it merely revealed what had been the latent weaknesses of Britain as a world power: to rule was too burdensome, to reform was too expensive, to secure the lasting cooperation of politicians outside Britain to the idea of an Imperial Commonwealth too impractical.

India, literally and figuratively, was the outpost of the Empire, a phrase which correctly suggests its remoteness, inefficiency and material deficiency. In 1922 there were few serviceable machines in the country and personnel were 'rotting through discouragement and lack of practice'.[1] The army was relatively immobile, under-armed, and unfit to take the field against an opponent with up-to-date weapons. India produced no power tools, motorised vehicles, electrical equipment for army supply. Before 1940 there were no transportation services; the railway was overstrained by domestic use, while lines did not exist to defend the Burma frontier. There were only a few inadequate munition factories, no aircraft industry or anti-aircraft defence, no reservoirs of fuel.

The security of the Commonwealth in the Far East was

[1] S. Kirby, *The War Against Japan*, Vol. I, 1957, p. 237.

posited in the great naval base at Singapore. Built hesitatingly during the inter-war period, and still incomplete at the outbreak of war, the base used up most of the energy of service chiefs and politicians. India played no part in the Singapore defences, providing neither supplies, money nor men. India's sizeable army, about 180,000 in 1939, was calculated to guard its own disturbed frontier and buttress the country against internal disorder. The Indian army was known to be incapable of defending India against attack from a great power, though it might restrain the enemy until 'Imperial reinforcements arrived'. Marauding tribes, a vulnerable western frontier, and insurrection marked the extent of India's defence obligations, so much so that when modernisation began in the late 1930s it was still based on the needs of the North-West Frontier. Government committees believed 'the defence of India and the defence of the Empire cannot be dissociated' but observed that there was little practical Imperial strategy for global defence.

Nor did the Indian army prove a training ground for the British army. It was suggested that, after a tour of duty in India, British soldiers had to unlearn inefficient habits.

Already drafts from the British army from the United Kingdom on arrival in India have to be retrained in the use of obsolete weapons and outworn tactical methods, while British units on leaving India have to be taught afresh before they can take their place in British field formations.[1]

When Wavell came to India as Commander-in-Chief in July 1941, he found 'no pagoda tree'. He was appalled at India's lack of equipment; there were no tanks or armoured cars, no aircraft capable of meeting the German or Japanese Air Force in the air. His greatest difficulties were the confusion and division of the eastern command. Strategic decisions were taken by the War Cabinet and the chiefs of staffs, though tactical authority was given to the Commander-in-Chief, China, Vice-Admiral Sir Geoffrey Layton, and to the Commander-in-Chief, Far East, Air Chief Marshal Robert Brooke-Popham. The Air Chief Marshal's command spread from Burma to Singapore. This left the Indian commander with administrative duties but

---

[1] C. Mackenzie, *Eastern Epic*, 1951, p. 3.

no direct involvement with the defense arrangements in the Far East. Indeed, at no time in the middle months of 1941 was he consulted about broad military decisions.

Assigning an Imperial function to India proved as difficult for British politicians as winning the lasting cooperation of Indian national leaders for new constitutions. Defence, like constitutional reform, had short-range perspectives because anything but cautious policies might make governing even more difficult than it was already. The internal instability and racial and religious differences of the country were used to justify the large defence budgets, but no doubt the vague fear of impending chaos and disorder among even the highest officers in the Indian Government led India to be regarded as a special and isolated defence problem. The Congress programme was committed to non-violence and the Party resented the size of the defence bill, for India bore the highest proportion of defence expenditure to total public revenue of any other country in the Empire. Statesmen with knowledge of the havoc the civil disobedience campaign had caused over two decades could reasonably doubt how much of an asset India would be when called upon to support Britain as she had in the First World War. Lord Willingdon very well expressed how feeble was his own and British confidence to weather many more crises. 'If we get into the soup, I shall feel like you [H. Butler] a determination that I shall disappear from the unequal contest and be very glad I am out of it all.'[1]

The war threatened to provoke civil disorder of the kind which had for a long time been a worry for British officials. It ended the precarious constitutional balance which the 1935 Act created and forced the Government of India to rely on its own powers of authority to keep India an ally.

Japanese conquests in China, the attacks on Hawaii, Malaya, and the Philippines by the end of 1941, brought an invading army to the borders of India. The fall of the bastions of defence in the Pacific—Singapore and Hong Kong—coincided with the Japanese invasion of Burma where a small Japanese force over-ran the British army. Japanese carriers and battleships raided

[1] Lord Willingdon to Harcourt Butler, 11 February 1934. Harcourt Butler Papers, IOL.

Ceylon, and threatened to cut off the allied shipping routes of supply from Australia, South Africa and the Middle East.

The World War, while changing the context in which Britain demanded obedience from Indians—for now Indians were asked to identify themselves with the Allied effort against totalitarianism—required of them a slavish submission to British authority which they resented. To placate Indian hostility concessions were offered. In 1940 the Viceroy pledged full Dominion status, self-government, and the right of free India to secede from the Commonwealth. The Viceroy's Council was expanded to include more friendly Indians. There were Indians on the Pacific War Council and Indian special advisers to the War Cabinet.

Though the dangers to India were substantial, they barely affected major political issues. The virtual suspension of the new constitution also marked the suspension of regular political intercourse, and with it the possibility of a mutually acceptable political solution. The war conveniently, from the British point of view, placed thorny constitutional problems as well as the matter of the duration of British rule beyond the scheduled future. 'After the war' became a refrain to every dispute. The British Government argued that no happy outcome could come from political bargaining during the war when there could be no opportunity to implement agreements. Discussions were superfluous. 'There is not going to be any kind of surrender or negotiations.'[1] The very dangers of war were taken as proof of the urgency to concentrate on the war effort. India's future, like her freedom, depended on the success of the Allies and therefore the country was expected to work towards victory not independence. Inevitably the letters between the Secretary of State, L. S. Amery, and Lord Linlithgow were filled with musing about the future, but even they realised there was something empty about such speculations.

> It is really rather absurd speculating about the constitutional future when there are so much more pressing immediate military problems before us.

From 1939 to 1945 a general state of confusion permeated

---

[1] *The Transfer of Power*. Vol. II, p. 391.

Indian political life. Amery gave some explanation of why
Cabinet meetings floundered. 'The Gandhi discussions were, as
most Indian discussions are, hopelessly confused, because
Winston, without giving one time ever to explain the situation,
or ever really reading the papers himself, sails in with a
monologue, and nobody else gets a chance of really setting out
their point of view.'[1] The War Coalition, with members of the
Labour Party wanting some new initiative in India, could not
undo the effects of bad relations between British and Indian
leaders. Mutual distrust had become too engrained. Since
Britain offered *eventual* self-government to India, the integrity
of promises given in the present for a later date was a potent
factor in all discussions. But leaders of the Congress questioned
British sincerity. Gandhi wrote in 1942 whether after the war
would be any different from the present. 'Has this offer any
reality about it?'[2] His doubts were not unjustified. The men
most concerned with India, the Prime Minister, the Secretary
of State, and the Viceroy were averse to plan far into the future
and could see no way out of the welter of difficulties. Major
changes would only create more problems. What also complicated matters was the lack of plenipotentiaries. The War
Cabinet, the Prime Minister, the Secretary of State and the
Viceroy acted with varying degrees of authority, so that often
in the middle of negotiations one would intervene over the heads
of the others. Nor was it clear who was the authoritative
Indian voice. The Congress high command included a number
of different points of view; indeed they referred to themselves as
the Congress Committee, but Gandhi exercised exceptional
influence though he was not even a member of the Congress
Party. However, the British Government did not recognise the
Congress as the party or group which spoke for all of India.
When Stafford Cripps came to India with a new offer from the
Cabinet he interviewed some thirty odd Indian leaders whose
views had to be considered. The number of would-be negotiators
and interested parties, as well as the many-faceted aspects of
every issue, made it impossible for conclusions to be arrived at
in a single series of negotiations. Discussions were protracted
because so many parties had to be consulted. Though there were

[1] *Ibid.*, Vol. II, p. 489.   [2] *Ibid.*, Vol. II, p. 704.

many dramatic events in India during the war, and feelings ran high, it is only a slight exaggeration to suggest that nothing happened in British India, or that nothing happened that had not already happened.

The dislocation caused by the war added extra tension to the already very complicated political situation. For Britain, the war justified her desire not to settle with an implacable opponent and a reason for controlling and suppressing hostile Indian opinion. Press censorship and war propaganda, an accepted right of governments in modern war, gave the Government of India special powers to squash critical public comment. The telegrams headed 'appreciation of the situation' sent by the Viceroy to Washington, Chungking, Kuibyshev and London were important instruments to influence allied opinion. Thus, Britain was able to withdraw into the narrow confines of allied war needs in order to justify the continuation of British rule.

What also became the source of confusion during the war was the degree to which political intercourse was put aside. Since constitutional questions had gathered all the essential disputes between the parties for the past three decades, the end of any need for the British Government to justify itself to Indian political leaders, wrecked what political institutions there were and threw the country into turmoil. As Churchill explained to Attlee in a 'hush-most secret' letter written in January 1942, there was no reason to trust Congress politicians or believe the war effort would gain as a result of reforms aimed at winning their cooperation.

> I hope my colleagues will realize the danger of raising constitutional issues, still more of making constitutional changes, in India at a moment when enemy is upon the frontier. The idea that we could 'get more out of India' by putting the Congress in charge at this juncture seems ill-founded. Yet that is what it would come to if any electoral or parliamentary foundation is chosen. Bringing hostile political element into the defence machine will paralyse action. . . . The Indian troops are fighting splendidly, but it must be remembered that their allegiance is to the King Emperor, and that the rule of the Congress and Hindu Priesthood machine would never be tolerated by a fighting race.[1]

[1] *Ibid.*, Vol. I, p 14.

Political stalemate, deadlock and impasse were the logical effects of this attitude which emphasised that fighting soldiers were more necessary in a war than quarrelsome politicians.

From 1942 to 1945 British policy towards India preferred to sustain the confused and unsettled situation. This was done by placing requirements that Indians had to meet before any devolution of British authority. Rather than make things simpler, the requirements touched India's pandora's box, the long-standing and unresolved problems of three decades, matters on which no one agreed. India easily gave the impression that it was a place where no one agreed on anything. While the British Government abdicated direct responsibility for providing solutions to India's many problems, it did not relinquish its right to set requirements for a just settlement.

> The fact is that there are here in this situation none of the materials for agreement or settlement. We may find ourselves forced to recognise that publicly a little later on but at the moment our policy must continue to be to refuse to accept the responsibility for a state of affairs that is none of our making and that it is wholly contrary to our expressed and specific policy.[1]

Gandhi, contemplating these layers of difficulties, saw them as a concomitant of British rule which he called 'orderly disciplined anarchy'.[2] British 'requirements' only disguised the disorder and confusion which British rule created. Asserting the ultimate nationalist aspiration, Gandhi conceived of chaos as freedom if it was of his own country's making. 'I tell the British, give us chaos. I say in other words, leave India to God.'[3]

What were the specific requirements Britain set India before self-government could be granted? To phrase this question so boldly is in many ways to digress from the main concerns of officials. To be sure the requirements were real, they were discussed in official letters, and the subject of special Cabinet missions. But the war, and the foreknowledge that the Congress absolutely opposed the principle that Indians needed to satisfy British demands before a grant of independence could be made, pushed the requirements into the background, rather to be

---

[1] *Ibid.*, Vol. III, pp. 262–3. [2] *Ibid.*, Vol. II, p. 96.
[3] *Ibid.*, Vol. II, p. 130.

stored than used in discussions with Indian political leaders. At the same time British leaders—Churchill, Amery and Linlithgow, and later Wavell—had little fondness for the Congress Party, its principles or leaders. Linlithgow called the Congress leadership a 'collection of declining valetudinarians,'[1] while the Secretary of State agreed, 'one will have to plough through the old gang down to better and younger stuff.'[2] In these circumstances it should be appreciated that the British Government and the Government of India were not eager to discuss, negotiate or settle the Indian problem. British policy, Lord Linlithgow aptly explained, was 'sympathetic but yielding nothing.'[3]

There were five conditions Indians had to satisfy before Britain could feel it could quit the country with justice and honour: (1) Indianisation of the civil service should occur to such a degree that the function of government could be carried on; (2) Agreement between Hindus and Muslims as to the respective powers of the two communities with guarantees to other minorities; (3) Signs that law and order could be maintained; (4) The obligations and treaties the British Government had given to the separate Native States would be respected; (5) India should be kept within the Empire.

Since it was a foregone conclusion that agreement on or realisation of one or all these points was quite impossible, there was a natural inclination among British officials to remain within familiar constitutional and political policies. An extreme form of pragmatism functioned in the years from 1942 to 1945, when in the face of demands in which 'everyone wants someone else to do the work and carry the responsibility',[4] the Secretary of State neutralised pressures from every direction by making the Government think in terms of 'a long period of *status quo*'.[5] During the war, no matter what was said or implied by official government statements, Britain had not yet decided actually to transfer power.

Seen in this context, the Cripps Mission, the most important government initiative during the war, was doomed to fail. The British Government, under pressure from the Allies and

---

[1] *Ibid.*, Vol. I, p. 60.   [2] *Ibid.*, Vol. I, p. 633.
[3] *Ibid.*, Vol. III, p. 178.   [4] *Ibid.*, Vol. III, p. 410.   [5] *Ibid.*

concerned about the threat of a Japanese invasion igniting a
rebellion within India, thought it prudent to make proposals to
unite the country behind British leadership. But the distrust and
hostility the Cabinet had to dispel in India were the very
attitudes which leading ministers had, especially towards the
Congress Party. The draft declaration approved by the War
Cabinet tried to avoid introducing interim changes which might
prejudice the ultimate position. Close ties between India and
Britain were expected after the war.[1] The draft declaration
which Cripps took with him had a familiar dichotomy between
'now and later'. Under the section 'immediately upon the cessation of hostilities', the Government offered the election of a body
to frame a new constitution, the participation of the Indian
States in the constitution-making body, and the right of any
province not to accept the new constitution. But 'during the
critical period which now faces India' the British Government,
accepted full responsibility for defence and the conduct of war,
which meant complete authority. Indian politicians who were
outside the existing Government were invited to participate in the
vital task of winning the war, but they had to be satisfied to
wait for the next constitutional advance. Once again, the
present was ransom for the future.

These proposals offered no profound change in government.
It was another 'sincere offer', made more credulous perhaps
because it was delivered by Stafford Cripps, an old friend of
Nehru and the Congress, and a politician of puritan honesty.
But it was Churchill who guided these moves, as he managed
the war. No matter how much the Prime Minister left details
to others or allowed broad discussions within the Cabinet, he
strongly influenced events. Churchill was not seriously worried
by the Japanese threat to India for the cool season was to end
soon, and the oncoming monsoons would make a large-scale
invasion impossible. He thought little would probably result
from the Cripps Mission, but the attempt was necessary to
show the Allies, and some critics in Britain and India, that the
Indian problem was the making of impractical Indian politicians.

---

[1] The carefully worded preamble referred to the new Indian union as 'associated
with the United Kingdom and the other Dominions by a common allegiance to the
Crown'.

Fully confident of his powers of persuasion, he believed Roosevelt and Chiang-kai-shek could be brought round to his point of view, for ultimately he could (and did) plead that it was improper for the Allies to meddle in Britain's right to govern India. Finally, Churchill was confident that law and order could be maintained because British authority was as capable as in the past of dealing with civil disobedience. Thus, India's participation in the war and continuing support were not dependent on constitutional reform. Of course, it would be convenient to have a united India behind British leadership, but Churchill like many other Conservative politicians had been accustomed to an imperfect state of affairs in India.

Cripps arrived in India on 3 March 1942. He met British officials and a number of Indian political groups. Crucial negotiations took place between him and the Congress Committee headed by Azad and Nehru. Cripps was joined by Colonel Johnson, President Roosevelt's special adviser in India. The Congress leaders wanted immediate concessions in the form of control over defence and the reduction of the powers of the Viceroy, making him similar in authority to the King in Parliament.

These negotiations took place over a week, from 3 April to 10 April. When Cripps requested Cabinet approval for the changes in the original draft, he was sharply warned by Churchill not to exceed the original proposal agreed by the War Cabinet. The Cabinet could not understand what was the new position. Churchill wrote:

> There can be no question of want of confidence and we sympathise with you in your difficulties, but we have our responsibilities as well as you. We feel that in your natural desire to reach a settlement with Congress you may be drawn into positions far different from any the Cabinet and Ministers of Cabinet rank approved before you set forth. . . .

> In your para. 13 you speak of carrying on negotiations. It was certainly agreed between us all that there were not to be negotiations but that you were to try to gain acceptance with possibly minor variations or elaborations of our great offer which has made so powerful an impression here and throughout the United States. As a fair-minded man you will I am sure try to realise how difficult it is

for us to see where our duty lies amid all these novel proposals and in the absence of clear and simple explanations.[1]

Cripps' 'novel proposals' became an embarrassment. Azad wrote to Cripps making further suggestions which Cripps interpreted as a complete rejection of his original offer, which they were not. Without Cabinet approval, there was little he could do. Azad wrote to Cripps on 11 April in some surprise. 'What we were told in our very first talk with you is now denied or explained away.'[2]

Before the Cripps Mission Churchill kept Roosevelt apprised of Indian affairs. The President was diffident in making suggestions: 'For the love of heaven don't bring me into this.' At first he drew a broad historical analogy between the problem of the newly independent thirteen American colonies and their need to create a federation, and the Indian problem. He recommended in a very gentle way a temporary Dominion government representing different Indian groups, similar to the Articles of Confederation. Irritated at the breakdown of talks between Cripps and the Congress, and the possible harm it would cause to the war effort, Roosevelt wrote to Churchill via Harry Hopkins on 12 April 1942: 'It is impossible for American public opinion to understand why, if there is a willingness on the part of the British Government to permit the component parts of India to secede after the war from the British Empire, it is unwilling to permit them to enjoy during the war what is tantamount to self-government.'[3] But Churchill knew how to deflect the President from opinions which might rupture their friendship. 'Anything like a serious difference between you and me would break my heart.'[4] he wrote. He also reasserted arguments which Roosevelt could not easily reply to: (a) Moslem loyalty had to be retained since they made up the core of the Indian army; (b) new reforms might not be to their liking, which could throw the country into chaos on the eve of invasion; (c) the defence of India was the responsibility of the British Government which could not be delegated.

Chiang-kai-shek and his wife visited India in February 1942 to survey the military situation and meet Nehru and Gandhi.

[1] *The Transfer of Power*. Vol. I pp. 721–2.   [2] *Ibid.*, Vol. I, p. 744.
[3] *Ibid.*, Vol. I, p. 759.   [4] *Ibid.*, Vol. I, p. 764.

Churchill at first opposed the meeting lest it spread the 'pan-Asiatic malaise through all the bazaars of India'.[1] Eventually a way was found for Chiang to meet Jinnah and Gandhi and Nehru. Like others before him the Generalissimo 'though anxious to do good he did not know how to achieve it'. He left India fully convinced of his earlier belief that the Congress Party was the effective political voice of the country and that some efforts should be made to win their participation. To this end he wrote to Roosevelt most confidentially via the Chinese Ambassador in Washington in July 1942, suggesting that the United Nations and the United States become guarantors of India's independence. It was an indication of the friendship between Churchill and Roosevelt that this strictly confidential letter was sent on to London. The Prime Minister in reply repeated the arguments which had been effective in the past and advised the President to dissuade Chiang-kai-shek from his completely misinformed activities. There could be no argument with British policy so long as the Government of India could maintain order and secure India's maximum contribution to the war effort.

> The Government of India have no doubt of their ability to maintain order and carry on government with efficiency and secure India's maximum contribution to the war effort whatever Congress may say or even do, provided of course that their authority is not undermined.[2]

The Government's ability to maintain order was soon tested. After the 'abortive' Cripps Mission the Congress Party would accept no compromise. 'The British desire our help only as slaves.' Angered by the affair and emboldened by Britain's recent military defeats, Gandhi and the Congress prepared to start a mass civil disobedience campaign by adopting a resolution which called on Britain 'India's immediate aggressor' to 'Quit India'. The highly efficient government intelligence service was forewarned of Congress's intentions, and Gandhi and the Congress leaders were arrested on the day the resolution was passed, 8 August 1942.

The arrests precipitated widespread disorder and rebellion,

the extent of which worried and surprised the Viceroy. 'I am engaged here in meeting by far the most serious rebellion since that of 1857, the gravity and extent of which we have so far concealed from the world for reasons of military security. Mob violence remains rampant over large tracts of the countryside and I am by no means confident that we may not see in September [1942] a formidable attempt to renew this widespread sabotage of our war effort.'[1] Statements in the House of Commons admitted there were 538 firings by military and regular police, 1,028 killed and 60,229 arrests. Government buildings, post offices, and railway stations were the main objects of attack, and telephone and telegraph communications were cut so that for a time large tracts of India were isolated from one another.

The seriousness of the rebellion and the extreme demands of war led the Government of India to adopt some of the methods of the tyrant. There was heavy censorship on the extent of the violence. The B.B.C. and press releases were used to create the impression that the country was more calm than it was. For example, when Arthur Moore, editor of the Indian *Statesmen* since 1933, refused to print government propaganda and criticised government policy, the Viceroy put pressure on Lord Catto, owner of the paper. Moore was dismissed. There was machine-gunning from the air of 'saboteurs', and the punishment of whipping was applied to rioters, arsonists and saboteurs generally. The Governor of Bombay, Sir R. Lumley, wrote to the Viceroy to explain the situation under which whipping was allowed, as the Government was being criticised in Britain and the United States for its use. Officials did not feel the need to exercise normal peace-time restraints. 'Some thirty-three persons have been killed and several hundred including many policemen, injured in four days in Bombay alone. Introduction of whipping, which might be better termed corporal punishment, is a minor detail in a serious situation. It is the only enhancement of penalty so far introduced in this Province. At least three others have put into operation the enhancement of penalties ordinance [of 1942] which validates death for an even wider range of penalties (offence?).'[2]

[1] *Ibid.*, Vol. II, p. 853.   [2] *Ibid.*, Vol. II, p. 700.

The combination of repression, tight control over news, and the flagging energy of the protestors dissolved the would-be rebellion. Gandhi, imprisoned in the Aga Khan's palace at Poona, wrote to the Viceroy on New Year's Eve, 1942, from 'detention camp', to announce a fast for three weeks or 'to capacity' in protest against the measures of repression adopted by the Government of India during the rebellion. Believing that the 'law of *satyagraha* knows no defeat', he used the fast once again to gather world attention to India's struggle for freedom. He placed the British and Indian Governments in a difficult position, for they could neither give in to the threat of the fast by releasing Gandhi nor concede any of his arguments without loss of face in the eyes of the world. That such a loss of face was uppermost in everyone's mind, more important than whether Gandhi lived or not, is evident from the negotiations in the early months of 1943. Lord Linlithgow, following the suggestions of the majority of provincial governors and the unanimous opinion of his own executive council, suggested that Gandhi be released before the fast began, to be re-arrested when the fast ended. His aim was to absolve the Government of India from any responsibility for Gandhi's death. A fast in prison was a greater embarrassment than a private one. The Viceroy preferred to let Gandhi starve to death in principle, so long as no ignominy fell on his Government. On the eve of the fast the Cabinet rejected the essentially 'cat and mouse' method of the Viceroy's and wanted Gandhi to be released only when his life was in danger. Churchill wrote to harden the Viceroy's resolution in no uncertain terms. 'I earnestly hope you will weigh very carefully the overwhelming opinion of the War Cabinet and other ministers concerned before consenting to a step which is contrary to your own better judgement and that of the Commander-in Chief on the merits and which I fear would bring our whole Government both in India and here at home into ridicule and thus cloud the magnificent work which you have done in these seven anxious years.'[1] In the Cabinet meeting which decided to keep Gandhi in prison during his fast, Churchill was more passionate. It did not matter to him if all

---

[1] *Ibid.*, Vol. III, p. 619.

the Viceroy's council resigned. 'We could carry on just as well without them and this hour of triumph everywhere in the world was not the time to crawl before a miserable old man who had always been our enemy.'[1] Three members of the Council, Mody, Aney and Sarker, did resign even though Lord Linlithgow in defiance of Cabinet letters ('putting the telescope to his blind eye'), still offered Gandhi immediate release which the latter refused. Gandhi's fast from 10 February until 3 March agitated the minds of the British Government more than it caused agitation in India. The Government felt a glow of satisfaction that matters had turned out so well for it. Gandhi had not inspired another mass disobedience movement, American opinion was not unfavourable to the current tone of British policy and Congress and the Muslim League were no closer to an alliance than before.

From this position of strength, Churchill chose Sir Archibald Wavell, the Commander-in-Chief since 1941, as Lord Linlithgow's successor as Viceroy. Churchill thought Wavell 'tired and lacking in drive'[2] and certainly unsuited for military command. Churchill sometimes unfairly taunted Wavell and was highly critical of him, a fact of which Wavell was well aware. Nevertheless, Wavell combined high military prestige, a broad cultural outlook, and little political experience. He would be less likely to play the big man against the Cabinet. He was known to oppose constitutional advance during the war. This suited Churchill, for he told Wavell that he would expect him to take over as Viceroy for the war only, 'for say three years'.[3]

Wavell was unprepared for his new political responsibilities. Even he was surprised to learn at first hand the view of the Cabinet about India's political development. 'I do not believe these men face their fences honestly, they profess anxiety to give India self-government but will take no risk to make it possible.'[4] The more he saw of the politicians the less he respected them; they seemed to exist as a body to block any political progress. 'I have discovered that the Cabinet is not honest in its expressed desire to make progress in India; and

[1] *Ibid.*, Vol. III, p. 632.   [2] *Ibid.*, Vol. III, p. 1048.
[3] *Ibid.*, Vol. IV, p. 2.   [4] Wavell, *The Viceroy's Journal* 1973, p. 20.

that very few of them have any foresight or political courage.'[1] When Wavell had a long chat until 1 a.m. with the retiring Viceroy he had his impression confirmed. Lord Linlithgow after seven years' hard labour with the Indian problem succinctly put the reasons for the lack of real political progress: 'stupidity of the Indians and the dishonesty of the British.'[2]

However, Wavell had a commander's penchant for regarding his authority as unchallengeable, and for wanting to know 'quite definitely where he intends to lead' and 'what he means to accomplish'.[3] His past experience and training made him impatient of political meandering in Whitehall and desirous to clarify the political scene in India. With his military career over and with no political attachments, he was psychologically independent. The great weakness of Wavell's position was that neither the Cabinet nor Indian politicians had much reason to accept his opinions and take his advice. Wavell seemed to be aware of his expendability, but oddly this did not make him timid about expressing his views. As Viceroy-designate, he wrote a memorandum for the Cabinet on how to settle all India's disputes by calling ten leading Indians together, including Gandhi, Jinnah and Nehru. Like a jury the Indians were to cut themselves off from outside opinion, use the offices of the Viceroy as a depot of information and sit in conclave until a solution was reached which prepared India for self-government after the war. During the Bengal famine, Wavell pressed the British Government to send foodstuffs, and convinced the Governor of Bengal to introduce price-fixing and rationing.

In October 1944 he wrote to the Prime Minister with a plan for a new political move. He told the Indian Committee of the Cabinet in May 1945: 'At present we were professing a policy of freedom for India and in practice opposing every suggestion for a step forward.'[4]

These were the actions of a man who took on politics as he did a campaign: courage, the unorthodox approach and pushing forward were his means. In March 1945 he returned to London

[1] *Ibid.*, p. 23.   [2] *Ibid.*, p. 33.
[3] Earl Wavell, 'The Triangle of Forces in Civil Leadership', 1948, Walker Trust Lecture, *Lectures on Leadership*, 1950, p. 5.
[4] Wavell, *Viceroy's Journal*, p. 130.

to discuss with the Cabinet a way to end the political deadlock, which like the other deadlocks called for a practical initiative from the British Government. The time was particularly favourable. Two months earlier, in January 1945, Bhuabhai Desai, leader of the co-operating Congress party in the Central Legislative Assembly and Nawabzada Liaquat Ali Khan, deputy leader of the Muslim League Party, agreed in writing to a formula whereby the Congress and League would share equally a number of places on the Viceroy's Council, leaving a few others for minorities. The Viceroy, the Commander-in-Chief and the present constitution would remain as they were. The continuance of the war with Japan would also justify overall British control for the first few months of any new arrangement.

In June 1945, after the end of the war in Europe and the fall of the Coalition War Government and after the Caretaker Government had been installed, Wavell set out his proposals, agreed to by the Cabinet, in a radio broadcast. The new council was exactly as the Desai-Liaquat Ali Khan agreement had envisaged, with the finance and home ministries given to Indians. Members of the council were to be selected by the Governor-General after consultation with Indian political leaders. A permanent constitutional settlement would be made when members of the Government discovered 'the means by which such agreements can be achieved'. Interned members of the Congress working committee were released.

To implement the plan, Wavell called a conference of leading Indian politicians to Simla on 25 June 1945, a conference not very unlike his first suggestions as Viceroy-designate in 1943. Like his predecessors Wavell met individually Gandhi, Jinnah, Nehru, Azad and other politicians before the conference, but after setting out the two main tasks before them (agreeing on the composition and names of the council and the principles under which it would work), he left them to meet privately to see if they could come to an agreement. Here was the unique achievement of the Simla Conference. British requirement and the British interest were in practice suppressed (partly because Wavell was himself uncertain of what the British interest in India was), before the acknowledged larger issue of agreement between the Congress and the League. The conference lasted for nearly three weeks but the Muslim League refused to join the new council. Jinnah's position was indeed difficult. He claimed the right to select exclusively the five Muslims to sit on the council, but in a council of fourteen he could not be sure that the Muslim community would not be out-voted. If the Muslim Unionist Party of the Punjab (who opposed the Muslim League), headed by the Premier Malik Khizar Hyat Khan Tiwana, were given one of the Muslim places this would question the authority of Jinnah and the League to speak for the whole Muslim community, besides weakening their voting strength. Since the Wavell plan did not guarantee self-government for Muslims, in fact said nothing about this, Jinnah could see no reason to approve of changes that did not strengthen his position. Jinnah was dogged, legalistic and fastidious over details in all negotiations. It would have been rash for him to throw away for very little reward the position he had won for Muslims over the years. During the Gandhi-Jinnah talks and correspondence of September 1944, Gandhi complained that they never seemed to touch one another, that the talks ran along parallel lines, Gandhi at one point grumbling that Jinnah was too technical. But this rigid style of negotiating, always asking for more and more clarification and explanation of detail, was how Jinnah retained the integrity of the idea of Pakistan against compromise. Jinnah simply refused to give Wavell a list of names. The Simla Conference ended with Wavell somewhat unnecessarily accepting the blame for its failure. In fact he succeeded in impressing upon Indians the imminence of the transfer of power by trying to remove the Viceroy as an institution from the centre of political controversy.

SEVEN

DUSK

THE LABOUR MOVEMENT, like the rank and file of the other political parties, had a limited interest in India's constitutional problems. The Trades Union Congress, the Parliamentary Labour Party, and the Labour Party had few and informal contacts with Indian politicians, particularly when, during the war, Congress leaders were imprisoned as wreckers of the war effort. The prominent association of Attlee and Cripps in the War Cabinet Committee on India prevented unrestrained criticism, for by that association government policy was the same as that of the Party's leaders. Understandably, Labour like most people in the country accepted that Britain's Indian policy was necessarily shrouded in secrecy and best left to Indian experts.

The annual conferences of the Labour Party debated Britain's Indian policy in broadly patriotic and ideological terms: India was the victim of vicious exploitation, a discredit to the national honour. C. W. Bridges of the National Union of Railwaymen told the 1944 conference, 'We can be a great nation; our battleships can go from sea to sea; but as long as there is poverty, destitution, and this terrible situation remains in India, it is a blot on the whole community and on the whole Labour movement.'[1]

As the war came to an end and a general election drew near, it was natural for the Party to interpret discontent in India as a further, if exotic, indictment of Conservatism and Capitalism. By 1945 Britain's immediate domestic needs—housing, rationing, social services, industrial reconstruction, health insurance, pensions, employment—and the prospect of forming a government to introduce a broad programme of reform, absorbed the

---

[1] *Labour Party Annual Conference Report*, 1945, p. 185.

Party's energies. Aware of its inability to comment effectively
on the next stage of Britain's relationship with India, the 1945
conference merely reaffirmed its recommendation of the
previous year, and called for 'a generous policy'.

Like his party, Ernest Bevin paid scant attention to India's
frequent political crises. Before becoming Minister of Labour in
1940 he wrote and spoke about the bigger issue: the need to
transform the Empire into a collective partnership. 'Empires, as
we have known them, must become a thing of the past.'[1] The
Empire of racial arrogance and domination, which developed
an economic system to provide a kind of tribute to the mother
country, had to be replaced by a co-operative Commonwealth.
The self-governing countries in the Commonwealth would
come together as equal members in an association committed
to construct what Bevin called a 'balanced economy' by which
he meant an economic system which co-ordinated the skills and
resources of the commonwealth to raise the standard of living
universally. As Minister of Labour in the War Cabinet he
prevailed on the Viceroy and Secretary of State to approve a
scheme for the industrial training of Indians. Indian workers
were brought to England to work in a factory for six months
and live with English working-class families. They returned
to India with greater knowledge not only of their jobs but also
of English life and trade union methods.

Bevin and Cripps crystallised the idea of the progressive
commonwealth in a memorandum, 'A Social and Economic
Policy for India', written for the War Cabinet in December
1942. They assumed that India's foreign debt and interest
were being rapidly repaid by the accumulation of sterling re-
serves and that greater direct taxation on wealth would be possible on India's considerable war profits. This left funds available for a far-reaching policy of social reform and development,
capable of transforming an ancient society with a medieval
economy into a country of scientific agriculture. Drawing from
the experiences of Russia, Turkey and the United States' policies
in the Philippines, they proposed a programme estimated by the
Chancellor of the Exchequer, Sir Kingsley Wood, to cost

[1] E. Bevin, *The Job To Be Done*, 1942, p. 157.

between £400,000 and £500,000. The plan provided for more schools, adult education, model villages to show peasants improved farming methods, a road scheme, low rent housing estates, poor relief for the destitute, factory inspection, development of railways and sources of power.

The draft memorandum met with little support from Indian officials, for it was obviously incompatible with the traditions of Indian administration and the present stage of India's constitutional structure. The Viceroy, Lord Linlithgow, by way of a preface to his reply to the memorandum warned that 'schemes must in no way imply that we admit or apologise for any misconduct by us of India's affairs'.[1] He saw quite correctly how such a large-scale policy or social and economic improvement indirectly criticised the long history of British rule when no such proposals were made. Since Indians also complained of the lack of progress among the people during these years, the specific recommendations would give substance to the accusations of politicians and the popular press. The Viceroy saw that any kind of reform could not be divorced from the political and constitutional deadlock which had undermined his term of office and distorted every British intention. 'Though we should remain impatient to achieve quicker results, we cannot sweep aside merely by good intentions the constitutional, political and financial obstacles in our path.'[2]

L. S. Amery, though less critical than the Viceroy, nevertheless, in a long reply, procrastinated. The prestige of Cripps and Bevin in the War Cabinet was such that their ideas had to be thoughtfully considered. But Amery, while complimenting the authors on their efforts and showing some sympathy for their intentions, felt little of their sense of urgency for a country where everything was in a state of flux.

The Minister's memorandum recognises in its first sentence that during the last 40 years great advances have been made in the social and economic life of India, advances summarily described in a note already circulated by me. It is important always to bear this in mind, because the magnitude of what patently remains to be done is apt to obscure the progress which has been and is being achieved, and to

---

[1] *The Transfer of Power*, Vol. IV, p. 246.   [2] *Ibid.*, Vol. IV, p. 253.

imply that the situation presenting itself to us is a static one, which is far from being true.[1]

His alternative to their vast scheme was the creation of an Indian cultural centre in London for the study of oriental art and literature.

When the Labour Government was formed in June 1945 the Party's ideas about Indian reconstruction were useless. Britain could not afford any contribution to Indian social and economic reform when it needed all the country's resources and credit to finance its own post-war programme. Indians were still suspicious of British motives; even a welfare policy would be interpreted as a planned distraction from independence. In fact, any vigorous policy which the British Government endorsed, except self-government would simply be taken as an indication of Britain's unrelenting desire to hold on to India.

The Government's Indian policy, while not advancing any of the projects in the Cripps-Bevin memoranda, was indirectly influenced by them. Because the party had concentrated on planning, welfare and economic reorganisation during the years of intense political discussion about India since 1931, Labour leaders retained a doctrinaire attitude towards constitutional and political problems. The Party had no reason to admire the traditions of Indian administration and the political turmoil they created, since it contributed little to the history of British India. The socialist point of view, 'equality of status, equality of wealth',[2] led the Labour Government to find a policy not designed to solve India's communal or constitutional problems, for these had nothing to do with socialism, but one which would vindicate the efficacy, sincerity, and consistency of their ideology.[3]

[1] *Ibid.*, Vol. III, 530.

[2] C. R. Attlee, 'The Indian Report: The Labour Minority View', *New Statesmen, and Nation,* 24 November 1934.

[3] It is easy now to underestimate the importance of socialist ideology for the Labour Party immediately after the war. Yet, ideas about democracy, equality, cooperation pervaded the speeches of Labour leaders. Socialism was a government plan to humanise society; to find the most practical scheme was the Government's difficulty, its broad intentions were simple. No doubt the defeat of the Axis powers and their totalitarian creed made democracy seem a victorious principle, while the Labour Party's landslide victory in 1945 was domestic proof of the same concept.

Socialism led the Labour Government to refuse to coerce India, particularly when this country had no constitutionally acceptable mandate to do so. For the Labour Government, with its socialist principles, the fact that the British Government could not materially assist the advancement of the masses meant that it lost its right to govern. India had its own political parties, supported by large sections of the population. The British Government had no such support.

As a result the Government's Indian policy was transparent. (1) Britain would leave India. (2) Britain could make no requirements for Indians to fulfil, except, it was hoped that the final arrangements would make it possible for Britain to depart with honour and dignity. The Labour Government, like any government, had to show the country and the world it was discharging its affairs with propriety. (3) Negotiations up to and including the final withdrawal should not turn Indian leaders against Britain so that India might remain in the Commonwealth.

These relatively moderate purposes had significant implications for the last period of intense negotiations from 1945 to 1947. The Government was impatient to rid itself of political responsibility in India. The speedy termination of British rule filled official statements. Phrases like 'at the earliest possible date', and 'as rapidly as the complexities of the task permit', 'trying to make Indians feel their responsibility by announcing we were clearing out, within a definite period', indicate the determination of the Government to quit India.

Given the limited goals of the Labour Government's policy, partition had an inner logic. Just as the communal problem pre-dated British rule, so partition freed Britain from any blame for the repercussions of the policy. By giving Indian leaders the opportunity to decide for one country or two, the Government asserted on the prime issue of all discussions its abdication of authority. As in Ireland, Cyprus, and Palestine, the policy of partition was a compromise between rival communities which asserted Britain's unwillingness to decide for others. Independence or partition were less the policy of the British Government than the first decision of a free India.

Was this a policy of surrender, an immoral abandonment,

considering the heavy toll of human life this policy took from
1946 to 1948? In this vein Lord Salisbury wrote to the Prime
Minister on 18 December, 1946. 'Is this country to go down in
history with the badge upon her of betrayal? . . . And nothing
would excuse surrender, and what will appear betrayal, except
such weakness as leaves us no choice.'[1] Attlee courteously
replied,

> I agree with you that the position in India is grave. It has been so for
> a long time. The situation when the government took office was so
> serious that, but for the sending of the Government Mission we
> should in the opinion of those best qualified to advise us, have been
> involved in a major crisis. As I am assured on all hands, there is now
> general recognition in India and in the world that the difficulties in
> India are not due to any fault of this country, but to the failure of
> Indians to agree among themselves. The present position is the
> result of policies pursued by successive Governments over a long
> period of years, and of the impact of world events on the Indian
> situation. The declared aim of all parties in this country has been the
> progressive attainment of full self-government by the peoples of
> India. We have done, and are doing our utmost to ensure that the
> transference of power is made with the least possible friction, and
> with the greatest possible consideration for the rights of minorities.
> There has been no weakness and no betrayal, nor will there be, but
> there are limitations to our powers.[2]

Thus with remarkable simplicity Attlee was able to show the
contours of government policy. This very simplicity was
essential if the Government remained determined to transfer
power. The phrase 'but there are limitations to our powers'
indicates that the Government was aware how impossible it was
for them to act other than they did and still hope to achieve
their limited goals. Britain was no longer an imperial power. It
could not impose its ideas on India; to make the transfer of
power dependent on the Indian acceptance of British views
about the constitution, community relations, and India or
Pakistan would have involved the British Government in Indian

[1] Lord Salisbury to C. R. Attlee, 18 December 1946. Attlee Papers, University
College, Oxford.
[2] C. R. Attlee to Lord Salisbury, 21 December 1946. Attlee Papers, University
College, Oxford.

negotiations to a degree which it had firmly decided not to be involved. Of course the smoother the transfer of power the more satisfactory it would be to the British Government. But in the negotiations, the British Government could not hope to influence the Congress and the Muslim League by making demands, particularly when their demands over the main issues would have further delayed Indian self-government.

A host of other factors by 1945 contributed to the Government's decision to leave India. The war-time policy of 'wait until the end of the war' meant that when the war ended the British Government was expected to initiate some new constitutional policy which would lead to self-government. The climate of world opinion and the chaotic state of affairs in India in 1945 made it impossible for the British Government to conceive of trying to write another constitution for India. With many Indian leaders stilll in prison, there was little practical reason to believe that some new initiative would make any improvement on former initiatives. The Cripps offer of 1942 stood as a basis for discussion between the British Government and Indian leaders making superfluous the thought of devising new proposals.

Britain could not impose its will on India after the war because the Indian structure of administration was disintegrating. The extent to which British rule in India simply collapsed after 1945 is a subject still to be exposed by historians. Even during the war it proved difficult to fill administrative posts with Europeans. 'I doubt if you can have any idea of the poverty and paucity of material for running institutions or arrangements in this country.'[1] Military officers were employed to assist because of the shortage of qualified civilians. It was even difficult to find men of the first rank to accept the highest offices in India. The appointment of Sir William Spens as Chief Justice of India in June 1943 dismayed the outgoing Chief Justice.[2] The last two Viceroys, Wavell and Mountbatten,

---

[1] *The Transfer of Power*, Vol. IV, p. 65.

[2] Sir M. Gwyn wrote to the Viceroy: 'I dare say that the person appointed is as competent as the average King's Counsel may be expected to be; though with reference to the Lord Chancellor's opinion that he is of the quality to be a High Court Judge in England, I cannot refrain from observing that no Lord Chancellor

were appointments of non-political men partly because leading politicians refused the office.

However definite the Government was on India's future in the long term, the problems they had to face were immediate. Their difficulty was to find a means in the present to achieve their intentions for the future. This proved troublesome because there was no regular method within the machinery of the government of India to settle differences of opinion among Indian political leaders. Yet without some agreement among Indians themselves, if only about the actual taking-over of power, Britain could not leave India. Since for a long time it just seemed possible that such an agreement between Jinnah and Nehru could be made, the Labour Government was drawn into protracted attempts to get Indians to accept the reigns of power in a co-operative spirit.

The failure of the Simla Conference, the election to office in June 1945 of the Labour Government, and the end of the war with Japan, began the last phase of British rule. Wavell returned from London and in September announced new elections on the existing franchise. The Labour Government declared its intention to make India self-governing; the problem was to find a process to create a constitution-making body to satisfy the major Indian parties. The British Government hoped the new elections would lead to talks between the representatives, including those from the Indian States, and the formation of a political executive council, an executive council made up of the leaders of the major parties. The elections showed the major divisions of the parties and the overall superiority of the Congress. In the central legislature it won 57 of the 102 seats while the Muslim League won 30. In the provincial legislature, Congress had a majority in eight provinces, including two provinces designated by the League for Pakistan. The Akalis, the party of the Sikh community, won two seats in the Punjab. As Jinnah realised, the superiority of the Congress was in a united India; the Sind, Bengal and Punjab were Muslim-majority provinces and elected the League to office. Control over these provinces and opposition to a united India became

has, up to the moment, thought of appointing him.' *The Transfer of Power*, Vol. III, p. 276.

the foundations of the Muslim League as a political party. They could not be compromised away without erasing the political influence of the Party.

While the elections were taking place, the Secretary of State, Lord Pethick-Lawrence, arranged to send to India a parliamentary delegation, composed of ten M.P.s from the three main political parties. This was the first of the three emissaries of the British Government who progressively achieved self-government for India. It took nearly a year of constant discussion and negotiations before the veracity of the Labour Government's statements was accepted in India, such was the general state of confusion. Indeed there had been so many statements of intent by British Governments in the past that words had nearly lost their power to convince. The delegation created a certain amount of good feeling by their general enthusiasm to learn, but they frankly acknowledged to the Viceroy how difficult it was to come to a swift conclusion over the Indian problem, given the intransigence of Jinnah and Nehru. It did not make a formal inquiry or write a report with recommendations.

The second emissary of the British Government was the more authoritative Cabinet Mission of three, Sir Stafford Cripps, Lord Pethick-Lawrence and A. V. Alexander. They arrived in March 1946 to interview the leading representatives of the main political parties. The Mission did not come with specific proposals for these leaders to accept; rather, they were to help in creating a form of government to replace the present regime, by persuading the leaders to agree on the machinery for making a constitution. On the whole the British Government favoured a united India, though Wavell and Alexander came to support the Muslims and their right to remain free of Congress dominance. Congress wanted a declaration from the British Government granting independence and the withdrawal of armed forces, leaving India then to settle its own affairs. The League opposed any formula which did not establish two constitution-making bodies for the peoples of Pakistan and Hindustan. Anything less would, the League warned, 'leave the Muslims no alternative but to resist such imposition by all possible means for their survival and national existence'. A conference was called in

May 1946 between the Mission, the Viceroy and four leaders from the two Parties. The British officials offered their own compromise. This consisted of what came to be named the 'three-tier system'. A central government with a legislature uniting British India and the Indian states would deal with foreign affairs, defence, communications, and basic rights, and have the authority to raise money for these functions; the separate provinces would be responsible for all other subjects; groups of provinces could establish their own executive and legislatures for the purpose of acting in common. An ingenious plan, it proposed a federation, a confederation, and a separatist alliance within both (the last was intended to allow the Muslim majority provinces to come together and manage their own affairs). The details of this formula proved so complicated, however, that they drew the intrepid opponents into discussions about implications. But these discussions fell far short of any fundamental compromise. After a week the conference ended in failure.

Though the two parties did not agree at Simla to accept the proposals, the Cabinet Mission with praiseworthy tenacity issued a statement in June elaborating what they believed to be the possible basis for a compromise. They recommended the three-tier system but added that bills affecting communal subjects debated in the central legislature would need a majority of both communities before they could be passed. Also, any province by a majority of one could call for a review of the terms of the constitution after ten years. The statement then concentrated on the machinery for creating a new constitution, quite a separate issue from the structure of the eventual Government.

The provincial legislature, more or less on the basis of one to one million of population, would send delegates to the Constituent Assembly. The Assembly would then divide into three groups, one for the Congress majority provinces, one for the Muslim majority provinces, and one from the disputed provinces of Bengal and Assam. Each section would draw up a provincial constitution, decide if and how a group constitution should be made, and finally the whole Assembly would meet to write the Union constitution. Specialist committees would aid

the Assembly on matters of citizen's rights, tribal areas and the
integration of the Indian States. An Interim Government to deal
with the food shortage and post-war social and economic
problems was also announced, and the names of fourteen
members were announced to serve on it.

Some hope of acceptance by the two parties existed, though
both made long statements raising objections, asking for points
of clarification, interpreting suggestions in ways to suit themselves, and recapitulating previous arguments. At first the
League accepted, but withdrew subject to Congress acceptance.
The Congress Working Committee met every day from 16 to
25 June. They rejected the June proposal for an Interim Government but accepted the one of May, the three-tier formula and
the Constituent Assembly. Thus, both parties initially agreed
to participate in the elections to the Constituent Assembly and
the freely interpreted long-term proposals for a settlement, but
refused to participate in an interim coalition Government. The
Cabinet Mission left India three days later on 29 June having
failed to settle anything, but having kept open the possibility
of an agreement in the next stage of negotiations. Since, however, an Interim Government was necessary whether or not the
major parties agreed to it, Lord Wavell was left with the
burdensome task of again opening negotiations to form an
Interim Government. In the meantime a caretaker Government
of officials was appointed. This was not Wavell's only burden.
The Congress in accepting the May proposal referred to a
previous resolution which said: 'While adhering to our view,
we accept your proposals and are prepared to work them with
a view to achieve our objective.' Wavell believed the Congress
acceptance was not genuine and the Cabinet Mission should
have had the courage to say so.

Nehru, in the months after the Cabinet Mission left India,
made a number of speeches which antagonised the League and
Muslims, particularly as he rendered his own interpretation to
what Congress's acceptance meant. On 29 July the Council of
the Muslim League rejected the Mission proposals which they
had previously accepted. Jinnah was also irritated at the com-
plicity of the Viceroy, though in truth the Viceroy favoured him
over Congress and Gandhi, in going back on an important

provision in his statement of June. Number eight said: 'In the event of the two major parties or either of them proving unwilling to join in the setting up of a coalition Government on the above line, it is the intention of the Viceroy to proceed with the formation of an Interim Government which will be as representative as possible of those willing to accept the Statement of May 16th.' Jinnah took this to mean that since the Congress had not completely accepted the May statement, he should have been asked to form a Government. By the Cabinet Mission's generous interpretation of the Congress's statement as an acceptance of the May proposals Jinnah felt he was duped by the Cabinet Mission and the Viceroy. Well might he think so since paragraph eight was inserted in order not to put Jinnah at a disadvantage, for at the time of the June announcement the League had accepted the May statement and the Congress had not.

With Jinnah for the time outmanoeuvred, in September Congress formed an Interim Government of seven of their members, one Indian Christian, one Sikh, one Parsee and two non-League Muslims, with Nehru as Prime Minister. It was never Jinnah's tactics to let the field run away from him. He could not allow for very long the Congress to be seen throughout the world as the only cooperating party and the political voice of India. Without agreeing with the Congress, the Viceroy or any principles, five League members joined the Interim Government.[1] The League, however, still refused to join the Constituent Assembly.

It was meaningless to have a Constituent Assembly to frame a constitution in which a large section of the Indian population was not represented. In December 1946, after calling Nehru, Jinnah, Liaquat Ali Khan and Baldev Singh to London for talks, His Majesty's Government said it would not contemplate forcing a constitution upon any unwilling parts of the country. This was taken by the League as a significant indication of the Government's growing acceptance of their point of view, that the majority in India could not cancel the right of the minority to give its acceptance. This statement erased the distinction between majority and minority.

[1] There was little attempt by the Indians to make this Government work; each party looked to consolidate its own position before the run-down to independence.

The Constituent Assembly opened on 9 December without the participation of the Muslim League. The December session was short. India was proclaimed an independent sovereign republic, but this was not voted upon, nor did the Assembly divide into sections as proposed. By the beginning of 1947 the whole political scene was in considerable disarray. There existed an Interim Government with little interest in carrying on the day-to-day government of the country. A Constituent Assembly sat to draw up a constitution, but had not implemented the agreed procedure. The Muslim League, hostile and aloof, could see no way to achieve any of its aims through participating in the existing political machinery, and was irritated by the small rewards it had received through the incessant political talks and correspondence. The British Government, having failed through direct personal contacts, between the Cabinet Mission and the Government and leading Indian politicians, could only make statements of policy, half-knowing that such statements qualified and confused matters. Each new statement was intended to provide another basis for discussions, but more often unfolded something more to disagree or argue about. In a mood of frustration, Attlee announced in February 1947: 'The present state of uncertainty is fraught with danger and cannot be indefinitely prolonged.' He announced the transfer of power 'to responsible Indian hands' by not later than June 1948. If no constitutional agreement had been reached by that time, the British Government left itself free to decide then what was reasonable and in the best interests of the Indian people. It was Attlee's hope that the spectre of freedom would make the discussions between the Indian parties more urgent and conclusive.

Throughout the two-year negotiations between the British Government and Indian politicians the Viceroy was uncomfortable. His journals show a man ill at ease with the responsibilities he had to bear, increasingly downhearted at his inability to be effective in the discussions either with Indian or British politicians, excitable and frustrated. 'I am feeling stale and over-worked; not sleeping very well and waking up depressed and worried. I think the strain of seven years' heavy responsibility without a proper rest is beginning to tell on me. However,

I expect I shall manage to carry on, though without much enthusiasm for the work. Indian politics and Indian politicians are disheartening to deal with; and we British seem to have lost faith in ourselves and the courage to govern at present.'[1] Wavell several times in his journal referred to himself as a military man, by which he meant that the knowledge and principles he had learned in the army he considered enough to deal with every exigency. He thought the transfer of power analogous to a military retreat. 'I admitted that our position was weak and that we were conducting a retreat; that the first military rule in making a withdrawal was to show as much strength as possible, and that the weaker one was, the more important it was to keep up a strong appearance.'[2] Gandhi took the unusual step of writing a critical letter to Wavell which he asked to be sent on to the British Cabinet. He complained that Wavell's plea that he was 'a plain man and a soldier' was no vindication of his behaviour. 'Your language last evening was minatory. As a representative of the King you cannot afford to be a military man only, nor to ignore the law, much less the law of your own making.'[3]

Wavell disagreed with the British Government over important areas of policy. By temperament and training he could not restrain his disapproval and did not conceive of the office of Viceroy as merely an instrument to carry out the decisions of the Cabinet. He had no respect for the ability of Attlee and his Cabinet. Whereas the British Government, with a fair understanding of the Indian problem, would not dictate to India a constitution but rather tried through interminable discussions to assist some accommodation between the Congress and the League, Wavell was for a rigid policy which the British Government enforced without flinching, if necessary by a blockade to cut India off from essential supplies. This he suggested to the Cabinet Mission in the 'Big stick note'. He also favoured a province by province withdrawal which certainly would have appeared as abandonment. Wavell disliked the long discussions with politicians. He was virulently anti-Gandhi, 'the real wrecker', and preferred Jinnah and the League to the Congress. The British Government, as partition was to express,

[1] Wavell, *Viceroy's Journal*, p. 282.   [2] *Ibid.*, p. 240.   [3] *Ibid.*, p. 342.

favoured neither. The Cabinet merely wanted to find a way to quit India honourably on terms which would still make it possible for the new country or countries to remain in the Commonwealth. Partition was the only viable means by which the British Government could both transfer power and, relatively, not impose a political solution on Indians. On 31 January 1947 Attlee wrote to Wavell to dismiss him—'The Indian problem is entering a new phase, which will be very exacting and may be prolonged.'[1] Wavell's dismissal implied that he was not considered suited for this phase. This phase began with the appointment of Lord Mountbatten as Viceroy with the specific task of terminating British rule and handing over power with the least difficulty.

Lord Mountbatten, formerly Chief of Combined Operations and Supreme Allied Commander, South-East Asia, was a great-grandson of Queen Victoria and second cousin to the King. By nature ebullient, friendly, direct in his manner of dealing with people, and free from narrow prejudice, he was a fine choice to dignify the last phase of British rule. What the British Government needed was someone who by his personality and method of negotiating would be able to inspire Indian leaders to remain in the Interim Government and eventually accept the transfer of power. Not only must the ceremony of Britain's withdrawal be dignified, but orderly government should follow.

Eager to return to sea and resume his naval career, Mountbatten approached the Viceroyalty with directness. Before accepting the appointment he entered into full discussions with the British Government, from December 1946 to February 1947. He received assurances from the Prime Minister that Britain sought neither to perpetuate the viceregal system nor impose British arbitration, both of which he knew to be impractical. Keen to succeed, he discussed with the Cabinet the best means to achieve their aims. He persuaded them to fix a definite date to end British rule, June 1948, and to give him full power to negotiate. These decisions by the Government are an indication of the degree to which the Cabinet no longer felt itself directly in charge of events or responsible for their outcome.

[1] *Ibid.*, p. 497.

The major points of policy were communicated by Attlee to the Viceroy-designate in a letter which clarified the Governor-General's Instrument of Instruction. The objectives of the British Government were unitary government for British India and the Indian States, the continuity of the Indian army so that India could fulfil defence requirements, and if possible the integration of the new Indian Government into the Commonwealth. The Cabinet Mission plan was to form the basis of further discussions with Indian leaders, but the Viceroy was not to compel either party to accept it. The text of the letter as summarised by Mountbatten's press secretary, Alan Campbell-Johnson, shows how reluctant the British Government was to assert itself in the final stages of negotiations. Not only was Mountbatten granted full powers to reach an agreement with the Indian leaders, but he was also given the initiative to advise the Government on the next steps to be taken for the hand-over of power. The best indication of the Government's shyness to dominate future events was in the verbs Attlee used to indicate what Mountbatten should do. Thus: 'He was instructed to do his utmost in his powers to persuade all Parties to work together towards this end'; the keynote of his administration 'was to be the closest cooperation with Indians'. Given the barren results over the past years of discussions between British and Indian leaders, these terms of reference were less formidable than innocuous.

Lord and Lady Mountbatten arrived in New Delhi on 22 March 1947. A few hours before their arrival Wavell lunched with Mountbatten's new staff, who struck him as not really knowing 'very much about it or to have any very new or definite policy'.[1] Wavell and Mountbatten talked privately from 4.30 to 7 p.m. but the outgoing Viceroy felt little optimism that Mountbatten could succeed where he had long laboured. On 24 March Mountbatten was sworn in during a short ceremony where, for the first time, a Viceroy spoke, calling on the goodwill of the greatest number of Indians.

Lord Mountbatten wanted from others what he abundantly had. But goodwill is a predisposition and not a guide to specific disputes. As he was to discover in the next few months there

[1] *Ibid.*, p. 432.

were areas of the Indian problem that the most friendly and
rational influence could not affect. No matter how much
authority he had from the British Government, Mountbatten
worked under severe limitations which ultimately dominated
the course of events. Lord Ismay, who accompanied Mountbatten to India, described their situation as 'going out to the
last chukka twelve goals down'.[1]

The Cabinet's unprecedented delegation of authority to the
Viceroy left Mountbatten in the unwieldy position of having
both to create and to execute a policy which could only be
effectively implemented if agreed to by Indian leaders. The
distance from New Delhi to London was in a sense doubled,
for the Viceroy, unlike his predecessors, could not call upon the
Cabinet to support a policy preferred by him but unacceptable to
Indians. The near breakdown of government administration, the
result of the run-down of men and resources, shortened the
duration in which it was possible to convince implacable
opponents. There was no way for the Viceroy alone to counteract this deterioration, except by a massive infusion of British
men, money, and authority, none of which were available.
Nothing in the Instrument of Instruction gave him a way
forcefully to influence communal relations. A political agreement between the League and the Congress over the transfer
of power, be it in the form of a divided or united India, would
only indirectly relate to the warring communities. Not even
Indian leaders were sure they could control their followers.

Mountbatten inherited a fossilised political situation. The
'three-tier' Cabinet Mission Plan remained unacceptable to the
League; the Interim Government had not produced harmony
among the leaders or the communities; communal violence had
become so much a part of the background to discussions that
political decisions reverberated among the masses of people.
The frequent incidence of communal outrage, while creating an
explosive atmosphere, could not help in the final decisions.
Riots were both a justification for a strong, central authority to
combat them *and* an expression of the fundamental incompati-
bility of the communities.

Britain placed its hopes in unity because it was simpler, in

[1] Lord Ismay, *Memoirs*, 1960, p. 410.

other words more likely to lead to a smooth transition in government departments, the police, and the armed forces. The latter
were especially important. Partition of the services was opposed
by the Viceroy and the Commander-in-Chief, Field Marshal
Auchinleck, because it was impractical and potentially dangerous.
In a divided India Muslims would not likely obey Hindu
officers; by ending the present structure of command, service
morale and efficiency would be threatened. Disgruntled service-
men could become a revolutionary force. The practical problems
were also formidable. It was estimated to take at least a year
to divide men and equipment, during which time the military
units would be anything but an effective defence force.

Along with the powers of persuasion and reasonableness, not
necessarily the most compelling weapons in the highly emotional atmosphere of the times, Mountbatten had the choice of
date when Britain would leave. The choice, if not agreed upon
by the Indian leaders however, would become a threat to
force Indians to accept power and responsibility. The choice for
the date of Britain's departure could also be a flag of surrender,
an expression of Britain's incapacity to govern and exasperation
at the failure of Indians to agree.

Against the archaic structure of the Indian problem Mountbatten brought a format, a regular procedure to carry on
efficient negotiations. In the absence of useful institutions and
real power to make demands, these methods, and the fairness
they conveyed, did much to create a favourable reception. The
Viceroy's private staff were men who had experience with
Indian affairs or had worked with him during the war. Sir Eric
Miéville had been Lord Willingdon's private secretary from
1931 to 1936 and Secretary to the Executive Council of the
Governor-General from 1935 to 1936. He was the King's
private secretary from 1937 to 1945. Vernon Erskine Crum,
Ronald Brockman, and Alan Campbell-Johnson had been
Mountbatten's aides in the South-East Asia command. Though
leading Indian politicians could not be on the Viceroy's staff,
he had experienced Indian administrators in Sir C. Trivedi,
Sir B. N. Rau, H. M. Patel, Mohamed Ali Chaudhury and
V. P. Menon. Menon was brought into the daily staff meetings
and did much to write Mountbatten's final draft plan and

an additional plan for the integration of the Indian States. Careful records were made of important political meetings. Mountbatten would delay meeting one leader until he had related to a secretary the substance of the last. Reports of the interviews were circulated to his staff and were used at staff meetings. On some occasions Mountbatten even showed the summary of an interview he had with one leading politician to another, so open were his methods.

The Viceroy had some early successes. He convinced the Finance Minister, Liaquat Khan, to reduce his proposed tax on big businesses from twenty per cent to sixteen-and-a-half per cent. The high tax threatened to break up the Interim Government. Congress members of the government regarded the tax as a direct attack on a section of their support made by the Muslim minister to embarrass them. In an attempt to shore up the confidence of the officers in the Indian Civil Service and the British officers in the Indian army, Mountbatten was able to announce on 1 May that retirement compensation would be generous.[1] Since it was hoped that trained British officers and administrators would stay on after the transfer of power, the generous rates of compensation would be paid by the British Government when a person retired and not on the date when Britain relinquished her rule of India.

Mountbatten met Gandhi on 31 March and 1 April. The first encounter lasted for two hours but they did not talk about the immediate political situation. Instead the two men, joined by Lady Mountbatten for the first hour, reviewed the past, with Gandhi explaining his early life and political activities. The Mahatma left, impressed by the Viceroy's sincerity and nobility of character. On the following day Gandhi brought with him the young girl Manu. Gandhi asked if she might wander in the gardens of the palace while they talked.

[1] The rates of compensation were so high that Nehru was puzzled to know why the British Government accepted the expense. The largest payments were: officers in the Indian Civil Service with sixteen years' experience would receive £8,000; military and police officers in the political department retiring at thirty-nine would also receive £8,000; regular officers including warrant officers and members of the social and economic departments such as education and the veterinary service would receive £6,000 if retiring at thirty-nine.

'Certainly', replied the Viceroy. Then addressing Manu, he added: 'All this is yours; we are only trustees. We have come to make it over to you.'

'You can search her person for hidden arms,' Gandhi put in laughing.

'I am perfectly satisfied there can be no need for that in a disciple of yours,' replied the Viceroy with a smile.[1]

At this second meeting Gandhi put forward his plan. Jinnah should be invited to form a government of his own choosing. Congress would support him as long as the policies advanced were in the interest of India as a whole. The Viceroy, as referee, would decide if a measure was or was not in the interest of India. Gandhi, as in the past, hoped to disarm his opponent by turning over power to him, a power which would cause a sense of guilt-justice-truth and lead to mutual understanding. When Nehru and the Congress made clear they utterly opposed these suggestions, Gandhi put the opposite notion before the Viceroy on 12 April: the Interim Government should continue to function until the end of British rule and then power should be handed over to the Congress majority. While thanking Gandhi for his efforts, the Viceroy fully understood that India's spiritual leader could not rid him of his many practical problems.

For this he turned to the seasoned veterans of the Indian political arena. Mountbatten met Nehru on 24 March and frequently thereafter. The two men, besides sharing a patrician bearing and temperament mellowed by the common touch, saw India's future in similar terms. It was clear that the unity of India, the clear intention of the British Government, could only occur by strengthening the centre of government, giving to it such powers as to prevent both the complete separation of the Muslim provinces and the loss of a sufficiently strong authority, and to insure an impartial administration of law and order. This centre would also form the bridge between British India and the Indian States. The powers accepted at the centre by the diverse sections of Indian opinion could provide a natural means for cooperation for mutual advancement. In defence, communications, external affairs, and perhaps food administration and planning, the common interests of the sub-continent would find

[1] Pyarelal, *Mahatma Gandhi*, Vol. II, Ahmedabad, 1958, p. 78.

an opportunity to function, leaving what was at present the unbridgeable gaps between communities to work themselves out by granting to the individual provinces significant areas of autonomy. This was the intention of the Cabinet Mission Plan and the constitutional *raison d'être* of the Interim Government. As prime minister in that government and spokesman for the majority party in a united India, Nehru offered the most plausible policy for the British Government to realise its wishes. Nehru even accepted that India would join the Commonwealth, going so far as to suggest common citizenship between Britain and India.

It is not surprising, therefore, that Mountbatten found Jinnah cold when he came on 5 April. Just as Jinnah did not belong to the Interim Government, so he opposed all arguments which purported to justify central government. He wanted a 'surgical operation', by which he meant complete partition, including parition of the armed services. He argued that no plan for the centre could work in the hostile atmosphere which existed since the Cabinet Mission plan had been submitted. Nothing had happened over the past year to warrant a compromise by the Muslims. On 7 April Jinnah seems to have made reference to a minimal centre after his demands for Pakistan had been met, but significantly the discussions between Nehru, Jinnah and Mountbatten never really turned to this subject. Instead of debating the nature of the centre on which the unity of India depended, the discussions became primarily directed towards the implications of partition for the provinces. This was the turning point in all the negotiations, and proved to be a crucial factor which led to the partition of India.

The logical methods Mountbatten employed required that he face the proposals of the two major parties realistically. By so doing he hoped to show Jinnah the impracticability of his position: 'he has not thought out one single piece of the mechanics of his own scheme.'[1] For the same reason Mountbatten agreed in April to the formation of a defence committee to consider the reorganisation of the armed forces on the basis of partition. He thought that if the details of Jinnah's Pakistan were made plain, the problems would invalidate the extreme

---

[1] Hodson, *The Great Divide*, p. 228.

proposition of a totally independent Pakistan which Jinnah maintained. There were so many unnatural aspects to Pakistan that once they were specified Jinnah would logically accept some compromise.

The Viceroy's logic proved to be Jinnah's gain. The concern for the practical details of partition in the provinces pushed from the centre of discussion plans for unification. Since the existing provinces were the only basis of support for Pakistan, it was to Jinnah's advantage to keep the arguments directed towards arrangements in the provinces. By obdurately opposing the constituent assembly, and the Interim Government, Jinnah gained the tactical advantage of keeping the negotiations on terrain which best fortified his claims.

The Viceroy had to concentrate on the provinces not only because of the attitude of Jinnah, but also because it was in the provinces that the greatest tension existed. The intensity of communal rioting, the migration of populations, the incapacity of the police to maintain law and order, the fearful representations by the provincial governors to the Viceroy at the Governors' Conference of the danger to Europeans, all threatened to tarnish any political solution, particularly if that solution was long delayed.

The Congress leaders made counter-proposals for the provinces perhaps in an attempt to so diminish the size of Pakistan that the principle would seem insubstantial. They argued that if Muslims were given a separate state solely on the basis of religion and community, then logically areas with a Hindu majority, though claimed by Jinnah for Pakistan, should have the right to choose for India or Pakistan. This would mean the partition of not just India but also the partition of Bengal and Punjab. Jinnah obviously opposed this 'moth-eaten Pakistan' but was prepared to discuss and compromise over these provinces.

The Sikhs also made strong representations to the Viceroy for him to protect their interests. The nearly four million Sikhs in the Punjab opposed with arms as well as argument the prospect of Muslim 'tyranny' in the Punjab which partition would mean. In March 1947 the coalition government of Sir Malik Khizar Hyat Tiwana resigned, a government which

included Hindus and Sikhs, but excluded the Muslim League,
though the latter had the largest voting strength in the province.
The prospect of a Muslim government led to unprecedented
communal violence. The Sikh leaders Master Tara Singh and
Sardar Baldev Singh asked the Viceroy to divide the Punjab so
as to leave the Sikh community free of Muslim domination and
guarantee them security in the form of sufficient voting strength
in any future constitution. The independent Sikh states of
Faridkot, Nabha, Jind and Khalsia sought a confederation to
oppose Muslim domination. A number of Muslim attacks on
minorities in the West Punjab led to counter-attacks by the
Sikhs and left little prospect for peaceful compromise in the
Punjab. The Sikhs, with their capacity for militancy, were in a
middle position where they hoped to preserve the integrity of
their community, though they lacked sufficient numbers to
assure that integrity by constitutional right.

Before the Governors' conference of 15 April, Mountbatten
drew up an alternative plan to that of the Cabinet Mission.
The provinces voting through their legislatures were to decide
for India or Pakistan. The Legislative Assemblies of Bengal and
Punjab were to be divided on the basis of community for the
purpose of voting. If Bengal voted for partition the predominantly Muslim district of Sylhet would have the option to join
Pakistan. A referendum would be held in the North-West
Frontier Province. A boundary commission was proposed,
consisting of a British chairman, a Hindu and a Moslem, to
draw frontiers on the basis of Eastern Bengal and Western
Punjab in Pakistan, Western Bengal, including Calcutta, and
Eastern Punjab in India.

The actual plan was not shown to the Indian leaders but
general points were raised. In particular, Mountbatten impressed upon Jinnah and the League leaders that, if Pakistan
was conceded, a centre or supreme defence council would still
exist 'with practically the same subjects as the Centre envisaged
in the Cabinet Mission plan'.[1] In his personal report of 24 April
the Viceroy, sensing his diminishing capacity to oppose Jinnah,
vaguely hoped for unity, though little in his plan spoke of it.

[1] *Ibid.*, p. 292.

This is the one bargaining counter I have left, for it is just possible that when faced with the full stupidity of what they are doing, the League might make some gesture to accept a compromise Cabinet Mission scheme and Congress in their desire to retain some form of unity might also be more forthcoming. But I am afraid this is a very pious hope and there are no signs that I shall succeed.[1]

Lord Ismay and George Abell left New Delhi on 2 May with the Viceroy's draft plan to obtain Cabinet approval. The India-Burma Committee of the Cabinet met three times to consider the main features of the plan. According to Lord Ismay the Cabinet changes in wording and the draft he brought from New Delhi were identical in essentials. Mountbatten also thought the changes were minimal and for the better. The Cabinet stressed that the plan was not final; partition had to await the referenda and the advice of the boundary commission.

Nehru and Krishna Menon were staying as the Viceroy's guests in Simla. On 10 May Mountbatten showed the draft approved by the Cabinet to Nehru who violently objected to the proposals. Nehru opposed the plan's total acceptance of partition without any provision for the unity of India. It seemed to him that the draft plan wiped away the previous decisions and pledges of the British Government, making the Constituent Assembly and the Interim Government useless. He feared disorder would result from the absence of a central authority. The Indian States might also, following the principles of the draft plan, choose to remain outside the Indian union.

Though the Viceroy was greatly surprised by Nehru's passionate disapproval of his and the Cabinet-revised plan, in retrospect it is not at all surprising. Mountbatten had not shown Nehru the plans in detail before sending them to London. There had been general discussions with the Viceroy still hoping, as he explained in his Report to the Cabinet of 25 April, for a centre as envisaged by the Cabinet Mission. Nehru was right to be surprised by the absence of proposals about the centre in the present plan. Perhaps he shared with the Viceroy the view that the specific details for partition would show the League how unfeasible were their ideas. But the draft plan, instead of

[1] *Ibid.*, p. 293.

producing insurmountable practical problems against partition, made it seem imminent.

It was now imperative to find an alternative which Congress could accept. Since the Party firmly held the principle that a free India could not coerce a province to remain a part of it, there was room for compromise. Nehru was afraid that the Cabinet-revised plan would allow provinces now participating in the Constituent Assembly to leave; instead of providing for one division between India and Pakistan, the new plan implied any province could choose not to join India. The implications of this idea for the Indian States were plain. Instead of India becoming the successor power to the British Government, the Indian States, with whom negotiations had not yet begun in earnest, might also decide to separate themselves from an India dominated by Congress, the Party which was highly critical of the undemocratic and autocratic States. Much also seemed to depend on the sequence of events. Before the partition of India, a final plan had to allow for the *possibility* of unity no matter how remote.

At this critical moment Mountbatten pushed forward the date when the Government's plan would be formally shown to the Indian leaders to 2 June. He called on V. P. Menon, a member of the Viceroy's staff, a former Reforms Commissioner, and a friend of Sardar Patel. Menon, in one busy afternoon on 11 May, drafted an eight-point 'Heads of Agreement'. The first item left the final decision for unity or partition to 'the wishes of the people', voting in the Sind, Punjab, and Bengal in the provincial legislatures, by direct referendum in the North-West Frontier, and in Baluchistan by a vote of tribal leaders and the municipal councillors of Quetta. 'In the event of a decision that there should be two sovereign states in India, the central government of each state should take over power in responsibility to their respective Constituent Assemblies, again on a Dominion Status basis.'[1] It was at first hoped that Dominion Status would mean a common Governor-General to both Dominions, who could assist the two states with the many social, political, economic, and military after-effects of partition. The Governor-General would be a tangible link between the new dominions

[1] V. P. Menon, *The Transfer of Power*, 1957, p. 366.

and the Commonwealth. The armed forces were to be divided. A boundary commission was proposed to demarcate the two states. One of the attractions of this plan was that the transfer of power would be almost immediate.[1] If the Muslim League refused this final plan, negotiations would end, leaving the Cabinet Mission scheme as the basis of the transfer of power, in effect the handing over of complete power to the Congress-dominated Interim Government.

Menon's ideas were not new to Nehru and the Congress. He had discussed them with Nehru and Patel before Nehru saw the scheme approved by the Cabinet. Dominion status was at first conceived as the transitional method for the transfer of power. Patel, who as Home Member in the Interim Government had to cope with communal bitterness, was resigned to partition. When Nehru telephoned Patel in Delhi to explain the new plan Patel approved of it. He told Nehru he would carry the whole Congress party.

Mountbatten flew to London on 14 May to explain the new scheme to the British Government. He left India with a letter from Nehru generally accepting the principles, but Jinnah wrote nothing though in conversation he gave a cautious agreement. When Mountbatten warned of the alternative to this scheme, the revival of the Cabinet Mission Plan which would undermine the position of the League by delaying the simultaneous transfer of power to two separate states, Jinnah was remarkably calm and indifferent.

In London the Cabinet soon appreciated that this shaky agreement was as close as the Indian leaders could come to a compromise. Without much discussion the Cabinet endorsed the plan which was published in a Government statement on 3 June.

In the two weeks that Mountbatten spent in London events in India threatened to undermine the tremulous situation. Any attempt by either party to question the principles of agreement or make new demands might throw the already complex arrangements into a cauldron of uncertainties which negotiating procedures could no longer support. Jinnah, instinctively sensing that one way in which to ensure Congress acceptance of a plan fundamentally in his favour was to ask for more, released

[1] Sometime in the beginning of June that date of 15 August was discussed.

through the press a demand for an eight-hundred-mile corridor to link East and West Pakistan. Gandhi, desiring communal peace before partition, spoke out against the division of India: 'Dare the British impose Pakistan on an India temporarily gone mad?'[1]

The rival claims for a corridor and a united India in effect cancelled each other. Indian leaders were accustomed to frustrations. The achievement of the last Viceroy was that he made issues so narrow and concrete, the methods of negotiation so fixed, that few practical opportunities existed for retrogressive arguments or new claims. The important meetings at the beginning of June when final decisions were taken were a tribute to Mountbatten's methods.

On 2 June Mountbatten met Nehru, Patel and Kripalani for the Congress, Jinnah, Liaquat Ali Khan, Abdur Rab Nistar for the League, and Sardar Baldev Singh for the Sikhs. In the tense atmosphere he handed round the statement of the British Government which he had brought from London. The group disbanded to discuss the plan with their party committees. They met again on the following day formally to state their reactions. Again Mountbatten dominated the conference. He avoided open discussion, saying that he knew each party had grave objections, but that it would be pointless to discuss them now as they were well-known to him. Instead of presenting arguments the Indian leaders were asked to give their assent to the Cabinet statement. This they did in turn, Jinnah, reserved to the end, making only a nod. Dramatically, the Viceroy then placed before the assembled politicians a long document on the administrative consequences of partition which they were asked to consider.

With the alacrity of a salesman the Viceroy arranged for the Indian leaders to follow his radio broadcast that very evening, stating their acceptance of a final plan; the public broadcast, coming after long, tense and secret meetings gave a finality to the negotiations. 'With no joy in his heart', Nehru accepted the Cabinet statement which would probably mean the partition of his country. Jinnah, maintaining his reserve, said that he 'examined British Government statements coolly, wholly, and dispassionately'. Sardar Baldev Singh, somewhat cryptically,

[1] Pyarelal, *Gandhi*, p. 208.

referred to the strain of making historic decisions fraught with
suffering; 'The shadow of our differences has thrown its gloom
over us.' The partition of India was accepted by Indian leaders
not as a settlement or an agreement, but as a truce among
themselves, a cessation of hostilities.

At the end of June the provincial assemblies of Bengal and
Punjab voted for partition; the Sind assembly voted to join
Pakistan, and Sylhet voted in favour of attaching itself to East
Bengal.

Besides the administrative consequences of partition, it was
necessary for the actual boundary lines between the two
countries to be established on the basis of majority population.
Two commissions were created, Bengal-Assam and Punjab,
with Sir Cyril Radcliffe, a distinguished lawyer and Vice-
Chairman of the General Council of the Bar, as chairman of both
commissions with a casting vote.

The history of the Boundary Commission reiterates the
inability of Indian leaders, and indirectly of the machinery of
government evolved by Britain for India, to solve major problems. Even in the very last phases of foreign rule, an official of
the frequently despised foreign ruler was called upon to decide
for the different Indian communities the contours of their
domain. Hindus, Muslims, and Sikhs, like feuding families,
remembered and cherished past injustices and strengthened the
identity of their communities by remaining hostile to the
traditional enemy. The energy expended over the long years of
struggle for national independence had provided too little
opportunity for a natural relationship to develop among the
Indian communities. The momentous events which were taking
place in the present were unable to induce among Indian
politicians or their followers a sense of reason and cooperation.
The two Boundary Commissions made up of two Hindu and
two Muslims on each floundered on the same narrow self-
interest which necessitated partition and communal rioting.

The two Commissions began their meetings on 30 July, in
Lahore and Calcutta. Sir Cyril Radcliffe arrived in New Delhi
on 8 July, well after the proceedings began. Unable to attend
both Commissions at the same time, he visited neither. Instead
he read the record of the Commissions' sessions and their

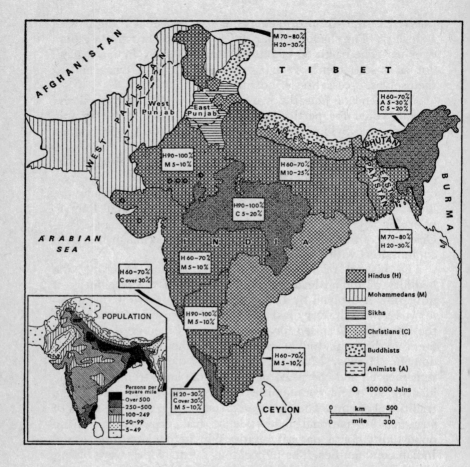

India and Pakistan, Religion and Population

respective reports. Since the two Commissions were divided
within themselves, and 'in the absence of any reconciliation on
all main questions affecting the drawing of the boundary itself',[1]
Sir Cyril, after meeting with the Commissioners, was left to
settle the boundaries himself.

The terms of reference for the Commissions required

[1] *Report of the Bengal Boundary Commission*, 17 August 1947

boundaries to be drawn on the basis of contiguous communal majority, with some consideration of social, economic, and administrative viability. His 'Awards'[1] gave Lahore to Pakistan, Amritsar to India in the Punjab, Calcutta to India, the Chittagong Hill Tracts and the whole district of Sylhet to Pakistan, in Bengal.

The Partition Council, created to facilitate partition, agreed to accept the decision of the Boundary Commission. As the time approached for the publication of the Awards, however, Indian leaders became covetous of every person or land belonging to their nation; Pakistan claimed the Ourdaspur district in the Punjab, India the Chittagong Hill Tribes in Bengal. The Viceroy thought the announcement of the actual boundaries might disturb the independence day celebrations. He sought to postpone publication until after 15 August. But Sir Cyril told the Viceroy that he would not delay beyond 13 August. The Viceroy accepted the Awards on that day but 'arranged' to leave for Karachi before reading them, thus assuring that they would not be published until the 15th or later. Though pleasing no one, and highly criticised in the press, Sir Cyril's Awards were as fair a decision as anyone could make in just over a month, without extensive consultation or negotiations with interested parties, and without highly accurate maps. The Boundary Commission Awards like the last stages of British rule in India were hurried, impartial, well-intentioned, but incapable of preventing communal massacres.

The desire of the British Government for a speedy end to their Indian responsibilities, a desire which made the Cabinet sitting in London impartial but somewhat casual about the effects in India of their decisions, was the single most important factor which made the last stage of British rule different from the previous decades. Mountbatten's insistence on a fixed date before accepting the Prime Minister's offer of the Viceroyalty plus the deadlock in India over the Cabinet Mission Plan did much to disengage the Cabinet from the Indian problem. Before 1945 Anglo-Indian relations had taken place in an open-ended context, a long afternoon, where the slow pace of change made the goals of constitutional advance become

[1] See Map 2, opposite.

lost. The indefinite constitutional future allowed for a wide variety of dissenting opinion and criticism. As long as the British Government avoided direct negotiations with Indian leaders by delegating considerable authority to the Government of India or *ad hoc* parliamentary commissions, the Cabinet was slow to conceive of the present as a time to grant self-government. Successive Governments were in the habit of basing their Indian policy on a traditional assertion: Indians had to satisfy certain pre-conditions before self-government could be planned. Since this never happened or was likely, there were few dramatic changes in Government policy before 1945. The revolutionary tactics of the Congress Party were in part attempts to create a sense of urgency about India which the structure of government and administration in India and the London-made constitutions deliberately tried to prevent. But after 1945, and particularly in the last few months before the transfer of power, the long afternoon became dusk as Indians were expected to plan their own future. In a brief time major controversies of the past were, if not settled, at least temporarily suspended so as not to prevent Indian independence. That so much was arranged in such a short time helped to cast the Raj's departure and the founding of two nations in a penumbrous glory.

The integration of the Indian States, like the fixing of the boundaries between India and Pakistan, was completed in the shortest possible time. The policy of the British Government was to end paramountcy, terminate the Political Department which had virtually dominated the States through its Agents and Residents. The States were asked to establish a basis for their existence by entering into negotiations with the two new successor governments of British India. Some of the Princes led by the Maharajas of Birkaner and Patiala joined the Indian constituent assembly, but others led by the Maharaja of Bhopal sought to assert independence with the lapse of paramountcy.

Lord Mountbatten met the Princes or their representatives on 3 June 1947. It became clear that His Majesty's Government would not confer Dominion status on any State which declared itself independent. Since most of the 565 Native States fell within the territory of India, Nehru wished to make the new

Indian Government the successor to paramountcy; in other words, India would take over the powers of the Political Department. He opposed the claims put forward by some of the States that they had a right to independence and sovereignty, particularly since he had long been a critic of the undemocratic and irresponsible form of government which existed in the States.

At a meeting of party leaders called by Mountbatten on 13 June it was decided to form a States Department, divided into two sections, India and Pakistan. On 5 July V. P. Menon assumed charge of the department and went to work to create a document which, by conciliation, would win the support of the Princely Order. Using Lincoln's First Inaugural Address for inspiration, and indeed phrases, Menon devised a document which asked the States to cooperate with either India or Pakistan in defence, external affairs and communications, precisely those areas of authority which the States had relinquished under paramountcy. The States were to join the new nations on terms identical with the ones they had accepted under British rule. There were no new financial arrangements. The Negotiating Committee of the States met the States Department at the end of July and in a week drafted an Instrument of Accession and Standstill Agreement, by which arrangements between the Crown and the States would continue until new agreements between the States and the new Governments were made. With the important exceptions of Kashmir and Hyderabad all the States signed the Instrument of Accession.[1]

The long and intricate history of the negotiations which led to the partition of India give little indication of the dissolution and chaos which prevailed in these years. By the end of the war, the Government of India had lost confidence in its ability to rule. It was impossible to replenish the Indian Civil Service with the best people. There were hardly any British politicians who wanted to accept high office in India. As the end of British rule grew nearer, officials found it difficult to reward or punish. Lord Wavell doubted whether the police and the native army would remain loyal if asked to quell a serious rebellion. He

[1] For a detailed account of the history of the integration of the Indian States, see the authoritative V. P. Menon, *The Integration of the Indian States* (1956).

lamented, 'We have lost nearly all power to control events.'[1] It was difficult for British officials to see what duty they had to perform except to depart. A. P. Hume wrote in his diary in April 1947:

> The whole thing is tinged with melancholy for me. One cannot escape the sense of an inglorious end to a great enterprise which seemed to have and should have had so splendid an object. The great Indian empire crumbling amid the strident shrieks of little-minded people squabbling and pushing about in their futility.[2]

There were many indications of the crumbling empire. In November 1945 members of Bose's Indian National Army who had deserted the British Indian Army stood trial. At the time it proved difficult to find them guilty since they were praised by the Congress as national heroes. Large-scale rioting, aimed at getting members of the army released, occurred in Calcutta in February 1946. Mutiny in the Royal Indian Navy in Bombay and Karachi and in the Royal Indian Air Force at Bombay among the crews occurred also in February 1946. Sympathetic strikes and demonstrations were held in Bombay, and in the clash between the protesters and police 200 people were killed. Strikes, communal violence, food riots continually worried British authorities. On 16 August 1946, the Muslim League observed a 'direct action day' and Muslims were enjoined to strike in support of Pakistan. The Muslim League Government in Bengal called a public holiday and communal rioting lasted for several days in Calcutta. At least 5,000 people were killed and 15,000 injured. Rumour and atrocity stories spread through the country. As the Muslim League did not accept the Constituent Assembly as a means to realise their hopes for Pakistan, Muslim para-military organisations were formed in East Bengal and Hindu communities claimed that Muslims murdered, looted and wantonly destroyed property. Hindus retaliated.

On 10 November 1946, Sir Malik Firoz Khan Noon, formerly Indian representative to the British War Cabinet and member of the Punjab Provincial Legislature, visited the devastated areas of Bihar. His memorandum which reached the

---

[1] Wavell, *Viceroy's Journal*, p. 402.

[2] A. P. Hume, Diary, 1947 (unpublished), IOL. A. P. Hume was District Magistrate in Benares.

British Government dwelled on the horrors of communal violence. Reports of scenes like this could only make British officials feel increasingly helpless. It was impossible to assess blame in the normal legal sense. Noon visited the Muslim parts of Nagar Nausa which was besieged for six days by a crowd estimated at 40,000.

> Not a house was left intact, nor a soul anywhere. Smell of dead bodies recently burnt. The firing was on the 6th. A house was still burning. The Hindus after looting the deserted houses are continuing to burn them. Not a policeman here yet! We saw many heads of burnt bodies in the little room on the right and the left as you enter the mosque. The door had been smashed and destroyed. The open ground at the back was littered with pieces of the Quran. . . . One dead body lay burnt in the compound. The Congress workers told us that the cattle of the Muslims who were absent were destroying other people's crops. We had reports from other sources that crops belonging to Muslims were in the process of being destroyed already. With a cup of tea at Fatwa we got back at 7.30 p.m. the smell of burning corpses in our nostrils.[1]

Towards the end of 1946 around 50,000 refugees were maintained in relief camps. Official statements and reports were far from thorough or complete. At Garhmuktesar in the United Provinces a quarrel among pilgrims led to the killing of Muslims. In a neighbouring village Muslims retaliated by killing every Hindu. In 1947 the Punjab, relatively free of communal violence, erupted when the Muslim League called for direct action, which eventually precipitated the fall of the provincial ministry. Violence between Hindus, Muslims and Sikhs brought the province near to civil war with around 1,000 killed. Eventually the Governor had to take control of the Government. As the time for the departure of British authorities drew near, incidents of violent crime were daily events in the larger cities, while in the countryside such displays of communal war were obscured by their remoteness. Nine of the eleven provincial governments were run by direct ordinance. Immediately after the Raj departed, from August to November, migration and massacre in Bengal, Assam, the Punjab and the

---

[1] Sir F. K. Noon, *Memorandum on a recent Tour of Bihar*, 10 November 1946. Attlee Papers, University College, Oxford.

North-West Frontier Province led to the death of perhaps 200,000 men, women and children.

These events vindicated what the leaders of the Indian National Congress had always preached: the price of freedom was high and suffering was a medium of exchange. Yet Partition gave something to everyone: Pakistan to the Muslims, freedom to India, a ceremony of honourable departure for the British, and the achievement that both new Dominions joined the British Commonwealth.

The people of India in their variety found ways natural to themselves to celebrate the coming of their freedom on 15 August 1947. In Mysore a Dakota airplane flew over the city and showered multi-coloured flowers on the heads of humanity below. In Trivandrum students held a cycle rally with national flags on their bikes. Prisoners in Chochin were released. In Coimbatore the mill owners association gave each of their workers five rupees. In Bodinayakanur sweets were distributed to children. The Dowager Zamindarani of Bod waived the collections of monies owed to her in arrears. Gandhi invited everyone to a day of fasting and extra spinning.

SELECTED BIBLIOGRAPHY

I. PRIVATE PAPERS

King George V. The correspondence between the Viceroys of India and the King, 1912–22. By kind permission of Her Gracious Majesty, Queen Elizabeth II. Royal Archives, Windsor Castle.

Lord Attlee. Great Missenden and University College, Oxford.

Thomas Attlee. Truro, Cornwall.

Lord Birkenhead. India Office Library.

St John Brodrick. IOL.

Sir Spencer Harcourt Butler. IOL.

Cecil of Chelwood. British Museum.

Lord Chelmsford. IOL.

Stafford Cripps. Nuffield College, Oxford.

Lord Dalton. London School of Economics.

K. Eates, 'Memoirs Grave and Gay of Crimes, Criminals and Court', (unpublished). IOL.

Sir A. Godley (Lord Kilbracken). IOL.

Lord Goschen. IOL.

Sir Hamilton Grant. IOL.

Lord Hardinge. IOL.

Sir Arthur Hirtzel. IOL.

A. P. Hume. Diary. IOL.

Lord Irwin (Lord Halifax). IOL.

George Lansbury. London School of Economics.

Lord Lawson. Chester-le-Street, Co. Durham.

Lord Linlithgow. IOL.

J. R. MacDonald, loaned to D. Marquand, M.P. By kind permission of Malcolm MacDonald.

Lord Meston. IOL.

Lord Minto. IOL.

Edwin Montagu. IOL.

Lord Morley. IOL.

Lord Reading. IOL.

Viscount Templewood. IOL.

Lord Willingdon. IOL.
Sir Guy Fleetwood Wilson. IOL.
Lord Zetland, (Lord Ronaldshay). IOL.

II. GOVERNMENT REPORTS 1900–1947

1. *Constitutional Reform*

Papers relating to the Reconstitution of the Provinces of Bengal and Assam; 1905, Cd. 2658, lviii, 201.

Further Papers; 1906, Cd. 2746, lxxxi, 631.

Resignation of Sir J. B. Fuller, K.C.S.I., C.I.E., Lieutenant-Governor of Eastern Bengal and Assam; 1906, Cd. 3242, lxxxi, 885.

Proclamation creating an Executive Council in Bengal; 1911 (26), lv, 627.

Proclamations for delimiting the Presidency of Bengal; for constituting the Province of Bihar and Orissa; and for forming Assam into a Chief Commissionership under the immediate authority and management of the Governor-General in Council; 1912–13, Cd. 6189, lxi, 757.

Proclamation creating an Executive Council in the Province of Bihar and Orissa; 1912–13 (320), lxi, 753.

Papers relating to an Imperial Advisory Council and Provincial Advisory Councils, the Enlargement of Legislative Councils, and the Discussion of the Budget; 1907, Cd. 3710, lviii, 451.

Proposals of the Government of India and Despatch of the Secretary of State (in continuation of Cd. 3710 of 1907), Vol. I; 1908, Cd. 4426, lxxvi, Pt I, 1.

Replies of the Local Governments, Etc., Vol. II, Part I (Enclosures I to XX); 1908, Cd. 4435, lxxvi, Pt I, 55.

Replies of the Local Governments, Etc., Vol. II, Part II. (Enclosures XXI to XXX); 1908, Cd. 4436, lxxvi, Pt II, 1.

Representation of Muhammadans on Legislative Councils; 1909, Cd 4652, lxii, 759.

Regulations, Etc., for giving effect to the Indian Councils Act, 1909; 1910, Cd. 4987, lxvii, 617.

Revised Regulations; 1913, Cd. 6714, xlvii, 1.

Regulations and Rules relating to the Constitution of a Legislative Council for the Central Provinces, and of certain Amendments in the Imperial Council Regulations; 1914, Cd. 7370, lxiii, 1.

Report on Indian Constitution Reforms (Montagu-Chelmsford Report); 1918, Cd. 9109, viii, 113.

Addresses presented in India to the Viceroy and the Secretary of State; 1918, Cd. 9178, xviii, 469.

Correspondence regarding (1) Constitutional changes to be made in Assam and Backward Tracts. (2) Champaran and Kaira Cases; 1919, Cmd. 271, xxxvii, 915.

Views of the Government of India on the composition of Grand Committees; 1919, Cmd. 228, xxxvii, 905.

Letter from the Government of India, dated 5 March, 1919, and Enclosures, on the Questions raised in the Report on Indian Constitutional Reforms; 1919, Cmd. 123, xxxvii, 581.

Recommendations of the Government of India regarding demarcation between Central and Provincial revenues; 1919, Cmd. 334, xxxvii, 943.

Government of India's Despatch, 20 September, 1930, on Proposals for Constitutional Reform; 1930–31, Cmd. 3700, xxiii, 679.

Despatches from Provincial Governments in India containing Proposals for Constitutional Reform; 1930–31, Cmd. 3712, xxiv, 1.

Communal Decision; 1931–32, Cmd. 4147, xviii, 965.

Proposals for Indian Constitutional Reform; 1932–3, Cmd. 4268, xx, 997.

Resignation of Ministries in Bihar and The United Provinces, 1938; 1937–8, Cmd. 5674, xxi, 323.

Memorandum by the Secretary of State for India regarding the Bill to make further provision with respect to the Government of India; 1919 Cmd. 175, xxxvii, 955.

Rule limiting the Secretary of State's powers of superintendence, direction, and control in relation to transferred subjects; 1920 (217), xxxv, 579.

Statutory Commission: Interim Report (Review of the Growth of Education in British India by the Auxiliary Committee), September, 1929; 1929–30, Cmd. 3407, x, 535.

Report of the Commission. Vol. I. Survey; 1929–30, Cmd. 3568, xi, 1.
Vol. II. Recommendations; 1929–30, Cmd. 3569, xi, 443.
Vol. III. Reports of the Committees appointed by the Provincial Legislative Councils to cooperate with the Statutory Commission; 1929–30, Cmd. 3572, xii, 1.

Proceedings of the Round Table Conference (1930–31); 1930–31, Cmd. 3778, xii, 91.

Statement by the Prime Minister at the conclusion of the second session on 1 December, 1931; 1931–2, Cmd. 3972, xviii, 957.

Proceedings during the second session, 7 September to 1 December, 1931; 1931–2, Cmd. 3997, viii, 1.

Proceedings during the third session, 17 November to 24 December, 1932; 1932–3, Cmd. 4238, xi, 169.

Report of the Joint Committee. Report and Proceedings; Evidence, Appendices, Records and Indices; 1932–3 (112), v, 661, vi, vii, viii, ix, 1.

Report, Proceedings and Records; 1933–4 (5) vi, 413, vii, viii, 1.

Lord Privy Seal's Mission: Statement and Draft Declaration by His Majesty's Government with correspondence and Resolutions connected therewith; 1941–2, Cmd. 6350, viii, 1.

Statement by the Cabinet Mission and His Excellency the Viceroy; 1945–6, Cmd. 6821, xix, 127.

Correspondence and Documents connected with the Conference between the Cabinet Mission and His Excellency the Viceroy and Representatives of the Congress and the Muslim League, May, 1946; 1945–6, Cmd. 6829, xix, 145.

Statement by the Mission dated 25 May in reply to Pronouncements by the Indian Parties and Memorandum by the Mission on States' Treaties and Paramountcy; 1945–6, Cmd. 6835, xix, 165.

Correspondence with the Congress Party and the Muslim League, 20 May–29 June, 1946; 1945–6 Cmd. 6861, xix, 177.

Papers relating to The Sikhs, The Indian States, and The European Community, May–June, 1946; 1945–6, Cmd. 6862, xix, 137.

Statement of the policy of His Majesty's Government made by the Secretary of State for India on 14 June, 1945; 1944–5, Cmd. 6652, ix, 653.

Statement of 20 February, 1947; 1946–7, Cmd. 7047, xix, 7.

Statement of 3 June, 1947; 1946–7, Cmd. 7136, xix, 11.

2. Crime and Sedition

Report of the Indian Police Commission and Resolution of the Government of India; 1905, Cd. 2478, lvii, 657.

State Prisoners: Return showing the Names of the Persons in India who are now detained under the provisions of Bengal Regulation III of 1818, and Kindred Regulations: their Caste, Race and Nationality; the grounds for, the Place, and Nature of, and the Date of Commencement of their Detention; 1909 (330), lxiv, 511.

Return of Prosecutions, for Seditious Speeches and Writings, instituted in East India since 1 January, 1907, showing the Names and Descriptions of the Persons charged, the Courts which tried them, and the precise character of the charge and the decision in each case; 1909 (50), lxiv, 1.

Similar Return, since 1 January, 1909, with further Information regarding such Prosecutions, Etc., in 1907 and 1908 (in continuation of No. 50 of 1909); 1911 (50), lv, 657.

Correspondence relating to the Attempt on the Life of the Viceroy, on the occasion of the State Entry into Delhi, on 23 December, 1912; 1912–13, Cd. 6642, lxi, 829.

Return showing the Number of Death Sentences passed in India during 1911, giving each province separately; the Number of these Sentences subsequently modified by the highest judicial authority; and the Number commuted by the Government; 1913 (158), xlvi, 509.

Report of the Committee appointed to investigate Revolutionary Conspiracies in India; 1918, Cd. 9190, vii, 423.

Report of Sir N. Chandavarkar and Mr Justice Beachcroft on Deternees and Internees in Bengal; 1918, Cd. 9198, viii, 105.

Report of the Commission appointed by the Government of India to inquire into the Conditions and Prospects of the University of Calcutta. Vol. I. Part I. Analysis of present conditions; 1919, Cmd. 386, xiv, 1.

Vol. II. Part I. Analysis of present conditions; 1919, Cmd. 387, xiv, 471.

Vol. III. Part I. Analysis of present conditions; 1919, Cmd. 388, xv, 1.

Vol. IV. Part II. Recommendations of the Commission; 1919, Cmd. 389, xv, 341.

Vol. V. Part II. Recommendations of the Commission; 1919, Cmd. 390, xvi, 1.

Reports on the Punjab Disturbances, April, 1919; 1920, Cmd. 534, xiv, 931.

Report of the Committee appointed to investigate the Disturbances in the Punjab, etc.; 1920, Cmd. 681, xiv, 1001.

Correspondence between the Government of India and the Secretary of State for India on the Report of Lord Hunter's Committee (in continuation of Cmd. 681 of 1920); 1920, Cmd. 705, xxxiv, 649.

Statement by Brig.-General R. E. H. Dyer, C.B.; 1920, Cmd. 771, lxxxiv, 677.

Report of the Indian Jails Committee, 1919–20; 1921, Cmd. 1303, x, 363.

Civil Disobedience: Telegraphic Correspondence regarding the Situation in India; 1922, Cmd. 1586, xvi, 579.

Measures taken to counteract the Civil Disobedience Movement, and to deal with the Terrorist Movement in Bengal, Ordinances Nos II to V of 1932, with Official Statements and Correspondence relative thereto and Ordinances Nos IX and XI of 1931; 1931–2, Cmd. 4010, xviii, 973.

Report of the Committee appointed to consider Racial Distinctions in Criminal Procedure, with the Bill introduced in the Indian Legislature on the basis of the Committee's Recommendations; 1923, Cmd. 1923, x, 627.

Judgment of the High Court of Judicature at Allahabad in the Revolutionary Conspiracy Case; 1924–5, Cmd. 2309, xi, 1.

World War II: Statement published by the Government of India on the Congress Party's responsibility for the Disturbances in India, 1942–3; 1942–3, Cmd. 6430, ix, 827.

3. *Indian Social Conditions*

Plague Commission (1898–9). Vol. I. Evidence, with Appendices; 1900, Cd. 139, xxxi, 1.

Vol. II. Further Evidence, with Appendices; 1900, Cd. 140, xxxi, 1.

Vol. III. Further Evidence, with Appendices; 1900, Cd. 141, xxxii, 1.

Vol. IV. Indices to the Evidence; also Glossary, Maps and Summary of the Report and Appendices; 1902, Cd. 809, lxxii, 55.

Vol. V. Report, with Appendices and Summary; 1902, Cd. 810, lxxii, 223.

Reports and Papers relating to the Famine and Relief Operations in India during 1899–1900. Vol. I. British Districts; 1900, Cd. 205, xxvii, 387.

Vol. II. Native States; 1900, Cd. 206, xxviii, 1.

Report of the Indian Famine Commission, 1901, and Papers relating thereto; 1902, Cd. 876, lxx, 545.

Papers regarding the Land Revenue System of British India; 1902, Cd. 1089, lxxi, 527.

Statement showing the number of Processes issued against Land Revenue Defaulters during 1901–02; 1904, Cd. 2015, lxiii, 503.

Review of Progress of Education in India, 1897–8 to 1901–02. Vol. I. Fourth Quinquennial Review; 1904, Cd. 2181, lxv, 1.

Vol. II. Maps and Tables; 1904, Cd. 2182, lxv, 517.

Progress of Education in India, 1902–07. Vol. I. Fifth Quinquennial Review; 1909, Cd. 4635, lxiii, 1.

Vol. II. Maps and Statistical Tables; 1909, Cd. 4636, lxiii, 357.

Progress of Education in India, 1907–12. Vol. I. Sixth Quinquennial Review; 1914, Cd. 7485, lxii, 1.

Vol. II. Appendices and Tables; 1914, Cd. 7486, lxii, 409.

Progress of Education in India, 1912–17. Vol. I. Seventh Quinquennial Review; 1919, Cmd. 256, xxxviii, 1.

Vol. II. Appendices and Tables; 1919, Cmd. 257, xxxviii, 287.

Report of the Indian Irrigation Commission, 1901–03. Part I. General; 1904, Cd. 1851, lxvi, 1.

Correspondence regarding Measures for the Prevention of Plague; 1907, Cd. 3516, lviii, 693.

Return of the Memorandum of the Royal College of Physicians in July, 1905, on Plague; 1907 (169), lviii, 747.

Return of Papers containing the Results of an Inquiry into the Origin of Certain Deaths from Tetanus in the Punjab, consequent on the employment of Dr Haffkine's Prophylactic against Plague; 1907 (106), lviii, 753.

Report of the Indian Factory Labour Commission. Vol. I. Reports and Appendices; 1909, Cd. 4292, lxxiv, 545.

Vol. II. Evidence; 1909, Cd. 4519, lxiii, 541.

Return showing the Number of Deaths, and the Death Rates per million living in India for each of the last 30 Years from Plague, Cholera, Enteric, or Typhoid Fever, and Small-pox respectively; 1908 (160), lxxiv, 497.

Measures for promoting the growth of an Independent Medical Profession in India; 1909, Cd. 4666, lxii, 763.

Correspondence regarding the Indian Medical Service and the Medical Profession in India (in continuation of Cd. 4666 of 1909); 1914, Cd. 7547, lxiii, 85.

Return showing the following particulars for each year in respect of which Records have been kept for each Province of British India and for British India as a whole; Ratio of Successful Vaccinations for 1,000 of the Population; Small-pox Death Rate per 1,000 of the Population at all ages; Percentage of the Total Deaths from Small-pox occurring at the following Ages; under One Year, One to Ten Years, and over Ten Years; 1912–13 (106), lxi, 837.

Return showing the Cases of Deaths from Small-pox occurring amongst Officers, Women and Children, respectively, with the British Troops in India, and amongst British and Native Officers, respectively, with the Indian Troops, together with the Ratio per 1,000 of the strength in each case for each year during the last Ten Years for which the Returns are available; 1912–13 (3), lxi, 835.

Report of the Indian Industrial Commission, 1916–18; 1919, Cmd. 51, xvii, 1.

Evidence, Vols I–IV; 1919, Cmd. 234, Cmd. 235, Cmd. 236, Cmd. 237, Cmd. 238, xvii, 541, xviii, xix, xx, 1.

Report of the Royal Commission on Agriculture, Cmd. 3122, 1928.

Report of the Royal Commission on Labour in India; 1930–31, Cmd. 3883, xi, 571.

III. EUROPEAN SOCIAL LIFE 1881–1905

D.J.A., *Notes on an Outfit for India*, 1903.

S.F.A. and G.G., *Complete Indian House Keeper*, Edinburgh, 1890.

Anglo-Indian Life. *Glimpses of Anglo-Indian Life*, Madras, 1901.

W. S. Burrell and E. E. Cuthill, *Indian Memories*, 1893.

C. T. Buckland, *Sketches of Social Life in India*, 1884.

H. E. Compton, *Indian Life in Town and Country*, 1904.

H. Drury, *Life and Sport in Southern India*, 1890.

Hon. C. Dutton, *Life in India*, 1882.

L. Emanuel, *Jottings of a Bengal 'Qui hye!'*, 1886.

Geofry, *Our Hill Stations in Southern India*, Madras, 1881.

J. D. Gordon, *Work and Play in India*, 1895.

K. Guthrie, *Life in Western India*, 2 vols, 1881.

S. Heron, *Anglo-Indians and Eurasians*, Simla, 1881.

C. F. Keary, *India: Impressions*, 1903.

E. A. King, *Diary of a Civilian's Wife in India, 1877–82*, 2 vols, 1884.

R. M. King, *Diary in India*, 2 vols, 1884.

Macleod, afterwards Wilson, A. C., *After Five Years in India*, 1895.

J. E. Mayer, *Humour and Pathos of Anglo-Indian Life*, 1895.

P. Millington, *In Cantonments*, Allahabad, 1897.

A. C. Newcombe, *Village, Town and Town life in India*, Edinburgh, 1905.

H. J. Reynolds, *At Home In India, 1856–89*, 1903.

I. Savory, *A Sportswoman in India*, 1900.

L. J. Shadwell, *Notes on the Internal economy of Chummery, Home, Mess and Club*, Bombay, 1904.

M. Thornhill, *Haunts and Hobbies of an Indian Official*, 1899.

A. C. Wilson, *Hints for the first Year's Residence in India*, 1904.

IV. SPEECHES AND PUBLISHED DOCUMENTS

Lord Curzon, *Lord Curzon in India*, selection from his speeches as Viceroy and Governor-General of India, 1906.

Speeches by the Earl of Minto, Viceroy and Governor-General of India, Calcutta, 1911.

Speeches of His Excellency the Right Hon'ble Baron Hardinge of Penhurst, Madras, 1919, 2 vols.

Lord Irwin, *Indian Problems. Speeches by Lord Irwin*, 1932.

E. Montagu, *Speeches on Indian Affairs*, Madras, 1917.

Viscount Morley, *Speeches on Indian Affairs*, Madras, 1917.

Speeches by the Marquess of Linlithgow [*as Viceroy of India, 1936–43*], 2 vols, Simla, 1944.

Speeches by Earl Wavell, From 26 October 1943 to 21 March 1947, 1948.

Speeches by His Excellency Rear-Admiral Earl Mountbatten of Burma, New Delhi, 1949.

The Transfer of Power, Vol. I, January to April 1942, 1970.

The Transfer of Power, Vol. II, April to September 1942, 1971.

The Transfer of Power, Vol. III, September 1942 to June 1943, 1971.

The Transfer of Power, Vol. IV, June 1943 to August 1944, 1973.

B. L. Glover, *British Policy Towards Indian Nationalism*, Delhi, 1967.

G. Allana, *Pakistan*, Karachi, 1967.

A. C. Banerjee, *Indian Constitutional Documents*, 4 vols, Calcutta, 1965.

D. Chakabarty and C. Bhattacharyga (ed.), *A Collection of Congress Resolutions*, Calcutta, 1935.

V. MEMOIRS

Lord Attlee, *As It Happened*, 1957.

A. K. Azad, *India Wins Freedom*, 1959.

A. Campbell-Johnson, *Mission With Mountbatten*, 1951.

R. Casey, *An Australian in India*, 1947.

N. Chaudhuri, *The Autobiography of An Unknown Indian*, 1951.

D. Das, *India*, 1969.

Marchioness of Dufferin and Ava, *Our Viceregal Life in India*, 1890.

M. Gandhi, *The Story of My Experiments With Truth*, 1949.

S. Ghosh, *Gandhi's Emissary*, 1967.

Lord Halifax, *Fullness of Days*, 1957

Lord Hardinge, *My Indian Years*, 1948.

Lord Ismay, *Memoirs*, 1960.

Aga Khan, *Memoirs*, 1954.

Lord Pethick Lawrence, 'Last Years', *Gandhi*, ed. by H. S. L. Polak, 1949.

Earl Lytton, *Pundits and Elephants*, 1942.

V. P. Menon, *The Integration of the Indian States*, 1956.

V. P. Menon, *The Transfer of Power*, 1957.

Countess Minto, *India, Minto and Morley, 1905–10*, 1934.

E. Montagu, *An Indian Diary*, ed. by V. Montagu, 1930.

Viscount Morley, *Recollections*, 2 volumes, 1917.

Earl Mountbatten, *Reflections on the Transfer of Power and J. Nehru*, 1968.

J. Nehru, *Autobiography*, 1936.

Sir M. O'Dwyer, *India as I Knew It*, 1925.

Viscount Simon, *Retrospect*, 1952.
Viscount Templewood, *Nine Troubled Years*, 1954.
Wavell, *Viceroy's Journal*, ed. by P. Moon, 1973.
Earl Winterton, *Orders of the Day*, 1953.
Lord Zetland, '*Essayez*', 1956.

VI. GENERAL BOOKS

R. Agarwala, *The Hindu-Muslim Riots*, Lucknow, 1943.
G. Ashe, *Gandhi*, 1968.
K. Aziz, *Britain and Muslim India*, 1963.
N. Banerjea, *Psychotherapy of India Riots*, Calcutta, 1941.
G. Bearce, *British Attitudes Towards India 1784–1858*, 1961.
B. Bhatia, *Famines in India*, 1967.
Lord Birkenhead, *F.E.*, 1936.
Lord Birkenhead, *Lord Halifax*, 1967.
J. Coatman, *Years of Destiny*, 1932.
I. Colvin, *The Life of General Dyer*, 1931.
A. R. Desai, *Social Background of Indian Nationalism*, Bombay, 1951.
M. Edwards, *Bound to Exile*, 1969.
M. Edwards, *Nehru*, 1971.
E. Erikson, *Gandhi's Truth*, 1970.
Sir K. Fitze, *Twilight of the Maharajas*, 1956.
L. Fraser, *India Under Curzon and After*, 1911.
Sir B. Fuller, *The Empire of India*, 1913.
R. Furneaux, *Massacre at Amritsar*, 1963.
J. Glendevon, *The Viceroy at Bay*, 1971.
Ram Gopal, *How India Struggled for Freedom*, 1967.
S. Gopal, *The Viceroyalty of Lord Irwin, 1926–31*, 1957.
Sir P. Griffiths, *History of the Indian Tea Industry*, 1967.
Sir P. Griffiths, *The British Impact on India*, 1952.
H. V. Hodson, *The Great Divide*, 1969.
Sir T. W. Holderness, *Peoples & Problems of India*, 1920.
A. Kapur, *Constitutional History of India*, New Delhi, 1970.
A. B. Keith, *A Constitutional History of India*, 1937.
S. Kirby, *The War Against Japan*, Vol. I and Vol. II, 1958.
E. Lumby, *The Transfer of Power in India, 1945–7*, 1954.
R. Lutyens, *Sir Edwin Lutyens*, 1948.
C. MacKenzie, *Eastern Epic*.
R. P. Masani, *Britain in India*, 1968.
P. Moon, *Divide and Quit*, 1961.
P. Moon, *Gandhi and Modern India*, 1968.

M. Mujeeb, *The Indian Muslims*, 1967.

G. Myrdal, *Asian Drama*, 3 vols, 1960.

B. Nanda, *The Nehrus*, 1962.

H. Nicolson, *King George V*, 1952.

B. Pandey, *The Break-up of British India*, 1969.

Pyarelal, *Mahatma Gandhi*, 2 vols, 1958.

Lord Reading, *Rufus Isaacs*, 1945.

K. Sayeed, *Pakistan*, 1968.

A. Seal, *The Emergence of Indian Nationalism*, 1968.

P. Sitaramayya, *History of the Indian National Congress*, 2 vols, Bombay, 1969

O. Spate and A. Learmouth, *India and Pakistan*, 1967.

I. Stephens, *Pakistan*, 1963.

E. Stokes, *The English Utilitarians and India*, 1959.

D. Tahmankar, *Lokamanya Tilak*, 1956.

Thompson and G. Garrat, *Rise and Fulfilment of British Rule in India*, 1937.

S. Wolpert, *Morley and India*, Los Angeles, 1967.

INDEX